Conversations with Andre Dubus

Literary Conversations Series
Peggy Whitman Prenshaw
General Editor

Conversations
with Andre Dubus

Edited by Olivia Carr Edenfield

University Press of Mississippi   Jackson

www.upress.state.ms.us

The University Press of Mississippi is a member of the Association of American University Presses.

Copyright © 2013 by University Press of Mississippi
All rights reserved
Manufactured in the United States of America

First printing 2013

Library of Congress Cataloging-in-Publication Data

Dubus, Andre, 1959–
    Conversations with Andre Dubus / edited by Olivia Carr Edenfield.
       pages cm. — (Literary Conversations Series)
    Includes index.
    ISBN 978-1-61703-785-6 (cloth : alk. paper) — ISBN 978-1-61703-786-3 (ebook) 1. Dubus, Andre, 1959– 2. Authors, American—20th century—Interviews. 3. Fiction—Authorship. I. Edenfield, Olivia Carr, editor of compilation. II. Title.
    PS3554.U2652Z46 2013
    813'.54—dc23
    [B]   2013003147

British Library Cataloging-in-Publication Data available

Works by Andre Dubus

Collections of Short Fiction and Novellas

Separate Flights. Boston: David R. Godine, 1975.
Adultery and Other Choices. Boston: David R. Godine, 1977.
Finding a Girl in America: A Novella and Seven Short Stories. Boston: David R. Godine, 1980.
The Times Are Never So Bad: A Novella and Eight Short Stories. Boston: David R. Godine, 1983.
We Don't Live Here Anymore: The Novellas of Andre Dubus. New York: Crown Publishers, 1984.
The Last Worthless Evening: Four Novellas and Two Stories. Boston: David R. Godine, 1986.
Selected Stories. Boston: David R. Godine, 1988.
Dancing After Hours. New York: Alfred A. Knopf, 1996.
In the Bedroom. New York: Vintage Contemporaries, 2002.

Novella

Land Where My Fathers Died. Winston-Salem: Palaemon Press, 1985 (limited edition).

Novels

The Lieutenant. New York: Dial Press, 1967.
Voices from the Moon. Boston: David R. Godine, 1984.

Collections of Essays

Broken Vessels. Boston: David R. Godine, 1992.
Meditations from a Movable Chair. New York: Alfred A. Knopf, 1998.

Edited Work

Into the Silence. Cambridge: Green Street Press, 1988.

Contents

Introduction

Andre Dubus was a generous man. He enjoyed people and good conversation. He was warm, gregarious, engaging, and smart. He liked to tell stories and to talk about the art of telling stories. He liked to write and to talk about the art of writing. For these reasons and because people—students, journalists, other short-fiction writers—found him approachable, he gave forty-two interviews (thirty-six print and six audio) over the course of his writing career, half of which are collected here. Andre was easy to be with, perhaps because he showed an interest in the person before him. He was curious about where folks came from, how they saw things, what their angle was. And he was happy to tell you his opinion on his various characters or his politics or his taste in music. He was happy to share, happy to help along the various and many people who came to visit and to write down what he had to say about the American short story and his place in that great genre. Andre Dubus was a generous man.

Generosity of spirit, a willingness to help, is what led him to stop along I-93 in Wilmington, Massachusetts, just after midnight on July 23, 1986, to aid Luz Santiago and her brother, Luis, who were stranded after running over an abandoned motorcycle. While assisting the two across the highway, he and Luis were struck by a car driven by Nancy Anthony, a young woman from Woburn, who he was eventually able to forgive through prayer, as he would later tell Stacey Chase ("Interview"). In early January of 1997, Dubus spoke frankly of this night in an interview with Chase, reporter for the *Lowell Sun*. As he recalled the events, he explained that he had no memory of the impact and he expected that he never would. Luis had died instantly while Dubus would go on to suffer great pain and a long rehabilitation as he learned to navigate without the use of his legs. The impact of the car going fifty-eight miles per hour crushed his right leg and necessitated the removal of his left leg above the knee. He would never be able to support his weight and so could not master the prosthetic he hoped for.

When Chase met with him only five months after the accident, however, his inability to walk was not what was worrying him. What had him in a state of despair that led to tears was his struggle to write. He shared with Chase that there was "no energy" and that he could not "get into it." As he explained, "They say I am just concentrating on getting well and have no energy left to write. I don't know why I can't write." The fact that he could not was a heavyweight, and when the tears came, he admitted, "I get the blues a lot. . . . I am crying because I can't walk and I can't work" ("Accident"). When the two would meet again two years later, Dubus was still suffering, only this pain was from a separate tragedy, related, of course, but new. His wife Peggy Rambach had left and taken their two young daughters, Madeline and Cadence, with her. Dubus was learning to live alone in the wake of learning to live with daily pain and a frustrating disability that robbed him of his physical energy and temporarily stole his ability to write the fiction that he and his readers depended upon. "If it weren't for prayer, I'd be fucked," Dubus would tell Chase. "When you grow up with the Passion of Christ as an example, I mean, you know at least there's a membership of suffering. And you get the focus that you're not the only one in the world who's got things rough" ("Interview") Stacey would write that while Dubus was clearly grieving over this loss of his family, the man she spoke with that day compared to the man she had met two years prior was a very different person, as "this time, the thick-chested, salty-tongued Southerner and his hard luck looked to be an even match." Dubus had recently received the $5,000 Jean Stein Award and a $310,000 MacArthur Foundation Fellowship, news which, he admitted, left him with "insomnia and loose bowels for about three days" but feeling "incredibly blessed" ("Interview"). These blessings continued to come with the publication of essays and stories as Dubus found his writing voice again.

It is impossible to pick up a recent article regarding Dubus's fiction and not find a lengthy reference to the accident. Scholars and interviewers both remark on the significance that night had on Andre's life. However, prior to that January 1986 evening, Dubus had already published eight books—four collections of short stories, two novels, a collection of novellas, and a novella published separately. While formidable, the experience would come in the latter half of his career. By the time he was injured, Dubus was already recognized as one of the masters of the genre and was generally compared to other contemporary giants in the field such as Raymond Carver. Vivian Gornick linked Dubus to Carver and Richard Ford, tracing each back to Ernest Hemingway: "Just behind the leanness and coolness of the prose lies the open—but doomed—expectation that romantic love saves. Settings vary and regional idioms intrude, but almost always it is men and women together that is being written about" (1). Gornick concludes that Dubus is the "the most complex and least well known," but "the most articulate in the matter of men and women together" (32). Likewise, other critics and reviewers found connections to Hemingway, in both style and spirit, in the emphasis on ritual and redemption, in the importance of the sacrament and the everlasting peace that comes from grace. Andre, too, would acknowledge his debt to Hemingway in many of the interviews that he gave over the years. He discussed Hemingway's objectivity and clarity of voice, his descriptive language. And he remarked as well on the importance of ritual in writing, another similarity to Hemingway.

In May of 1970, in fact, Dubus opened his conversation with Corinne Peace by telling her, "Discipline is the thing." He referenced Hemingway twice, stating that he was his favorite writer. Asked to give "three rules for writers," Andre started with the importance of ritual, of writing every day. In May of 1982, meeting with Harvard students Christopher Caldwell and Adam Cherson, Dubus would again bring up Hemingway and all that he had learned from him: "People don't give Hemingway enough credit for what he went through, what he taught us. . . . I like what Anthony Burgess said in a little biography commissioned by Scribner's. Everybody said Hemingway was ill tempered as a young man, but people should remember that he was walking around Paris fighting nineteenth-century prose, trying to think of one perfect sentence." This way of writing would mark Dubus's craftsmanship as well. He would tell Dev Hathaway in the spring of 1983 that he was learning to write slowly, to take on one sentence at a time, revising each step of the way to ensure the perfect sensory experience. Writing "Anna" changed the process for him, as he would tell Hathaway. "Now until that time, my method of writing was to try for a thousand words a day; whether the pages were there or not I wrote them. Right? And I averaged something like five drafts per story, sometimes six. . . . But for 'Anna' I couldn't write 'horizontally,' I couldn't write moving ahead, because I didn't know who she was. So I told myself write vertically. Do not leave a sentence until you know how she feels. And I went like that at that pace, and then I knew her." From that moment on, his rituals changed as he wrote more carefully, more slowly, while still averaging his typical three stories a year. Andre would record his word count at the end of every writing session, thanking God for each word there, every day, "Thank you." He learned from Hemingway as well to stop in mid-sentence, to quit writing in mid-thought, almost, so that, returning the next day, he could pick up right where he had left off, warming up with the familiar.

He would also share details from his childhood with his many interviewers. With Caldwell and Cherson, he was frank about his own perceived inadequacies as an undergraduate: "I hadn't read a whole lot by the time I got out of high school. I thought Hemingway was a movie director. . . . I showed a story to a teacher who said, 'Your Negro dialect needs work; why don't you read Faulkner?' I said, 'Who's that?,'" a story he also shared with Hathaway. But Andre was a quick study and had early on distinguished himself as a gifted writer. When his father met with his teachers in the spring of 1954 as he was preparing to graduate from the Christian Brothers School in Lafayette, Louisiana, Andre Sr. learned that his namesake had talent for writing. In a conversation with his son, though the two were often strained with one another, he would tell his boy that he thought there was a living to be made there. Andre later shared with Bonetti that, hearing this, his heart "leaped," but he would not feel free to pursue writing full time until he received news of his father's death in 1963. In the interim, he would graduate in 1958 from McNeese State College in Lake Charles, Louisiana, and marry Patricia Lowe in February of that same year; he would father four children, Suzanne in 1958, Andre III in 1959, Jeb in 1960, and Nicole in 1963; he would join the U.S. Marine Corps, where he would earn the rank of captain before his resignation at the news of his father's death. He would tell Bonetti of his and Pat's decision to leave behind their life in the military. As Dubus told it:

> I had a wonderful first wife. We saw what was happening to the barracks and over a beer in Bellingham, Washington, we decided that's it, we're getting out. And it's "we" in the military. It is "we." She was in the Marine Corps too. Our marriage didn't make it because we were nineteen and twenty-one in the fifties. She was pregnant; we got married. You will notice if you look closely that the ex-wives in my stories are wonderful because they're all based on her. Because we had a splendid divorce. And she was a strong woman. I mean, she had a child in '58 at nineteen, '59, '60, and then '63. She had four kids, and that was it. And well what can I do now? I don't know. And she said, call Mark Costello. And I said ah, no, I'm not going to teach. And I didn't know what teaching was like, I thought you become dry and abstract; I had an image of a tweed coat. I called him. He said, I'll get you to Iowa because I had a story in the *Salon Review* by then. And about a year later in Iowa I'm walking down this street, and I said, yes, your father set you free. You would not have left the Marine Corps with four children to go to graduate school if your father were alive.

Dubus joined the M.F.A. program at the University of Iowa in 1964, becoming part of the prestigious fiction workshop. It was at Iowa that he would meet his longtime mentor Richard Yates, who served as his teacher and friend until his death in 1992. Kurt Vonnegut was his neighbor on Brown Street, and Andre III told me, when we talked in Newburyport in July of 2011, of Vonnegut coming down the hill to their house each weekday afternoon to watch *Batman*. In March of 1966, while he was still a graduate student, Dubus sold his novel *The Lieutenant* to Dial Press. He told reporter Phyllis Fleming of the *Cedar Rapid Gazette* that the celebration party went on until 4:00 a.m. As it turned out, Dubus was "the first student to ever write and sell a book while still a workshop student" (8B). After graduation Dubus accepted a teaching job at Bradford College with the starting salary of $17,200. As he would explain to Mimi Read, he was comfortable in New England, at home with the people. Read would conclude, "In short, Dubus doesn't write about the breakdown of regional affiliation or the mutterings of a land with a complex, dark history and an uncertain future; instead, he writes about what happens afterward, when the man leaves the South and doesn't look back as he struggles to create his own unit of warmth and meaning, his own family." When Read met with Dubus on a rainy day in July of 1984, he was living happily with third wife, writer Peggy Rambach, and their two-year-old daughter, Cadence. By 1984, he had published seven books, four of these collections of the stories that would secure his reputation. And while Read was making reference to Andre's life, she might have been summing up his characters in his many short stories dealing with the failure of marriage and the breakdown of the family, themes he discusses in many interviews over the years. Before the accident he felt that he was in his last marriage, as he told Robert Dahlin in July of 1984. He believed that he and Peggy had a relationship that was balanced and equal. He went on that next spring to tell Jesse Kornbluth that when he and Peggy met at Godine, "I was forty-one, she was nineteen," but she "didn't need to be entertained." They married in December of 1979. When Kornbluth interviewed him, Dubus was teaching classes at Bradford, writing good stories, and in love with his wife and new baby daughter.

Dahlin described Andre Dubus as "happily loquacious," a man "more at ease with talking than with listening." In his interview with Andre, Kornbluth focused on Dubus's physical presence: "In his book-jacket pictures, Dubus is a kindly, round-faced man with a salt-and-pepper beard. In person, he's something else. He wears a large gold cross around his neck, a maroon corduroy shirt, blue jeans with a wide leather belt, and cowboy boots. His manner is hearty in the extreme, as is his candor." He was at ease with his company, though sometimes interviewers detected an underlying shyness beneath the talkative exterior. He was an attentive host, as each interview suggests, and a good many of the conversations take place in Dubus's home over food that Dubus served.

When Dubus wrote, he wrote longhand into notebooks, usually hard-covered notebooks with stitched bindings. He double-spaced, giving himself room to edit. He counted his words and recorded the amounts in the margins and tallied them at the end of each day's work. He would tape record each draft, he told Hathaway:

> Yes. And I count that in my log book that I keep about daily exercise and how many words I write. . . . [The taping] counts as much as another draft. I think the difference is not so much how the story sounds, but that after reading the whole thing over every day the way I do, you've gotten to where you've read it a hundred times and you don't really *read* it anymore. Then when you read it aloud you're doing something physical, which makes you concentrate. I'm sure that's why I tend to cry when I read aloud. The body's involved now, and words start to jump at you that you've been looking through.

He would maintain this attention to detail throughout his writing career, in his essays and in his short fiction that followed the long hiatus of recovery and rediscovery. Dubus would begin writing short stories again by focusing on a character much like himself who has to learn to navigate in a world broken by physical and spiritual disability. When "The Colonel's Wife" appeared in the February 1993 issue of *Playboy*, it was clear that Dubus was back to the genre for which he was renowned. In the meantime he had published *Blessings* in 1987; *Selected Stories* in 1988; and his first collection of essays, *Broken Vessels*, in 1991, a runner-up for the Pulitzer Prize. "The Colonel's Wife" would become a part of the critically acclaimed short-story cycle *Dancing After Hours*, published by Knopf in 1996. Dubus had signed with Knopf due to mounting medical bills. The larger house could pay more than David R. Godine, the small Boston press that had been Dubus's home since 1977, when they had published his first collection of stories, *Adultery and Other Choices*. In 1998, Knopf would also publish Dubus's second collection of essays, *Meditations from a Moveable Chair*. The next year, he would die at his home in Haverhill from heart failure.

Shortly before he died, he split the one beer in his refrigerator with his son Andre III and watched the end of the De La Hoya fight on television. Andre III had walked away from his sister Suzanne's house that evening without finishing the remodeling work he had intended to complete before leaving town. Andre told me that he had felt drawn to go over to his father's house in ways he cannot explain. His pop had called him on his cell phone, over and over, five times, Andre would tell me later, urging him to come see the fight, that he would regret it if he did not. Andre emphasized this word, *regret*, and this is what made him leave mortar in the bucket, tools on the floor, what made him drive to his father's house to split that last beer and watch the fight. He was catching a plane the next day to kick off the book tour for his novel *House of Sand and Fog*. He needed to be at home with his family, he told me. He needed to pack, to sleep, to have finished the work for his sister. But he sat there with his father.

Having dinner with Andre III and his family in July 2011, I listened to Andre talk about cellular connection, about our all having come from the same genes—all the way back—and how our cells were all connected because of that. That cellular connection makes us bound by energy, bound by the protons that give to us a collective consciousness that we were not made to understand, but hopefully recognize. This energy, this cellular understanding was what pushed Andre to go to his father that night.

In the interviews following the two with Stacey Chase, the accident is typically highlighted. Even the one Amy Schildhouse conducted in June of 1986 is edited to open with descriptions of the accident: "Andre Dubus ended up on the trunk of the woman's car; his right hip fractured, a broken bone in his right hand, broken ribs, two compressed fractures of the vertebrae, a compound fracture of the femur in his right leg, a compound fracture of the tibia in the same leg, a gaping hole in his left thigh, and his left tibia nearly decimated. The force of the impact tore off his cowboy boots, and a quarter that was in his right pants pocket was bent neatly in half." From the moment Nancy Anthony's car hit Dubus, he would be forever thought of in reference to his injury.

Schildhouse's conversation takes place at the Indiana University Writers' Conference late one afternoon. The interview is a recording of Dubus's mannerisms, his method of running a workshop, his energy, his good humor and easy manner with the participants. They "grow accustomed to Dubus's method," she writes. "He heaps anecdote upon story, bandies about names . . . and quotes from countless memorized stories—all the while interrupting his patter to tell more stories of his own." At the end of the first night, Dubus goes out for Mexican food and margaritas with the group. The last image she has of him, he is walking towards a cab, where he laughingly engages the driver before the two shake hands, gets into the front seat, and drives away.

Tim McCarthy sees Andre's recovery after the accident as a testament to his will to write. While his daily rituals had changed, as he told McCarthy, the struggling to write was still part of his day. What had also remained constant in his life was his deep Catholic faith. Dubus took communion daily. He told McCarthy that in the spring of 1998, he swooned when "the Eucharistic minister anointed him at home. He would lie there on the bed with his eyes closed, unable to move. And sometimes he had visions of Mary. . . . Another time she hugged him and he felt really loved. All the visions were tactile, sensual," a descriptor that McCarthy links to Dubus's fiction, the "prose he shapes it with." Susan Larson called Dubus's Catholicism the "enduring legacy of his Louisiana upbringing." Dubus would tell Lori Ambacher in March of 1993, when asked if he was comfortable calling himself a Catholic writer, "I can only see the world as a Catholic." Dubus gave his final interview the day before he died. On the afternoon of February 23, 1999, Greg Garrett met with Andre to discuss his fiction. Things quickly got around to his faith: "I've been a Catholic all my life. That's the way I see the world. We all share in the universals, but my worldview is shaped by my being a Catholic." Faith shaped his worldview and gave him the courage to write, to come back from the blues.

When I met with Andre Dubus in February 1993, I was most taken with how determined he was that I stay safe while I was visiting. There was a lot of snow on the road, and it had been years since I had driven in it. I had to call him from my hotel room after we had dinner to let him know I had made the drive safely. This connection to others is present throughout the twenty-one interviews collected here. Of the twenty-one, twenty are print interviews. The one audio interview included is a complete transcription of the conversation Andre had with Kay Bonetti in April 1984. It appears here in its entirety for the first time. There are valuable interviews, both print and audio, that Dubus gave that for various reasons are not collected here. Some already appear in a variety of resources. Some permissions were simply not negotiable. The interviews that follow span Dubus's career and give a wide range of perspectives on his life and art and remind us constantly of the joy he found in a good story told. I am indebted to the Dubus family and to my own for their love and support.

OCE

Works Cited

Ambacher, Lori. "A Conversation with Andre Dubus." *Image* 3 (Spring 1993): 40–55. Reprinted in *Leap of the Heart: Andre Dubus Talking*. Ed. Ross Gresham. New Orleans: Xavier Review Press, 2003. 215–34.

Bonetti, Kay. "Andre Dubus Interview with Kay Bonetti." American Audio Prose Library. April 1984. Printed in *A Leap of the Heart: Andre Dubus Talking*. Ed. Ross Gresham. New Orleans: Xavier Review Press, 2003. 51–59.

Caldwell, Christopher, and Adam Cherson. "A Conversation with Andre Dubus." *Harvard Advocate* 115.3 (1982): 7–8, 32.

Chase, Stacey. "Accident Robbed Author of Desire to Write." *[Lowell, Mass.] Sunday Sun* 11 January 1987: A2. Reprinted in *Leap of the Heart: Andre Dubus Talking*. Ed. Ross Gresham. New Orleans: Xavier Review Press, 2003. 148–53.

Chase, Stacey. "An Interview with Andre Dubus." *Puerto Del Sol* 25 (Summer 1990): 108–19. Reprinted in *Leap of the Heart: Andre Dubus Talking*. Ed. Ross Gresham. New Orleans: Xavier Review Press, 2003. 154–65.

Dahlin, Robert. "Interview with Andre Dubus." *Publisher's Weekly* 12 October 1984: 56–57. Reprinted in *Leap of the Heart: Andre Dubus Talking*. Ed. Ross Gresham. New Orleans: Xavier Review Press: 2003. 72–78.

Fleming, Phyllis. "Andre Dubus Knows What Happiness Is, He Sold Book." *Cedar Rapids Gazette* 8 May 1966: 8B.

Garrett, Greg. "Interview with Andre Dubus." *Art and Soul* 23 February 1999. Reprinted in *Leap of the Heart: Andre Dubus Talking*. Ed. Ross Gresham. New Orleans: Xavier Review Press, 2003. 276–77.

Gornick, Vivian. "Tenderhearted Men: Lonesome, Sad, and Blue." *New York Times Book Review*, 16 September 1990, 1.

Hathaway, Dev. "A Conversation with Andre Dubus." *Black Warrior Review* 9.2 (Spring 1983): 86–103. Reprinted in *Leap of the Heart: Andre Dubus Talking*. Ed. Ross Gresham. New Orleans: Xavier Review Press, 2003. 27–50.

Kornbluth, Jesse. "The Outrageous Andre Dubus." *Horizon* 28 (April 1985): 16–20.

Larson, Susan. "Profile in Courage." *Times-Picayune* 28 July 1991. Reprinted in *Leap of the Heart: Andre Dubus Talking*. Ed. Ross Gresham. New Orleans: Xavier Review Press: 2003. 200–202.

McCarthy, Tim. "Andre Dubus's Knuckler Keeps Him in the Game." *National Catholic Reporter* 13 July 1990: 1, 16–17. Reprinted in *Leap of the Heart: Andre Dubus Talking*. Ed. Ross Gresham. New Orleans: Xavier Review Press, 189–99.

Peace, Corinne. "Former Resident Is Writer and Teacher in Massachusetts." *[Lake Charles] American Press* 30 May 1970: 8. Reprinted in *Leap of the Heart: Andre Dubus Talking*. Ed. Ross Gresham. New Orleans: Xavier Review Press, 2003. 6–7.

Read, Mimi. "A Redneck Intellectual at Home in New England." *Dixie Roto Magazine* (of the *Sunday Times-Picayune*) 15 July 1986: 30–31. Reprinted in *Leap of the Heart: Andre Dubus Talking*. Ed. Ross Gresham. New Orleans: Xavier Review Press, 2003. 68–71.

Schildhouse, Amy. "Our Dinners with Andre." *Indiana Review* 10.1/2 (1987): 9–20.

Chronology

1936   Born on 11 August to Andre Jules (16 November 1904) and Katherine (Burke) Dubus (2 January 1903) in Lake Charles, Louisiana. Welcomed by two older sisters, Kathryn Claire (3 November 1930) and Elizabeth Nell (26 October 1933).

1944   Enters the Christian Brothers School, Lafayette, Louisiana.

1954   Graduates from the Christian Brothers High School.

1958   Earns B.A in English and journalism from McNeese State College, Lake Charles, Louisiana. Marries Patricia Lowe, 22 February. Commissioned as lieutenant in U.S. Marine Corps. Birth of daughter Catherine Suzanne Dubus, 16 August.

1959   Birth of son Andre Jules Dubus, III, 11 September.

1960   Birth of son John Ethan Burke Dubus (Jeb), 29 November.

1963   Birth of daughter Nicole Mignon Dubus, 3 February. Death of Andre Sr. Publishes "The Intruder" in *Sewanee Review*. Resigns commission from U.S. Marine Corps as captain.

1964   Enters M.F.A. program in fiction, University of Iowa, Iowa City, Iowa.

1965   Completes M.F.A., University of Iowa. Accepts lecturer position in English, Nicholls State College, Thibodaux, Louisiana.

1966   Accepts teaching position with the English Department at Bradford College, Bradford, Massachusetts.

1967   Publishes *The Lieutenant* with Dial Press.

1970   Divorces Patricia Lowe Dubus. Publishes "If They Knew Yvonne," selected for *Best American Short Stories, 1970*.

1975   Publishes *Separate Flights*. Receives *Boston Globe* Laurence L. Winship Award. Marries Tommie Gale Cotter in June.

1976   "Cadence" selected for *Best American Short Stories, 1976*. Receives Guggenheim Fellowship.

1977   Publishes *Adultery and Other Choices*. Receives a Guggenheim Fellowship.

1978   Receives National Endowment for the Arts grant. Divorced from Tommie Gale Cotter in June. "The Fat Girl" selected for annual Pushcart anthology.

1979   "The Pitcher" selected for *Prize Stories: The O. Henry Awards*. Marries Peggy Rambach, 16 December.

1980   Death of Catherine (Burke) Dubus Watkins, age seventy-eight. "The Winter Father" selected for *Best American Short Stories, 1981*. Publishes *Finding a Girl in America: A Novella and Seven Short Stories*.

1982   Birth of daughter Cadence Yvonne Rambach Dubus, 11 June.

1983   Publishes *The Times Are Never So Bad: A Novella and Eight Short Stories*.

1984   Retires from Bradford College. Publishes *Voices from the Moon*. Publishes *We Don't Live Here Anymore: The Novellas of Andre Dubus*.

1985   Receives National Endowment for the Arts Literature Fellowship. Publishes limited edition of *Land Where My Fathers Died*.

1986   23 July, on his way home from Boston's Combat Zone where he was conducting research for a story, struck by car driven by Nancy Anthony of Woburn, Massachusetts, on Route 93 in Wilmington, Massachusetts, after stopping to assist an accident victim. Lost his left leg above the knee with extensive surgeries on the right leg to follow. Did not regain ability to walk. Reprints *The Lieutenant* as paperback with Green Street Press. Receives Guggenheim Fellowship. Publishes *The Last Worthless Evening: Four Novellas and Two Short Stories*.

1987   Birth of daughter Madeleine Elise Rambach Dubus, 10 January. Wife Peggy Rambach moves out of the couple's Haverhill home with daughters Cadence (six) and Madeline (two) in October. Publishes *Blessings*.

1988   Suffers a mild heart attack, 30 October. Receives the Jean Stein Award from the American Academy and Institute of Arts and Letters and the MacArthur Foundation Fellowship. Publishes *Selected Stories*. Publishes an edited collection of stories, *Into the Silence*.

1991   Receives the PEN/Malamud Award for Excellence in Short Fiction.

1992   Publishes *Broken Vessels*, runner up for Pulitzer Prize.

1996   Winner of the Rea Award for the Short Story. Publishes *Dancing After Hours* with Alfred A. Knopf.

1998   Publishes *Meditations from a Moveable Chair*.

1999   24 February, dies of heart failure at home in Haverhill. Buried 13 April 1999, Fenway Park's Opening Day. Sons Andre III and Jeb dig the grave. The Red Sox beat the Chicago White Sox 6-0.

2001   Todd Field adapts "Killings" into the film *In the Bedroom*, nominated for five Academy Awards, including Best Picture. Posthumously publishes *In the Bedroom*, a selection of previously published stories, including "Killings."

2004   Screenwriter Larry Gross adapts "We Don't Live Here Anymore" and "Adultery" into the film *We Don't Live Here Anymore*.

Conversations with Andre Dubus

Former Resident Is Writer and Teacher in Massachusetts

Corinne Peace / 1970

From *[Lake Charles] American Press* 30 May 1970: 8. Reprinted in *Leap of the Heart: Andre Dubus Talking*. Ed. Ross Gresham. New Orleans: Xavier Review Press, 2003. 6–7. Reprinted with the permission of the *American Press*.

"Talent is cheap. Discipline is the thing."

This is the appraisal of the writing game by Andre Dubus, author of the novel, *The Lieutenant*, and a McNeese State College graduate, class of 1958. He is the son of Mrs. H. Moss Watkins of Lake Charles.

Dubus has had a number of short stories published also. He has sold his third story to the *New Yorker* which will be published this summer.

During a visit to Lake Charles last week, Dubus said he was particularly pleased that one of his short stories, "If They Knew Yvonne," has been selected for inclusion in the anthology, *Best American Short Stories, 1970*, edited by Martha Foley and published by Houghton, Mifflin of Boston.

The story first appeared in the *North American Review* published by the University of Northern Iowa.

Dubus, in talking about the necessity of a writer disciplining himself, said, "I write five pages every morning in longhand five days a week. I throw most of it away, but I keep writing. It's my life."

He teaches modern fiction and creative writing at Bradford Junior College in Bradford, Massachusetts.

He said that his classes are in the afternoon, so after he has done his writing in the morning, he goes out and runs or jogs for about five miles. "This relaxes me and makes me forget writing so I'll go to class with a fresh mind," he said.

Asked what makes a writer, Dubus replied, "The writer is the product of some disorder and pain. You know Hemingway said that a writer is forged in injustice the way a sword is forged in fire."

Hemingway is his favorite author. Next come Chekhov and John Cheever. He feels that Cheever has written some of the best short stories in the world and particularly likes Cheever's "The Enormous Radio." One of his favorite Faulkner stories is "Golden Land," which deals with Hollywood and the "American dream."

"One of the limitations of my particular talent," Dubus said, "is that I work on incidents. I see something happen to a friend or to myself, or notice a news item in the paper, and I see it as a story. I sit on the thought for about a year and then later decide to try writing something."

He continued, "My book, *The Lieutenant*, is based on a particular incident. If I were writing it now, it would be about half as long. I've learned additional craft since then and I've learned a lot of it from teaching. I wrote the novel in Iowa."

Dubus received his B.A. degree in English from McNeese, and from 1964 to 1966, he attended the University of Iowa Writers' Workshop where he received his master in fine arts degree in creative writing.

He served in the U.S. Marine Corps from 1958 to 1964, during which he was stationed in California two years, served on board the carrier *Ranger* in the Western Pacific, and was stationed at Puget Sound. He came out of the corps as a captain.

Movie star Burt Lancaster's Norland Productions has an option on *The Lieutenant* which expires November 3, Dubus said. He met with Lancaster and was asked to do the screenplay.

Asked if he ever knew how any of his stories were going to end, he replied, "I've never heard of a writer who would say how it will end. As author Mary McCarthy said, everyone of her stories was a 'discovery.' It would be like telling a rose how to grow; all you can do is plant it."

Dubus said, "There's a time when a character 'takes over' your story. Like in *The Lieutenant*, there was one of my characters that I wanted to win, but two-thirds through the book, I realized he was not going to win. If a character can't end the story for you, there's something wrong."

Asked to give three rules for writers, he gave this bit of advice: First, work every day on a schedule like everyone else. Secondly, read as much as possible what other writers are doing and learn from that.

Thirdly, he advised, "Come to terms with the knowledge that no one cares whether you write or not and that no one will publish or buy it, and go right ahead and write anyway!"

Conversation with Andre Dubus

Christopher Caldwell and Adam Cherson / 1982

Harvard Advocate 115.3 (1982): 7–8, 32. Reprinted with the permission of Adam Cherson.

Andre Dubus was born in Lake Charles, Louisiana, in 1936. After graduating from McNeese State University, he served in the United States Marine Corps. He did graduate work at the University of Iowa Writers' Workshop, where he later held an assistantship. He now teaches literature and creative writing at Bradford College in Bradford, Massachusetts, where he lives with his family. Mr. Dubus is the author of three collections of short stories, *Separate Flights*, 1975; *Adultery and Other Choices*, 1978; *Finding A Girl in America*, 1980 (all published by David R. Godine, Boston); and one novel, *The Lieutenant*, 1967, Dial Press.

ADVOCATE: How did you start writing?
DUBUS: I used to tell myself stories; I'd always be making up stories and telling them to myself. I remember we had to write one story every year at my grade school, the Christian Brothers School. And I used to look forward to that.

After graduating from high school, I didn't know what I wanted to be. The day after I graduated, my father went to my teachers and asked, "What's he good for?" That's the way he said it. And he came back and told me the teachers said I was good at writing and English. I said, "Good, yeah." He said it was a good living and my heart leaped. I realized years later that that's what I had always wanted to do, but that I had wanted him to say it was all right. So I started writing right away, very seriously. I majored in journalism my first year, and, after that, because I was learning to write backwards, I switched to English and started sending out stories.

ADVOCATE: What made you decide to join the Marines after college?
DUBUS: When I went into the service, there was a draft. It was peacetime

and everybody went, that was all. People who went to college usually wound up in an officers' program. I chose the Marines for one practical reason and one psychological one. The practical one was that I was in the Army ROTC—you had to be—and the other people who were graduating were not very impressive. I thought, "Shit! I'm not learning anything, so I'll join an outfit that will teach me." I also wanted to prove myself a man to my father, because I knew that he loved me but thought I was a wimp. And he was right.

ADVOCATE: Did you have an eye for gathering material for your fiction?
DUBUS: No. Just to get out of Louisiana. To become a man among men. Which is a problem you don't have now, but back then if you weren't an athlete, it was hard to get a date with a good-looking girl. If you weighed 105 pounds, it was hard. So I tried athletics and wasn't any good at that. Everything was hard: making friends, finding a girl, all that shit. A lot of English majors joined the Marine Corps; Philip Caputo himself said he joined to show his old man he was a man. The nice thing is, they deliver, too.

ADVOCATE: What writers influenced you early on?
DUBUS: I hadn't read a whole lot by the time I got out of high school. I thought Hemingway was a movie director. I saw an advertisement in the paper that Hemingway's "The Killers" was coming to the theater. I didn't know he was a writer until his crash in the fifties. When I was in college, I showed a story to a teacher who said, "Your Negro dialect needs work; why don't you read Faulkner?" I said, "Who's that?"
I read a lot in high school. *The Three Musketeers*, stuff like that, John R. Tunis . . . he still gets mentioned a lot. He wrote baseball and football novels, and they were great. The first serious book I read was in fifth grade: *Asphalt Jungle*, I guess. Is that the one which ends with "Is this the end of Rico?" James Cagney was in the movie. Later, I read *To Have and Have Not* when I found out Hemingway wasn't a director.

ADVOCATE: What do you like to read now?
DUBUS: Realistic fiction, the shorter the better. In the nineteenth century: Chekhov, Zola. Tolstoy amuses and pisses me off more than he excites me, but I certainly respect him. For all his problems, he's a god. I still think the best thing he wrote was "The Cossacks," when he was young, didn't preach.
Under the Volcano. I was afraid to read it, because I'd been writing to Anton Myrer, who's a very popular writer now. I read a good war novel of

his called *The Big War* and started sending him letters while I was in the Marine Corps. I didn't let him know I was writing; I thought it would be nice for him to think a professional Marine was reading his stuff. But he caught on. He said, "I think you're writing; send me something." He's the one who suggested *Under the Volcano*; he was a friend of Malcolm Lowry's.

ADVOCATE: Poor Lowry.

DUBUS: Actually, I don't feel sorry for anybody who destroys himself. I guess I should, and it feels like hubris to say that, but I don't. Myrer had written me a lot of letters about tarot, and Marlowe's *Dr. Faustus*, and all the other things you "had to read" before reading this book. I read it twice and was scared to teach it, so I got Lowry's thirty-five-page letter to Jonathan Cape explaining every symbol. It's great as a letter between writer and editor, but it ruined the book for my class.

I don't like Joyce. (Richard) Yates and I belong to the "We Hate James Joyce" Fan Club. Dick said to me in a restaurant one day, "I think around the year 2000, everyone's going to catch on to Joyce, and all these assholes making a living off of him are going to be out of work. You know, Joyce said he could have written two conventional novels a year, but he wouldn't . . . while he was sitting in Trieste, living off rich people's money, writing that fucking unreadable *Finnegans Wake*."

I said, "*Portrait of the Artist* is a conventional novel . . . Remember, Dick, you had an interview in *Ploughshares* in which you said that two traps of the autobiographer are self-pity and self-aggrandizement? Well, what do you say about a novel that starts with a kid wetting his bed and ends with him becoming the conscience of the universe?"

I hate that. The last time I was teaching *Dubliners*, I threw it up in the air and said, "I'll never teach this book again." Chekhov should have written it. It's an arrogant book. It's an easy book. I admire the craft of all the stories, but—come on—Joyce only likes two characters: the little boys of the first two stories, because they're Jimmy Joyce. Every other character Joyce is removed from. There's no soul in that work. Joyce hates the Irish; he wrote a letter to his brother saying, "I'll get them back for what they did to me." What an egotistical prick.

ADVOCATE: How do you feel about Latin American literature, Márquez, for instance?

DUBUS: I haven't read much Márquez. I can't read Márquez. A friend of mine once said that the trouble with the Latin Americans is that they keep looking at Europe, when there should be a James Jones on every street corner of that continent. Somebody gave me *Autumn of the Patriarch*, and I had read halfway through it when I realized I didn't have to read the rest. There aren't any people in there and I know what the politics are by now. It's a nice surrealistic view, but . . . Look, I admire him. I'm just going on personal taste and that's not the same as having respect.

ADVOCATE: What is it about surrealism that annoys you?
DUBUS: I guess I'm a sentimental old guy. If I never get involved with the characters, then I can't remember the book.

Márquez had a great article, by the way, in the *New York Times* last summer, called "Meeting Hemingway." He mentioned the stop in mid-sentence, which I think is the best advice ever given a writer. Always stop while you still have something left to write; that way you never have to face a blank page. I wonder what it cost Hemingway to find that out.

People don't give Hemingway enough credit for what he went through, what he taught us. They see the asshole, and that was there, but I like what Anthony Burgess said in a little biography commissioned by Scribner's. Everybody said Hemingway was ill tempered as a young man, but people should remember that he was walking around Paris fighting nineteenth-century prose, trying to think of one perfect sentence. That can make a man ill tempered.

It occurred to me that the subtle influences of money might have shunted him away from his real strengths. Some of the later stuff gives me this impression. He would have been so good if he'd written more of those short stories and novellas and travel books. Then, of course, how do you turn to Mary in the 1940s and say, "My real form is the five-pager; we may have to give up some houses"?

ADVOCATE: Let's talk about your work. First of all, why do you write?
DUBUS: I write for myself. I usually write about something I'm curious about.

ADVOCATE: Then why publish?
DUBUS: For the completion of the act—the real pleasure. When I was trying to get a publisher, I used to say, "All I want is to see those books on my

shelf." That's still the pleasure. I never feel like a story is finished until I see it in print.

ADVOCATE: So you don't see any political purpose in your work?
DUBUS: No. I'm very glum about that. I don't think art affects anybody. The *Iliad* said war was hell, and what did that do? Do you think books affect people? Books affect people who want to be affected by books. *Go Down, Moses* convinced me the ownership of private property was evil. So what? I don't own any anyway. Art is good but it doesn't have an effect on the commonweal or on history. That is because it appeals to the part of us that is universal and human, the part that is always perplexed. Nobody who runs for office in this country reads anything. They're all dolts. I quit voting in 1980. I'm old enough to realize I am smarter than some people.

ADVOCATE: Do you feel comfortable in an academic atmosphere?
DUBUS: I really get snowed by it. We had a dean here who was from Yale, a big literary scholar. I was walking him home one day, trying to be friendly, and I said, "You know, I've just discovered Zola from reading an interview with Robert Penn Warren, and I love Zola." He said, "Oh, well, some people like that naturalism." And I thought to myself, "Funny, I never feel a concept when I read him. I don't feel naturalistic determinism any more than if I'm reading some other writer." I think people make that shit up.

ADVOCATE: Let's get back to your work. Each of your three story collections contains a novella. Is this a conscious program?
DUBUS: No, it's not conscious. What I would really like to do is write a book of three novellas because I think the novella is a wonderful form, but I can't do it because I can't plan to write a novella. I write a novella when a character won't stop.

ADVOCATE: What relationship do the stories in which the same characters appear bear to each other? Do you consider them continuations?
DUBUS: I guess not, because there was never a design. I wrote "We Don't Live Here Anymore" first. Now that there are three novellas with the same characters, I'm sorry I made one of them a teacher and one of them a writer. I don't like to be one of those who writes only about teachers and writers. I did it for pragmatic reasons. I wanted somebody whose work was so important to him that he didn't give a shit what happened, and I had the naive and elitist idea that if you want a sensitive character who is articulate, you've

got to make him a teacher or—God forbid—a lawyer, an idea I no longer hold. Both the stories in which Roy Hodges appears—"Waiting" and "The Misogamist"—were originally flashbacks in a hundred-page novella.

ADVOCATE: You've been praised for your ability to write from the perspectives of women and children in a way that few authors can. Do you find it natural to identify with women?
DUBUS: I don't find it hard. Maybe it's not accurate. It's as hard as becoming any other character except that there are certain experiences I cannot write about—childbirths and abortion have to take place offstage. Yet, Chekhov wrote about labor pains and received letters from women saying, "You're right."

ADVOCATE: Do you consider it an artistic mission to write about family dissolution, as you have in the past?
DUBUS: No. I hope I never write about marriage again. I think you write about things that bother you. In my case, things that bothered me years ago. Almost every friend of mine has been divorced, but I have no mission. I was just responding to my own questions about marriage and love and death. Wondering about the *relationship* between love and death. I reread Rollo May to get prepared for writing *Adultery*.

I'm working now on a lot of violence. I just finished a story where a woman gets a beating from her husband. The story before that is about a man who rapes and harasses his ex-wife. In the end, she shoots him. I've been gestating violence for a long time now. It comes from living in America. When I think of stories, I think of bad endings: armed robbery, shooting, hit and run.

ADVOCATE: Do you think about your future as a writer?
DUBUS: I was thinking last year that I've published three books of stories and that's enough. I could retire at seventy, I could say, "Yeah, I'm a writer."

ADVOCATE: Might you do that?
DUBUS: No.

A Conversation with Andre Dubus

Dev Hathaway / 1983

Black Warrior Review 9.2 (Spring 1983): 86–103. Reprinted in *Leap of the Heart: Andre Dubus Talking*. Ed. Ross Gresham. New Orleans: Xavier Review Press, 2003. 27–50. Reprinted with the permission of *Black Warrior Review*.

Andre Dubus is the author of a novel, *The Lieutenant,* published by the Dial Press; and three collections of short stories, *Separate Flights, Adultery and Other Choices,* and *Finding a Girl in America,* all published by David R. Godine, who will publish his fourth collection *The Times Are Never So Bad,* this spring. Dubus and his wife, Peggy Rambach, live, write, and teach in Bradford, Massachusetts.

The following conversation with *BWR* Editor Dev Hathaway was recorded in Tuscaloosa, Alabama.

D.H. Let's start with the state of the short story today. I was reading Hortense Calisher's introduction to *The Best American Short Stories 1981,* which includes your story, "The Winter Father." She says the short story is doing well, but that it's looked on as the orphan—or the chamber music—of literature; that people don't pay it much attention, it doesn't sell.

A.D. That pissed me off. When she says the chamber music and the orphan, she's talking the way Updike does when he says there's no place to send a short story—he said if the *New Yorker* turns one of mine down, I send it to *Playboy,* and after that, where? Well we know the answer—the literary quarterlies.

D.H. Where there aren't often big bucks.

A.D. Right. So Hortense Calisher's talking about *money,* as a gauge. And I think the short story is wonderfully flourishing, with many fine magazines to publish in. I find good short stories all the time. I subscribe to a half dozen quarterlies; I buy collections of stories wherever I can find them—I was just knocked out by Tobias Wolff.

D.H. *In the Garden of the North American Martyrs.*
A.D. Yes. Beautiful book. And Nancy Huddleston Packer's book from Illinois Press, *Small Moments*, I've been teaching to my students. I was reading a novel by a man I like very much, but I was getting tired of the sloppy prose. So I picked up *Southwest Review* and read "The Women Who Walk," which later got an O. Henry prize. I wrote Nancy Huddleston Parker a fan letter and sent the story to my editor, to try to get a collection from her. I told him, you know, if you really want to read good prose, read the short story.

D.H. Do you think novels naturally tend to be "sloppy"?
A.D. No, certainly not all of them, but many I read now. I was at Amherst once for a prose festival. Two of the other writers there were talking about the short story and the novel, saying that when you start working on a novel, you'd better forget about that perfect sentence—you'd never get a novel done. I don't know if that's true or not, but it seems to me that a lot of them read that way. Maybe that's why some of my favorite novels are like Kate Chopin's *The Awakening*, which is so beautiful . . . *line* after *line* after *line.*

D.H. So the sentence, the word, is all-important to you, like a poem.
A.D. Yes, like the poem. I think the short story is much closer to the poem than to the novel. Like that poem you read me earlier by Greg Pape—"My Happiness." My God, it was all there. I wish I could write a story like that. *He* should have written my story, "His Lover."

D.H. You mentioned the *New Yorker* and *Playboy.* I know about them having writers drop or change words in poems and stories.
A.D. I had a story in *Playboy* and had to drop all the brand names because of their advertisers. You don't get that from literary magazines, who are looking exclusively for excellence in the work. Anyway, at first it amused me, it didn't really matter whether the characters in this story drank a shot of Fleischmann's or just a shot of whiskey. I could change it in the book. I called them up and said are you sure you're not going to want some other changes? And they said no, no, we don't do that. Then at the very end, after the check, after the galleys, they called and said we have to drop some words, we don't have space. I said what words? So they went through—nothing that a reader

might detect; but I had worked so hard on that story, I had busted my balls for that story, and I'd changed my whole approach to writing while writing that story. And I said who in the hell is some layout person to drop something that I've busted my ass on, because she doesn't have room to get in her advertisement, because she screwed up. I said if I still had the $2,000 I'd send it back to you and send the story to *Sewanee Review*. They said well you'd have twelve hundred readers, we reach hundreds of thousands. I said I don't give a shit, I want my story, as I wrote it, to be in the magazine. For what I was trying to achieve in those sentences, those words came out of labor—

D.H. While they're seeing it as a piece of entertainment they can cut to fit, like a made-for-TV movie.
A.D. Right. And I'm sure to somebody who doesn't write, it looks like a quirk or a neurosis or an obsession. But to me it's a commitment you make to yourself writing, that nobody is ever going to take this away from you. The world is going to take everything else, but they can't touch my comma.

D.H. At least you have a publisher in Godine who gives your books the care and design—and marketing—that your work deserves.
A.D. I'm one of the luckiest short-story writers in America because of Godine. How many publishers would publish four collections of stories by a writer, without *one* novel?

D.H. It sounds like the *Playboy* experience is another extension of the general misconception about the short story, that it is "story" more than art crafted out of perfect sentences.
A.D. Yes, definitely.

D.H. You mentioned them changing "Fleischmann's" to "whiskey." It brings to mind Carver's story "Gazebo," how different the tone would start off, lacking a first touch or sorriness, if the woman wasn't pouring *Teacher's* on the guy's belly.
A.D. Exactly.

D.H. Or suppose your character in "The Misogamist," instead of blurting out his helpless "Fuck it," said . . . "Gosh."
A.D. Exactly . . . You've probably read wonderful novels that had terrible parts, some necessary, where you could see the novelist struggling to make

a transition or give some information. I found only two pages in Sholokov's *And Quiet Flows the Don* where I said well he's getting tired here, he has to abstractly *explain* what his character was doing in battle for a couple of days. That doesn't ruin a novel, but man one word can ruin a poem, and one line or a paragraph can destroy a short story. Sholokov's novel is one of the best I've ever read.

D.H. Any other examples of perils for the story?

A.D. Yes, I sent a story, "Townies," to George Core at *Sewanee*. He didn't want it. He had a very interesting thing—he said if I'd reverse the sections he'd take it. I thought about it and called Mark Costello for advice, and we decided the story should stay as it was. But Core also worried about the word "asshole"; he said, you know, we're letting you cuss in your stories; but could she call him something else? I wrote back no, because that's why she gets killed. Michael, in the story, knows he's an asshole. It was just the wrong word at the right time, because he felt like one.

D.H. But overall, Core has been very receptive to your work, publishing stories like "The Winter Father" without changes.

A.D. Core has been wonderful. I published my first story in the *Sewanee Review* in 1963, and couldn't place one there again till he took over and published "Cadence" in 1975. Since then he's published others, given a lot of pages to the novella, *Adultery*, and I even enjoy his rejections. He's intelligent, sensitive, and honorable. I know if I had agreed with him about the structure of "Townies," he would have understood my reason for using the word "asshole" and kept it in the story.

D.H. You know, thinking of the story, "Townies," for me part of how it works is in your having the section about the old campus nightwatchman first, so I get to accept his passive resentment, which comes from the same kinds of frustrations as the kid's, Mike's. I guess the compassion I'm willing to give Mike, the killer, gets won some before the ugly part. It would seem not as effective to have those parts turned around.

A.D. That's interesting. Because I based the story on a guy who was vicious to one of my students, and I hated him. Maybe the first section led me to that compassion, too. Maybe I couldn't have started with him.

D.H. You say you based that story on a real person. Do you think it's another way the short story gets misunderstood, people thinking of it as just disguised "true story"? They can miss the difference that characters (I think Eudora Welty said this) go through deep reckonings that we as *people* rarely do—certainly not in such compressed experience?

A.D. Yes, that's true . . . and it applies even more to novels. Your average TV-watching human-being American can read something like *For Whom the Bell Tolls* and enjoy it because it took you into another world and you got the action (the beautiful action) and the love and all that, and it made you sad—but never get down to the real themes that are in that book. That Robert Jordan decides to sacrifice earthly love for an ideal in which he knows he will lose. You can miss all that and still love the book.

Now you can read a short story like "A Clean, Well-lighted Place," and unless you are a person who has some culture, you don't understand the son of a bitch. And I think that might be what's going on with many readers—and publishers—because the short story is a *poetic* art form. You can't just pick that thing up and read it between innings or after a football game. And if the short story does suffer from a lack of readers, it's because we have a culture that makes people like Barry Manilow rich. I think that's closer to it.

D.H. You're saying a good story asks you to read it several times, like a poem.
A.D. Yes—

D.H. I agree.
A.D. And I don't think the story does that on purpose, just to be obscure, but that a good story, like a good poem, hits you one way the first time you read it—you say my God, like Pape's poem, which made me cry. That just hit me so hard, because it is tactile, as literary art has to be, and I became the man burned in the poem, and I became the boy watching him, pouring the cold water and watching his new stepfather saying oh Jesus oh Jesus, and his mother saying oh honey oh honey—I was there. But I could read that poem ten more times and it would get better and better because it would get deeper, past my immediate and sensory reaction to it. And I think a good story has to always do that. Probably good novels too. My point is, you can read a good novel and not understand how good it is and say that was *great*. I think that's why a lot of people who aren't very good readers do buy good novels and read them. They don't know what the fuck they're reading.

D.H. While in a short story you have to understand what you're given on the surface is the tip of a whole life underneath?
A.D. Yep.

D.H. Otherwise it won't resound afterwards; you won't know what the artistry is up to . . .
A.D. Yep.

D.H. What about the culture that doesn't appreciate these things?
A.D. I know I sounded scornful before. I don't think it's the fault of the people. And I'm not wise enough to understand this, but it seems to me, mostly from my year tending bar at the local pub, which is a working man's pub (and students go there too) and I drink there now and talk to guys who work with their hands and certainly wouldn't call themselves intellectuals. But the stories that you and I write are for them. I think somewhere along the way, in their childhood, they got a tacit message from somebody; this is not for you, ignore it, you are supposed to sit in front of a TV—which they don't really like! Somebody in this country who controls TV—and maybe editors too—has a very scornful attitude toward the human beings out there who are really ready to experience anything—

D.H. Something literary.
A.D. Yes, and it's not given to them. I think somebody cut them off. I've had rejections from commercial magazines referring to "our readers"—"this might be too hard on our readers." And you see I don't believe that, because those allegedly simple men I talk to in the bar are not simple. And they understand everything you and I do; they have a different frame of reference. If I mentioned "the . . . *Abyss*," they'd raise an eyebrow, what the hell are you talking about? But if we start talking about death, love, work, they know those things.

I had a gunnery sergeant in the Marine Corps, and he told me, Captain, I'd like to read that book *War and Peace*. I said why don't you borrow it, it's a wonderful book. But . . . he didn't. I know he was afraid to, and I know he would have loved *War and Peace*. I'm sure he thought how could he, a high-school educated Marine gunnery sergeant, understand this famous book. And *Tolstoi*, who wrote the thing, decided somewhere in his middle age—he said we're just writing for ourselves, for the aristocracy. Ninety-five percent of the country can't read. So he started schools for peasant children, and he and some friends got together stories and made books and sold them, for a penny. He said we've got to get the libraries in the poor people's houses. And the peasants bought the books. You know, if you could sneak in a good TV dramatization of a short story—not just on PBS—from 8:00 to 8:30 one evening, the viewers would like it. They're not dumb.

D.H. You mention the commercial magazines saying this would be too hard on "our readers." It makes you wonder what they would say about a story in which a man is fated to make love to his mother—to become literally a mother f—
A.D. There you go.

D.H. And then that people stab out their own eyes—
A.D. With knitting needles—

D.H. With knitting needles, in the mortification of finding out what they've done, and die all over the scene with woe and lamentations—
A.D. Right. Right.

D.H. Wasn't the idea that the people it might be too hard on—wasn't it the reverse, that they would understand that it was art, and that it would give them something that your character Hank Allison is in search of in "Finding a Girl"—catharsis?
A.D. Yes. Yes.

D.H. Pretty strange that the magazine gives you that response.
A.D. It might be goddamn evil, because—I'm getting very angry—here are those people wearing whatever clothes somebody told them to wear that year, making a decision that the readers of their magazines have never grieved over the death of a child, or brother, sister, father or mother or husband, have never suffered divorce, have never committed adultery, or been the victim of infidelity, never been through any pain—just live these dull lives out there, watching TV. That's not true. Those human beings are going through suffering; they recognize it, and it is cathartic to read a story about what you yourself have suffered—

D.H. Or can experience someone else suffering, like you reading Pape's poem.
A.D. Yes. And it's soothing. A poet friend of mine, Michael van Walleghen— I could not believe he did this. He met an old girlfriend whom he later married, and when he remet her, she was in the hospital with cancer; he brought her *Separate Flights*. And when I met her she said it was the first book she read after her operation. I said . . . my God. She said . . . it soothed me.

D.H. I'd like to push this even farther. I read a story like your title story,

"Separate Flights," which is just going down and down and down toward divorce, but I get the same good feeling from "Separate Flights" and your other novellas that, say, I get by the end of something like Flannery O'Connor's "Wise Blood"—
A.D. Wow.

D.H. I feel . . . exhausted, wonderfully, by everything that's been fulfilled, even though it's downward, because the story makes good on its promise. And I guess this is really about art and its goodness, that it's made something beautiful out of the terrible reckoning of the characters. And I don't mean it makes me a sadist or voyeur of the story—but that I feel *aesthetic* catharsis. It's a pretty goddamn exuberant feeling.
A.D. Yes. Yes.

D.H. And if that's hard on people, then a lot of our culture really has lost something valuable.
A.D. Again, when I was younger—I mean only ten years ago—I thought that the culture *had* lost that. But now I truly believe that it's been taken away from them by somebody.

I've got a line that I write on the board, at the first meeting of literature classes: "ART . . . is always affirmative, because it shows us that we can endure being mortal." If somebody can celebrate bleak lives that's *something*.

D.H. Bleak, like the killings stories that start off *Finding a Girl in America*.
A.D. Sure.

D.H. You know, when I first read those stories, reading the book through, . . . what bleak stories—
A.D. Right, put the violent ones first.

D.H. At first I felt myself being subjected to those killing stories, resisting them some, because they seemed to be going for my solar plexus—because they seemed, maybe melodramatic? But then as they resonated I realized how much you were making me see the real victim, the wrongdoer, and showing the side of him that was capable of compassion. Talk about crying, one place I felt it coming on me was in the scene in "Killings" where Matt goes into Strout's room—the room of the man he will kill, out of helpless vengeance—and notices, in his bureau drawer, the rolled up socks—
A.D. Yeah—

D.H. Folded underwear—
A.D. Yeah—

D.H. The simply made bed. Jesus, Andre, those plain details are so subtly loaded with Matt's softening, and then we see him have to lie to Strout, invent some cock and bull story about taking him to the airport (as though not taking him off to shoot him) to go through with it . . .
A.D. Yes, he's becoming human seeing that Strout is humbly human. In that car ride I didn't know if Matt was going to do it or not. I know this, that if Strout had not been proud and had begged don't shoot me, he never would have gotten shot.

D.H. I believe it. . . . Now, further, in the course of the book—and I'm seeing what you mean by celebration. After I got through those tough stories, I get to the beautiful, concluding title story.
A.D. Oh do you like that one? You don't think it's sloppy?

D.H. Oh, yes, I liked it. I'll call you on that "sloppy" in a bit.
A.D. Oh good. I love it. I hope you convince me.

D.H. Anyway, first I think celebration has to be earned.
A.D. You mean celebration in the sense of a happy ending?

D.H. I mean in your words about art, affirming life.
A.D. Absolutely.

D.H. Okay, so now I've read all the stories and I get to the last one, "Finding a Girl in America," with this guy Hank, who I've seen more and more as your kingpin character—not because he's a writer but because of the emotions he has to deal with, and the questions. And I don't like him very much, you understand, up to now. At times I've wanted to stand up and throw eggs at the son of a bitch.
A.D. Yes, me too. In the first two novellas, didn't like him at all.

D.H. But, finally, he brings home and makes true those first inklings of compassion I saw in Matt in "Killings." When he beats up the guy in the bar but later is able to imagine the guy going home—
A.D. To a woman—

D.H. Yes, who can give him tenderness and love the little boy inside him. What's wonderful, Hank imagines this and *feels* for the guy—this is what Matt could have done in "Killings." And, when Hank has to face his ex-girlfriend Monica's having had an abortion, he is anguished and angry but pulls his punches that are leveled at his girl Lori's stomach—womb—*pulls his punches.*
A.D. Uh-huh.

D.H. In the heat of frustration he is governed finally by feeling for some-one else: *there,* the whole book for me comes to where it's going to start celebrating, and I know that it will be affirmative. The urge to do violence, that comes from so many quarters in your stories, is put in balance with compassion.
A.D. Yes.

D.H. And I go all the way back to the young Paul, in those stories, who couldn't hug his father because his anguish was already making him resort to viciousness, so he even enjoys his friend Eddie getting beat up.
A.D. Yes, he worships the bully.

D.H. Just as the older Paul in "Cadence" can't give sympathy to his friend Hugh.
A.D. That's right. And Hugh has what Paul doesn't—*no* father, and a girl who's sensitive, takes him to art museums, and doesn't care if he can do push-ups.

D.H. Then here is Hank, who has been a designing son of a bitch with his wife—ex-wife—Edith, and like so many of the male characters in your sto-ries, thinking that the best part of him is in some self-contained activity—pitching, soldiering, writing—who discovers now a need for catharsis and to answer the truly best part of himself, the part that reaches out to affirm someone else's life.
A.D. Thank you. Yes, Hank finally learns that living and loving take the same discipline that writing does.

D.H. So, that's how I'm understanding your grand words about art.
A.D. Jesus, that's the best thing I've heard about that story.

D.H. Would you like next I should tackle technique?
A.D. Go on.

D.H. No, no. You talk. You said you thought you were technically sloppy in "Finding a Girl." Whose voice is saying Andre Dubus, you were sloppy in this story?
A.D. Ha, well, one friend read it in manuscript and said you know some of these things you could have done in an essay in *Boston Magazine*. About female liberation and Hank's and Jack's final discussion on the sexual revolution furthering the victimization of women. It looks awfully preachy. So, one voice in me, too, says let's compress all this and let the reader sense it; another voice in me says no it came from the gut, the ending is beautiful, and if you touch it it could be a good story but it won't be that story. So let it be a little loose and expansive and exciting.

D.H. Right. And when I first saw the title, and as the title of the book, well, there're overtones of . . . a social statement.
A.D. Yes . . .

D.H. But that says to me you chose to let it stand that way. And that's a little different issue than the one I meant when you said technically sloppy. Were you technically not as tight with this story as usual?
A.D. Yes. I would prefer to write a story that's more subtle. I get nervous about a man standing up at the ending and saying the theme. I ran into that trouble with "If They Knew Yvonne." What little boys and dead crabs have to do with masturbation and love making wouldn't be very clear without that confession scene. But in "Finding a Girl in America" what I felt cautious about was having so many of my own feelings come out in Hank's voice. It made me wonder am I just having some cardboard guy do my talking—or am I creating a character? But I think Hank is very much alive and his own person as a character.

D.H. And as long as the story stays in character. . . . It brings to mind Chekhov, of course, who always kept a story in character.
A.D. Yes. Chekhov's characters very often state the theme in those wonderful dialogues, and it's beautiful; but the great thing is you can never find Chekhov, no matter who states the theme.

D.H. Sometimes, though, I applaud finding the writer, at least in his milestone stories—not that he's necessarily making his statement but that in the world of his stories here is suddenly the opening where celebration breaks through. Like Chekhov's "Rothschild's Fiddle," or Carver's Cathedrals"—

A.D. "Cathedrals," yes. You should see his rewrite of "The Bath," from *What We Talk about When We Talk about Love*. He completely rewrote it, it appeared in *Ploughshares*, and it just won first place O. Henry. I think it's the best story he's ever written.

D.H. Boy I want to see that. . . . Or Updike's story in *Problems*, "Transaction," where the prostitute leaves the family man his dried condom on the motel table, with his other Christmas purchases—so sex finally isn't an enslaving mystery for an Updike commuter.

A.D. Jesus.

You know, I was telling Hendrie Updike's "Sense of Shelter" at 1:00 this morning. I love that story—it makes me wonder about the kind of people who teach literature, who really are not the type of people to teach literature, they're sort of bloodless, and passive, and . . .

D.H. Bookwormy—

A.D. Yes. And literature was written by very live people. I asked my friend the poet Kenneth F. Rosen why do so many teachers present literature as something you understand, package, and put away? He said because they treat it like an acquisition, and like all people who devote their lives to acquisition, they're cowards.

D.H. Sounds like the kind of teacher a commercial mag editor had who now fears something is "too hard for our readers."

A.D. *Yeah*. And I think Updike's story "A Sense of Shelter" defines that type for all time.

D.H. Something Eudora Welty said somewhere, when you get into this business of interpreting and teaching dry, what you're really doing is removing literature from experience.

A.D. Exactly.

D.H. I'd like to go back to Chekhov and some others. He comes up often in your stories, whether mentioned directly or in a fine tip of the hat like your story "The Doctor."

A.D. Thank you.

D.H And Hemingway, too. What has he meant to you?

A.D. Hemingway was the first one I read. I didn't read much in high school— I thought Hemingway was the director of the movie "The Killers"! My freshman year in college, I started writing stories and showed them to a teacher who said your Negro dialect needs improving, why don't you read Faulkner. I said who is Faulkner?

But Hemingway right away was an idol. The first thing I read was *The Sun Also Rises*, then *For Whom the Bell Tolls*, which still makes me weep. I read a lot about him, and learned about writing every day, stopping writing in half sentence, while you're still going well, then do physical exercise, come back to it the next day.

D.H. There seem some things Hemingway-like in a wonderfully realized way in your stories, and I don't mean imitation.

A.D. Of course, who could?

D.H. In the third-person stories especially, the narration reminds me of Hemingway, something so simple as pronouns repeated and repeated—*he* this, *he* that, *he* knew—that keeps a coolish distance from the character, on one hand. While, on the other, your characteristic way of putting a finger on the inside life, the emotions, of your characters and going after that life relentlessly.

A.D. That's where I like to work.

D.H. It shows. For example, this kind of sentence, from "Going Under": "Then he drove home through tears and again tried to prepare a meal and again could not eat; then he lay on his bed and submitted with curiosity and hope to the rape of grief." Boy, there's a lot of torque for me, between the objective distance in tagging with so many pronouns, and the closeness in identifying complicated emotions straight on. Anyway, it's pretty delightful, and I wish I understood how that works.

A.D. I've got a hunch that the effect you're talking about comes from something very simple, and that is trying to keep things tactile, I think.

D.H. All right, let me push you on that one and say that in some of these third-person stories where you get rolling on the life inside, I feel that the real particulars *are* inside, and the stream of tactile things the character perceives, though compelling, aren't as forceful for me as his emotions. So my attention, and I feel the writer's, is on how the character notices more than what—in these steamrolling stories anyway.

A.D. Oh yes, how he sees, more than what.

D.H. Yes. And of course you do have stories that operate very tactilely, a story conveyed wonderfully along the surface, like "Delivering." But it's the ones that roll for forty, fifty, sixty pages, hardly ever coming up for air, that give me that exhaustion I talked about earlier, and take me in a way, so . . . directly, like I don't know of any other writer doing, Andre.
A.D. Well, good. Good.

D.H. Something related, in these stories you seem to resist making any mileage from "symbols."
A.D. I hope so. Like the point in the novella, "Adultery," where Edith is carrying the shrimp to Joe's—

D.H. The priest, her lover, who is dying of cancer—
A.D. Yes, and she slips and falls on the ice. Of course that was intentional—vulnerability, mortality—you fall and you get up and you go again and again. Some of those teachers we were talking about would say that's symbolic, but really that is *falling down.* This symbol stuff is so stupid to focus on because it takes things out of proportion. Because our entire lives are full of symbols; we use them all the time. And then to talk about them as though they belong to the literary province alone is to falsify everything.

My father and I were never able to talk. He was dying of cancer, and he came home to die, and he was awake the last day, drinking bourbon and water and we were talking—not deeply talking, but we were talking. And at times during the day he asked me to feed him crushed ice. Now if some teacher saw that in a story he would say it was symbolic of their silent love, which it's not—it is their silent love.

Anyhow, I want Edith's love for Joe to be like that, what she does.

D.H. You dedicated that novella, "Adultery," to Gina Berriault.
A.D. That's right.

D.H. I remember a story of hers I used to read to my high school students, called "The Stone Boy." The boy Arnold who accidentally kills his brother, goes into shock and picks peas for an hour before telling his parents, who then give him the silent treatment for days.
A.D. Oh, yes.

D.H. Arnold puts me in mind of your character Paul, who becomes a "stone boy." And some other characters who envy or hate someone for something they don't have, or who can't bring all the parts of their lives together with someone, a lover, and so become viciously independent. Like "The Fat Girl." What about them?

A.D. I think, probably. Of course I didn't think any of it out before writing the stories, but made discoveries in the stories. For instance, in "The Bully" Paul kills the cat because the cat represents to him a part of himself which he hates—weakness. He needs his friend Eddie, but then Eddie is school and so forth, where Eddie and Paul are the sissies, the outcasts. And when the bully beats up Eddie, it's Paul's terrible need for manhood that makes him whore himself to this bully and praise him. Then he takes great delight in the bully's drowning, deceiving himself into praying for the bully's soul, while what he is enjoying are the images of the bully roasting in Catholic purgatory. And he doesn't understand this about himself. Of course what he needs in all the Paul stories, and many of my characters do I guess—is someone who would love all of him.

D.H. Especially the weak, vulnerable part.

A.D. Yes. So that part which could only be loved by his mother or sister—a woman—could be loved by a man. And there was no man to show him; his father was not . . . able, to go all the way and make Paul feel like he was . . . all right.

D.H. And he joins the Marine Corps to try to earn that love.

A.D. Definitely.

D.H. How about some of your other characters in the military who resort to violence or who are "stone boys"? I look at the character in "The Misogamist," Roy Hodges, who despairs of his limitations, his inability to be vulnerable—even with Sheila. She scares him because she's so sincere he doesn't have anything on her, resents having to lie to her, and stands her up at the altar.

A.D. Yes, he is a certain breed of professional soldier, who has that stunted development of a man who can't make the next step to total commitment, who just can't go all the way—and it is painful for him.

D.H. The creator of these characters sometimes observes that at the moment they can't make that next step, their bodies and souls become separated, as though they've lost the sacrament of living—if that's not reading in too much.

A.D. No, I feel that. Very much.

D.H. You desire sacrament, and salvation, for them, don't you?

A.D. Every one of them. I can't write about a character I can't love.

D.H. You know, Katherine Anne Porter said that none of her characters were tough enough to save themselves. Is that true for yours?

A.D. Ten years ago I would have said so; but now they've grown, through divorces and changes. They're learning to love, some of them. In the story you're running—in fact the concluding story in the new collection—"A Father's Story," Luke Ripley argues with God, about love. Where God accuses him of loving out of weakness, and he replies—In the same way You love me.

D.H. Yes, I thought that was wonderful.

A.D. You know, I realized he was getting from God what Paul Clement never got from his father.

D.H. You know, thinking of two other concluding stories—the novellas, "Adultery" and "Finding a Girl"—love gets the last word there, too.

A.D. Yes.

D.H. I'd like to talk about the novellas some more, where—I said this before—you get rolling. They are different from the shorter stories. Maybe how you feel writing them . . .

A.D. I think I know what you mean. It gets to a point where the character is taking off and I'm just hanging on for dear life—at a very slow rate, of course. Two to three hundred words a day, though sometimes when I get near the end I have gone all night. But yes, the rhythms start to change.

D.H. With longer sentences, lots of semicolons and lists in piled phrases— it was something like this I was wondering about when you said "sloppy" earlier. I mean I don't see it as sloppy, but rather the story going on instinct. Moving back and forth from past to present, accumulating characteristics about feelings and actions—*he* would, *he* liked to, sometimes *he*, etc.—then pulling back into a particular scene again.

A.D. Swooping, I call it. Yes. And it's a wonderful experience when it comes.

A rapturous experience. When I was writing "Finding a Girl in America," I kept coming out of the desk every day and saying to Peggy, this crazy bastard's . . . *moving*. And "A Father's Story," I kept coming out of the desk every day—I meant that, coming out of the desk, not out of the room—saying, I don't know what this guy's doing he's . . . *talking to God*.

D.H. You mentioned another story from the new collection, that changed the way you were writing, the story *Playboy* tried to snip.

A.D. Yes, "Anna." I've written differently ever since. The story was from a note I made years ago about a guy robbing a bank. He went to the phone booth in Boston and called his girlfriend in Florida; she told her lover to go next door and call the cops while she kept him on the phone. And so I gestated and gestated and gestated and said okay, I'm going to write a story about betrayal. So I finally got a couple, a young woman and a young man, and made them poor, the kind of people you buy your hamburgers from. . . . But what was bothering me was I had never known anybody like this, someone who robbed a drugstore. I was writing about a woman I knew nothing about.

Now until that time my method of writing was to try for a thousand words a day; whether the pages were there or not I wrote them. Right? And I averaged something like five drafts per story, sometimes six. "Adultery" was seven—seventeen months, four hundred typed pages. But for "Anna" I couldn't write "horizontally," I couldn't write moving ahead, because I didn't know who she was. So I told myself write vertically. Do not leave a sentence until you know how she feels. And I went like that at that pace, and then I knew her. And I found out that she and the guy loved each other.

D.H. So it wasn't a betrayal story?

A.D. Nope, not at all. It became about their love, after robbing the drugstore. But anyway, ever since then I've been writing that way. I write more slowly— if I get a hundred words I think that's good. Two hundred, three hundred. And now I write less drafts. "A Father's Story," the first hand-written draft was just about right. So I'm writing faster by going more slowly—well, still averaging about three stories a year. I think before, I wrote so many drafts because I wrote too fast and missed a lot of the story and had to go back.

D.H. Is it your sense that up until "Anna" you had known better who your characters were in the early going?

A.D. No, it usually took a draft or more. Now, by slowing down, I'm getting to know them sooner. Oh, one thing though, I still tape the penultimate draft.

D.H. Tape it, and play it back?
A.D. Yes. And I count that in my log book that I keep about daily exercise and how many words I write. I started doing that after reading a lot of John Cheever stories, realizing that most of his characters had this problem of saying everything is wonderful wonderful, while, say, they're driving to California—but we can see that the trunk is open and all their clothes are falling out behind them. They never see that. I thought, I better start keeping a log!

D.H. That's great. And the taping . . .
A.D. It counts as much as another draft. I think the difference is not so much how the story sounds, but that after reading the whole thing over every day the way I do, you've gotten to where you've read it a hundred times and you don't really *read* it anymore. Then when you read it aloud you're doing something physical, which makes you concentrate. I'm sure that's why I tend to cry when I read aloud. The body's involved now, and words start to jump at you that you've been looking through.

D.H. So do you hear things, too, maybe jangling?
A.D. Sure, a word will stand out that's repeated too often, or that interior rhyme you didn't want.

D.H. What you were saying before about how close the short story is to the poem, and maybe far from the novel.
A.D. Yes.

D.H. How about the novella, where does it fall on this scale?
A.D. That's a good question.

D.H. Is it just an extended story?
A.D. I don't think it's just length. Let's see. I would call Joseph Conrad's *The Nigger of the "Narcissus"* a novella. To me, a novella has the richness, the depth of a novel, and the poetic form of a story. I don't think I've ever read a good novella that was written with a clumsy hand. . . . I guess I'm saying it's longer than a story because it needs room to disclose more about a charac-

ter's life, but it doesn't ask to be pushed much past sixty to a hundred pages. The material dictates the form.

D.H. In your novellas also it seems you need to disclose things about more than just one or two characters (as in the stories)—typically three, or four. But that the novellas are still close to stories because they're sticking to a single dramatic conflict. Maybe that sounds too academic.
A.D. No, you're making sense. Maybe there aren't many novellas because they're written mostly by short-story writers who from time to time need room for another character or two. Maybe that's why good novellas have such beautiful form.

D.H. Story-like.
A.D. Yes, like Katherine Anne Porter—"Pale Horse, Pale Rider" or "Noon Wine." Chekhov's "My Life." A story writer.

D.H. Where like in a story, the form is determined by character.
A.D. Yes, like Chekhov. Jesus, when he got past thirty pages, no one could touch him. Still can't.

D.H. I'll buy that. . . . Is there a novella in your new book?
A.D. Yes, "The Pretty Girl" starts it off. The new book is called *The Times Are Never So Bad*. It's from a line from St. Thomas More, "The times are never so bad but that a good man can live in them."

D.H. More of that growing faith in your people being able to save themselves?
A.D. Yes, though there is also an epigraph from Flannery O'Connor, about violence bringing out essential qualities in a man that he will take with him to eternity.

D.H. We've talked some about violence in your work. There's more in these new stories?
A.D. There's a lot of violence in this collection. I think I'm just catching up with my notebook, with things that have been happening in this country. Like most of those "Killings" stories, they were based on things that really happened.

D.H. Beyond that, do you have the feeling O'Connor expressed, that the reckonings that come out of violence are crucial for the characters?

A.D. I never thought of it until I read that line this summer. But I chose it because it does apply to some of the characters in the book, whose violent actions bring out their qualities—and they're not always bad ones.

D.H. I usually get the feeling that even your worst characters have some good qualities.

A.D. I hope so.

D.H. One other way, too, that I feel your care for them, is in some of the mid-story point-of-view shifts you take, giving each character his due—like switching focus to Lori in "Finding a Girl."

A.D. You know, I don't think I ever planned to go to Lori's point of view, but it was just her finally pulling me over and saying it's time.

D.H. I like that.

A.D. I don't know, something happens when we love our characters and respond to them like that. We become better than we are. We become like God. We enter that character, and we understand that character, and we forgive that character, and write about somebody we maybe could not spend ten minutes with over a beer. And we can read about somebody the same way—in Chekhov, we can love this person, feel like we could embrace the whole universe. Cry . . .

D.H. More power to you, Andre.

A.D. Thank you.

Andre Dubus Interview
with Kay Bonetti

Kay Bonetti / 1984

American Audio Prose Library. April 1984. Excerpt printed in *A Leap of the Heart: Andre Dubus Talking*. Ed. Ross Gresham. New Orleans: Xavier Review Press, 2003. 51–59. This is a print version of a recorded interview produced by the American Audio Prose Library, Inc. Used by permission. © American Audio Prose Library, Inc. All rights reserved.

DUBUS: I suppose, as with all autobiography, you begin by writing about something that was painful to you, and then by the time you write the story, certain actions have changed because the characters become themselves and they're no longer you, so by the time the story is over—and each of those Paul Clement stories is based on an actual incident which was painful for me—you no longer remember which really happened, and you end up having a different perspective.

BONETTI: So those Paul stories are autobiographical?
DUBUS: They're about as autobiographical as I ever get. When I finished writing a story called "Contrition"—all of those are written after my father's death; he died in 1963—I was here in Massachusetts, and I called my mother and said, "I just forgave Daddy." She said, "For what?" I said, "I've been writing about those French horn lessons and just saw something." And you know, that, for me, was the epiphany of the story. I think at the end the sister comes to comfort Paul and he realizes for just a few moments what it's like to be his father. And I forgave him, as the writer. As a child I didn't. So those are really the only autobiographical stories. Of course, autobiography is a strange thing to talk about. I read to the faculty last fall at the president's house, and one woman said, "Well, everything we do as artists is really autobiographical because of course it is our soul which comes out." I'd read them "A Father's Story." There's nothing in there—no action in there—which has

anything to do with me. I don't even know much about horses. But I had to give the narrator a job. I've always fought writing autobiography—I've felt that there was something wrong with it. Richard Yates said there are two traps in writing autobiography: self-pity and self-aggrandizement. I guess in my early twenties I was worried then that if I spent too much time writing autobiography I'd lose touch with the world to learn a lot about me.

BONETTI: Too self-absorbed.
DUBUS: Yeah.

BONETTI: Didn't you put your finger on it when you said that Paul in the Paul Clement stories is no longer you, once the story is finished?
DUBUS: Yeah, I guess the closest he gets to being me is that I realize things in the process of writing which he didn't at that point in his life. So in "Contrition," for instance, he's a little wiser than I was at age ten, but I can honestly say I don't impose things on characters, because if they don't come through for me, the story doesn't get finished. They are the ones who tell the story. But there is a joy in it. I separate joy from happiness. I think joy is a mingling usually of pain.

BONETTI: You're saying, I take it, that there is a joy that surely comes from looking at a work well-made?
DUBUS: Yeah and actually doing it, too, as there is a joy in certain exercises of the body which are difficult but by chance I'm having fun, but there is a joy there. I think in both exercising and in writing it is one of the few things you do, few actions you perform in a day or in the evening that absorbs all of you and demands the most of you.

BONETTI: What is your discipline? Do you have a routine?
DUBUS: Well, when I'm working on something I write every day and work out every day, and if I can get those two done, then usually nothing can mess me up.

BONETTI: Do you divide your writing life in terms of, oh, you know, the Hemingway model that everybody knows about where they used to say he would create in the morning, revise in the afternoon—do you have that kind of—I don't mean that identical schedule, but do you have a comparable regime that you go on when you're working on a piece?

DUBUS: I do, and it's interesting you mentioned Hemingway because I read hardly anything in high school. I thought Hemingway was a movie director [laughs] until his plane crashed in the fifties, because I saw a billboard in town or a marquis saying, "Hemingway's *The Killers* is playing at the movies." Then when he crashed in Africa in the fifties and I was in high school, I thought he was a writer. I got to college, I began, I had started writing stories as soon as I got out of high school. I get to college and my freshman English teacher said, "You should read William Faulkner to improve your negro dialect." This was in 1954.

BONETTI: [Laughs]
DUBUS: I said, "Who's William Faulkner?" He said, "You're kidding me. He lives in the next state, Mississippi. He's our greatest writer." I said, "Oh." So then I started reading about these people, and I guess I did a research paper, something on Hemingway, and learned something that was very good, when I was about nineteen. The discipline he kept talking about, the discipline is you have to write every day and you have to exercise afterwards to clear your mind, and you should not think about the work again unless it's your subconscious doing it. And I followed that rule all my life as a writer, and it's a wonderful rule, and I've learned that anytime you think that, anytime I think of other stories, all I do is exhaust energy and nothing I've thought about helps in any way. I also learned something else from Hemingway I keep passing on to students, and they don't believe me. He's saying that you should always stop writing for the day when it's still going well and you should stop in mid-sentence. And I've done that always, except a couple of times. I was too excited and I finished a scene and it was terrible because the next day I could not start. So I always stop in mid-sentence, and mid-scene, with notes in the margins so that next day I come in and I read everything I've written up to that, and then the sentence is already waiting to be completed and the scene is waiting to go and pretty soon the story is moving.

BONETTI: That's a mystery to me. I really am puzzled by that.
DUBUS: But doing it the other way frightens me and I'll tell you why, and this is what I tell students. You write for two or three hours or whatever you have, and maybe thirty hours go by before you get back to it and a lot of things have happened to you in those thirty hours, and if you have finished a scene, then you don't know too well what's coming next. Those thirty hours of sleep, action, movies, crises, whatever are liable to interfere and knock you off the course. You come back to it the next day, and you can't feel,

which I think this is very important, feeling every day this story you're getting tired of. So I'd rather stop it in mid-breath, so to speak. You come back the next day and just start breathing with it.

BONETTI: Do you have a revision ritual?
DUBUS: Yeah I do. I came up with a new method of writing—not a new method, new for me—in 1980. I was writing a story called "Anna." Like many of my stories, the story began to be about one thing, and it ended by being about something else. So "Anna" began in my mind as a story about a young woman who would become frightened or something by the escalation of her and her boyfriend's robberies and would turn him in. However I had a very hard time writing the story because I have never known anybody who held up a drugstore. Maybe I do, but I don't know that I know them. You might've iced a few drug stores. And I decided not to leave a sentence until I knew exactly how Anna felt sensuously about whatever was happening at the time, so I began to concentrate on her senses, which you're supposed to do anyway, but I concentrated even more and decided to be satisfied if I wrote a hundred words a day. Now I used to shoot for a thousand a day, and I would get out of that my usual three stories a year, no matter if I'm teaching or not, three stories a year. But I would write five, six, seven drafts. "Adultery," for instance, was seven drafts, four hundred typed pages to get the final sixty, over a period of years.

BONETTI: Years?
DUBUS: Yeah. Eighteen months of actual writing time, but I wasn't working all the time because it kept throwing me off the saddle.

BONETTI: But back to "Anna."
DUBUS: So then I began concentrating, and I did it physically—I'd sit at the desk, and I'd hunch my shoulders inward and say, "Write vertically; do not think about the next page," and I realized I had been writing horizontally. I'd been writing a scene to get to the next scene. When I wrote "Anna," I didn't think about the next scene. I thought about the sentence, the moment. How does this tequila feel? And it was done in one draft. So by writing more slowly, I wrote more quickly. That sounds Oriental, I don't know. But what happened to change the story was after the hold-up, they go to these bars I used all the time based on Robby D's, a local bar in Bradford, and as they were talking, I realized they were in love. I said, my God, it's a love story.

There's no betrayal here. It became a very old-fashioned story saying materials don't make happiness, right? But it was a love story, and I found that out by knowing how she felt. That is not unique. That is how I always wrote stories, but by going more slowly, I took less wrong roads. Of course I realized what I had been taking while I hurried: "I will write a thousand words a day." Of course it would be five drafts. Now, ever since then, knock on wood [knocks], I've written—that's probably not wood—I've written one longhand draft, and then I have taped it, which I've done always my whole career, to the next-to-last draft. I prefer that than the ultimate. I tape that and play it back, and I always consider that a draft because I read the entire manuscript from beginning to where I end, every day, so there are passages I've read hundreds of times. Now when I read them aloud, when I read that handwritten manuscript aloud, it involves my body, and I think it makes me feel it more. Which is why I often cry—almost always cry—when I read aloud. And then hearing it back I hear things, repetitions, a line of dialogue that's not necessary. And then from the tape I make pen and ink changes. I skip a line and I write double-spaced in longhand and I type the final draft. Until then, until 1980, it was a matter of, say, four handwritten drafts, each one getting closer to the story, each one we're trying to find the story, and I used to simply consider the first draft something painful I had to go through to find out what the story is and then I can start over.

BONETTI: Let's use the story that you read for us today.
DUBUS: Okay.

BONETTI: "A Father's Story." Of how that came to be.
DUBUS: I started it in the summer of 1978 simply because I was interested in the question of hit-and-run. I know what the civil law says, but what is the moral responsibility? If you hit a person and the person is in fact dead, there's not much you can do, so why turn yourself in? That was the premise I started with. That was not an answer. That was the question. I start most stories with, "What if?" And then I go after it and find out what if. So I wrote the opening scene, and it was a very bad beginning because the opening scene was the actual accident, which was a stupid device on my part, be- cause you've got an accident but you don't know who the driver is.

BONETTI: Told from whose point of view?
DUBUS: Yeah, who did it? It was the young girl's. I wrote the last one, I mean the final one, in the spring of '82. By then I'd been gestating this story

for four years, and at one time I thought I'll make it a young man, and then I thought no, because I wanted it to be about the father, and if it's a woman the father will treat her differently than he would a son. I didn't know how. I just decided to make that part of his conflict. I wanted to write about a man of faith. And one day I was walking and I thought why not make the man of faith the father of the hit-and-run girl. And that excited me. I said now I might have a character. But I still didn't get to work—well, I got to work, but not writing. Then I bought William James's *The Varieties of Religious Experience* and I read that. And then I taught Kierkegaard's *Fear and Trembling* with a woman named Peggy Walsh, who teaches philosophy here at Bradford. We did a free open seminar like four Tuesday nights in a row, anybody who wanted to read it. I really did it to reread *Fear and Trembling*. Then I started the story, after getting him a job. I have a daughter named Nicole, who's at the University of California, Santa Cruz, and when she was younger every Sunday we would go to these stables for her riding lessons, so I thought well, I'll make him the owner of the stables.

And that's how it started, and I knew something else, except I kept telling Peggy, my wife, when I'd come up from writing, "He won't stop talking. There's no action in the story. He is still talking." Then the action started, and I was just hanging on for dear life. I said, "Now he's talking to God. I don't know what's going on." He took over; he told me the whole story, and told me why it was wrong not to confront the family and confront what had happened, and he told me a lot of things about the Pope, and all sorts of things. I loved spending time with him. But that's a four-year period. No, seven to eight years. The actual writing, it was fast. It went about six weeks.

BONETTI: How do you feel about reader response to the story? Because I want to pursue that story. I want to talk about it. I have a feeling that the story you wrote is not the story you intended for me to read, in a funny way, but I might be wrong about that.
DUBUS: Well, that's interesting. Let's go for it.

BONETTI: Well because the moral responsibility in that story, to me, is what the man did to his daughter.
DUBUS: I agree.

BONETTI: That story, to me, is a sketchbook of the evils of patriarchy. Is that the story you intended?

DUBUS: No, because as a father I know I would have done the same thing. But I like it when people see something in a story which is not as important to me as it is to them. I've noticed as a teacher over twenty years that often a student will be affected by a part of a story, not a story by me, that does not affect another student. The other student is affected by something else, and all of those are in the story. And no one can deny that a reader is going to bring her or his own soul to that story and be angered or shocked or joyful because of something that goes right by someone else. So I think you're right. See, I don't feel that way, but I also know that the way many of us men are with our daughters is not good.

BONETTI: And moreover it is not good for you as a father. I mean, he has, in abusing her the way he has, in locking her into a relationship with him forever, which will probably cripple her as a woman for the rest of her life in terms of being able to deal with the world that we now live in. He has also injured himself All the elements are there. When he, the father, goes through her purse and talks about the trappings of responsibility in this world, he makes the statement that they're like so much sand.
DUBUS: Yeah, that was a very sad passage for me, when he wrote it for me. I feel a deep sadness about what's happened in America because of my experiences as a teacher, so I've seen twenty years of eighteen- to twenty-year-olds. That's a long time. And there are so many of them who have never been given any philosophical values. And so as Luke Ripley went through her purse, I grew very sad with him because he said, "These are the rites of passage." Car keys? Checkbook? Money? Cigarettes?

BONETTI: Kleenex.
DUBUS: Yes. And I know what he's saying is that there should be something of value, of spiritual value in her life. Now, back to what you were saying about your criticism of him. It excites me that we're talking about this character who doesn't exist, so I feel very good as a writer. And I love it that we're talking about what Luke Ripley should have done. I don't agree with you that she's crippled forever. That doesn't make you wrong. It's just my view of the world. It occurred to me some time ago—this has nothing to do with writing short stories—but I prefer reading short stories or novellas because too often a novel tries to tell you that this is the whole story. And I think now in my late forties that our lives are really a collection, a huge collection of short stories, and that is how we communicate with each other. The collection has sad stories and bleak stories and joyful stories and foolish stories, and some

of them we never understand anyway while we're doing them. But it is our lives. So that we'll have a friend and you say, "How are you doing?" and she can tell you a terrible story, and that is her, that day, and she can tell you why this happened and this happened, and we tell stories. Only the people who aren't your friends say, "Fine." She tells you a story. You call her Saturday, "How are you?" and she is a different person, and she tells you a story and she's feeling good because this happened and this happened. And both of those are stories. So when I read a story and write a story, unless somebody dies at the end or there's really, really an ending, I think that is a time in that person's life. And I might come back to that, if I'm the writer of the story instead of the reader. I might come back to that character years later to find out how that person is doing. I just finished reading François Mauriac's *Therese*, and I remembered something I read of him when I finally started reading in college and in the Marine Corps. He said, "I don't understand why people write long novels because you can always write another short novel about the same people." As a matter of fact, *Therese* ended sort of openly. She has tried to murder her husband, and finally she's exiled and she's lonely and she walks out into the streets of Paris. You don't know what's going to happen, but you know that this was a period in her life. So anyway that's why I don't agree she's crippled forever, although I would not argue with you that his treatment of her is not wise fatherhood. It is emotional, and he violates—I don't expect anybody to have noticed this, because it's buried in the story, but there's one sentence where he's remembering his marriage and he says, "We should have had ritual and subordinated feeling to action," he said, "for that is the essence of love." But when it comes to it, he goes on feeling with his daughter because of the way he cherishes and protects her, which I think is very much a part of fatherhood of a daughter. And I think, and this is not just me, other men I've spoken to, with sons we feel nearly the reverse, that it is our responsibility to nurture them so that they can be men, good men. And you know your daughter needs the same, but by God. A young graduate student said it better than this, better than I'm saying. We were—we went to read in Syracuse, for Tobias Wolff, wonderful, wonderful writer—and there was a party at Toby's house and there was this young graduate student who came up to me. "I have read 'A Father's Story,' as a matter of fact," he said. "I have a little baby daughter, and I am in love with her," he said. "I am modern. I am 1980s. But the first time some boy comes knocking on the door I'm going back to the fourteenth century," he says. "I know I will."

BONETTI: But the fact is that he's a classic case. You know in a way of the unreliable narrator and in terms of the craft of fiction because what he had—

DUBUS: Good, I've always wanted to write one of those. You think I pulled it off? I'm serious.

BONETTI: Well he is a classic instance of the unreliable narrator because he concludes the story deluded, you know, about the nature of what he's done. He has sinned against himself, and he has sinned against her, but the thing that's so magnificent about that story is that to take it from the standpoint of just saying well, all fathers treat their daughters differently is to have basically a rather superficial story. The precise thing that deepens the story is the fact that there's like a—I don't know what my technical term is—but there's like a sub-text. There's a story that's in that story. And the story that's in that story is what is now going to happen to that girl for the rest of her life. What kind of a human being is this sending her out at this point in the world to be? All those lost years of being a divorced father, of having his kids taken from him, being just a summer dad, all that was wiped out—he was able to restore his bond with his daughter, but the question that remains open at the end is, but at what price? At what price has he done that? You see what I'm getting at? The meaning of the story?

DUBUS: I do, I do. And I think a line in the story that refers to that is when he's talking about his sons, and he says they tried to make up reasons why they did something and why they shouldn't, he says, but he said what they were really working from was the awful solitude of the heart. And the moral conduct of the story is that he has all these rules to live by, but, and that is why, as a matter of fact, it has such a long beginning because I simply couldn't say, "There was a man with faith." I had to show that he really does have it, and one way to do that was to have his wife leave and he would not remarry and, therefore, would not see a woman so that he could go through this pain. And he had this nice certainty and this good spiritual love affair with God, but then when it came to the daughter, he was back on his heart again, acting—and it occurs to me, he acted as a father might in response to what he first thought—rape, murder—he attacked. Rather than doing what she thought he would do, which was call the police and then take her down. She's not a greatly developed character in the story because it is his story, but I think the grief she shows should imply that she does know those things that you're talking about. And also in support of your argument though, she is grateful she got off. I love old Luke. I love all my characters and end up feeling pretty badly for them.

BONETTI: Well the larger issue I think that we should talk about is in terms of the listener. It is a classic Andre Dubus story in that most of your major themes I think can be found in this story, and one of them is the one we've been talking about here. What you're dramatizing is in fact the crippling effects of ritual and faith in our time. That's the story that I read.
DUBUS: Hmm.

BONETTI: Well, here we have a decent man, you know, a moral man, a good man. His need for ritual has in fact denied him remarriage. It's that very flaw in his reasoning, you know, in his value system which is what leads him to behaving in a very largely irresponsible manner.
DUBUS: Yeah, but we have to also understand there are people—I'm not one of them—although I certainly was for a long time in the matter of birth control, who actually believe that this is the way one must live, and if it turns against you then you just carry that cross. I've known, they probably don't exist now, since people are thinking more for themselves, or whatever has happened in the Catholic church, but I have known people who were divorced, and that was it. And they just had to accept it; they cannot remarry.

BONETTI: But it's the very thing, though, that ends up, it seems to me, as a reader hoisting you, because his denial of what most of us would call a normal life and normal needs make him the kind of creature who I feel, you know, out of his deep loneliness, then could only respond on that level to his daughter. Real love sets people free. Real love frees people.
DUBUS: Yeah. I think had he still been married to Gloria he would've reacted that way, but the mother, as I'm sure you had wished, had not said, "Wait wait wait wait a minute, Luke. We can't cover this up, we have to call the police. This isn't helping anybody. We have to face the music. We'll stand beside her." And the father would be pacing up and down, smoking cigarettes.

BONETTI: You're going to end up writing another story after this interview.
DUBUS: But I do like this discussion. It reminds me of—

BONETTI: But do you see my point?

DUBUS: Oh sure, sure. I want to amplify on that. I used to team teach with a man who no longer teaches here, a wonderful philosopher, named Downing Bowler. And I recommended that he go see *A Man for All Seasons*, the movie with Paul Scofield, and the next day he said, "Oh, you bastard." He said, "That movie, I couldn't sleep." I say, "Why?" He says, "Because I realized, if I had lived in the time of Thomas More, they would've had to cut my head off. I would have had to lose my head for something as silly as not signing something that Henry VIII wanted," which says you can marry or whatever the issue was. I enjoy getting into characters' souls, Anna robbing a drug store, those who are living in a way that has nothing to do with me, and put them under scrutiny and let them grow and see what happens.

BONETTI: That to you is the business of what you're doing then.

DUBUS: At least in that story, yeah. I just finished a long story about child abuse because I wanted a story that's about a silent partner. The husband is doing it, and she knows about it. What excited me morally was his trying to understand why a woman would tell herself this wasn't happening. You see what I'm saying? I like what the character—and also as a reader of other stories, to read of other people who are living by a different standard. I think that's why I love *Heart of Darkness* so much, and I wonder how much of what I'm talking about was happening to Conrad as he wrote. I wonder if he started knowing that Marlowe would find out so much about not only civilization but about himself and would have this feeling of reverence and abhorrence for Kurtz. I'm suggesting that that was probably a very morally exciting novella for Conrad to write, and he must have made as many discoveries as Marlowe did by studying a man like Kurtz, who is so completely different, but is in some way as terrible as he is, has a radiance about him, a glory. He is out there doing something entirely different.

BONETTI: So that is what you see yourself as doing, is in the essential business of the short story, is getting inside the skins of characters, rendering them whole?

DUBUS: Most of the time, yes.

BONETTI: Making them into living beings. So that we can sit here and talk about them like—

DUBUS: Yes. And trying to feel what it's like, yeah. I tell students, I don't know much about acting, but I've read a little bit and saw a movie about method acting. I said I think a writer does what a method-actor does. I said the hardest part I'm finding a lot while writing "Anna" that the most difficult part of writing—I don't know why I didn't know this until 1982, or '80, 1980—is concentration. I do not mean that the phone distracts you or bills. It's not that. It is being able to write a sentence feeling that person rather than yourself. And when I attain that depth of concentration, I am no longer Andre Dubus. And that is the hardest part. You know, to get into that, and back to Conrad's wonderful preface to *The Nigger of the "Narcissus,"* best writing I've ever read about prose, he said that art is communication between one temperament and all temperaments and that communication must occur through the senses because the temperament is not amenable to persuasion. I break that down for students. I tell them what he means is if I tell you I'm sad, a good friend of mine just found out she has cancer—that's not true, praise God—you are not moved. I can't simply tell you I'm sad and make you sad. If I tell you about the friend and make her come to life for you and tell you stories and anecdotes about her and me, you can start crying because now you feel it through the senses. And that's the whole secret, and the whole magic of getting that two-dimensional white and black to become a person we're discussing, I would even say arguing about. But we're discussing what should he have done, and why did he do this. It's exciting. I say writing isn't fun, but it's exciting. Writing certainly isn't drudgery. I wouldn't do it if it were. But I'd do something else. Again, that Simenon article, he said, I guess the whole world knows by now that he would write five books a year in ten days.

BONETTI: Who are we talking about?
DUBUS: Oh, George Simenon. Simenon, he wrote I don't know how many hundreds of books. He said the way he did them was he'd emptied himself. He called it the state of grace and he meant it humorously. He said as a Catholic boy he's taught the state of grace that you can receive, and he meant it in a very humorous way, "I empty myself." Become completely empty. Get a name from a phone book—he has phone books from all over the world, including America where he lived for ten years—then he'd get a physical exam from his doctor, and he'd have his children get physicals, because if one of the children got sick while he was writing his book in ten days, he would tend to the child, and once he was interrupted he could never finish the book. Then he would go to his room for ten days, literally, and he said he would begin by walking up and down for an hour and a half or so, saying the name over and over, and starting to become this person. He said, "And

then I would think, 'What event would change this person's life?'" He said, "Then I'd have my first chapter, and I would sit down and let my character take over. And I would just remain that character." And the woman who interviewed him said, "Why have you never written longer novels?" and he said, "I can never bear to be those characters for more than ten days." What if you had come down?

BONETTI: Can you elaborate?

DUBUS: I can articulate as much of it as I can do to make it happen. Talking about religion and philosophy so much here that people are going to think I'm a theologian, but there's a connection. And the parallel in writing is that you have to work with sentences as precisely as a poet does. And you try to empty yourself, to get back to George Simenon, and let that character come in and fill you, much as these mystics waited for God to come fill them. So the process, which is analogous to those mystical religious experiences, is you first learn through work to write. You learn the craft. Then you use the craft as a means of working through the senses and getting into that character, or maybe opening yourself to the character. I guess that's more like it. And the rest is a mysterious process when a character finally enters you and possesses you, and again if it doesn't happen you can't force it. You have to wait, but it usually always happens. All writers, well I don't know about those experimental writers, but the writers who write about people all will tell you the same thing: a moment comes when the character takes over, and then the writer is led by the character, and that's when the writer knows the story is going to move now. All I need now is the discipline to report to duty every day and achieve that depth of concentration which will allow the character to become the flesh of Andre Dubus who no longer remembers that he has a name, and I think that is the whole process, which is so wonderful, because writing like that, and reading, really reading well, I think gives us, for the time that we're actually doing the writing or reading, the empathy, the perspective of God. In other words we can love a character in a story, and we finish the story. Whether we're writing the story or reading it, we finish the story and we're deeply moved. We've become that person. And we know that we cannot bear having lunch with that person because we would despise her or him, you know? And a wonderful writer like Chekhov can make you become a boring, shallow person and feel what it's like. I think that's wonderful.

BONETTI: Is this why you work in the short story, because you could not bear to be with these people? It's a simple issue with you.

DUBUS: No. Of course because of commercial pressures, yeah. I get asked very often, why don't you write novels? And matter of fact, I went through a very sad period which to me isn't sad anymore in memory. I think it's funny, but it wasn't funny then. Before I had Philip as an agent, I'm leaving off his last name on purpose, but before I had him, I was sending out a collection of stories. Now some publishers simply didn't like them, and I didn't mind that. I outgrew that long ago. I mean somebody doesn't like your work, that's alright, that's acceptable. I mean it happens. You can't expect everybody to love it. The ones that hurt me were the ones that said, "We will publish these if you write a novel." I was also moving more rapidly toward feminism, which I think I was moving toward when I was five years old anyway, having two older sisters and seeing what they experienced, how they had to live in the world compared to how I had to live as a boy, so nothing new. But I was moving more rapidly toward it as my female friends did too, and I told one of them, I know what you feel like. Whether you're a woman who wants to be a professional or whether you're one of those who does not want to be a professional but would rather raise her family, either way you get picked on, and I said, I feel like a woman. I sent a whole book of stories and they said we'll publish it if you write a novel. See but—I don't write novels, I said, I know exactly how you feel, said I just want to be what I am, but anyway I know why I don't because I get one idea at a time. And I don't think that's a novel. I have read novels which work with one theme, but to me they all should have been either stories or novellas.

BONETTI: Care to name some examples?

DUBUS: No, because I don't like to say things about writers in public.

BONETTI: What about a book like *Gatsby*, for instance?

DUBUS: Oh, that's a wonderful novel!

BONETTI: Yeah, it's a novel, yeah okay, but it's about—

DUBUS: But I don't think it could be a story. Okay, if I wrote *The Great Gatsby*, it would probably . . .

BONETTI: I guess the hit-and-run thing is what made me free-associate, but . . .

DUBUS: Forgot about that. That's right because yeah—that is what I would have thought. What if there's a man hopelessly in love with a woman and she had run over somebody and he'd take the responsibility. That would be my story. But Fitzgerald to me told a story of America. Yeah, the whole country. That's a stupid thing to say, everybody knows that, but my stories are not like that. I mean, to me there's a depth and a resonance, and he adds that by having Nick Carraway tell the story and having him react. I mean, I know *The Great Gatsby* says much more about the world than any of my stories.

BONETTI: No, I meant that it's the totality, that if you add up all of your stories. They are certainly about America. That's certainly what they're about.
DUBUS: I sure hope so.

BONETTI: And all of America is implied in that story in all these things we've been talking about. It's all implied. I mean, are we not the way we raise our children? I mean if you look at the world, it starts with the individual. It starts with the individual in relationship . . .
DUBUS: Oh, God, yeah. I'll take old Luke Ripley over a lot of fathers I've known through their children whom I've taught.

BONETTI: But it's, but I mean my point is we are all, we're all, first of all everybody is somebody's child, you know even if we're an orphan. That says something in terms of the relationship with one's parents—the fact that one does not have a parent. And then we, you move out of that. We are our culture, we are our religion, we are our family structure, so in a way, you could say that it's like with you in a way in the kind of short story you write. There's other stories implied by the story that you write, they move out—
DUBUS: Oh I do go for that when I write. Thomas Williams, the novelist, wrote a wonderful review of *Separate Flights*. He said he wants each of his stories to be great. He wouldn't say they're not all, right? How did he know that? Because I would like people to say about me what I tell my students about my favorite writer, Chekhov: "He didn't write novels because he didn't have to," I say, "because Chekhov could say so much and it's so easily misunderstood." That's what I would like to achieve. Chekhov can say so much, and I tell students when he gets over thirty pages long, nobody can touch him. When he writes something between thirty and a hundred pages, there is no one who goes more deeply and touches more bases than Chekhov. His novella *My Life* is the best thing I have ever read in all of literature. It's about ninety pages long, and it is just so rich.

BONETTI: So he's your model?

DUBUS: And compressed, yes, yeah. I was—

BONETTI: When did you discover him?

DUBUS: Well that's interesting, because that really launched my career as a short-story writer, and I reach Chekhov's "The Peasants"—no, it's just called "Peasants"—and I said, well, that's strange because he said he couldn't write narratives. How did he do this? Because it's a thirty-page story that covers one family and its peasant village, and one year, and by doing that also painted a big canvas of what peasant society was like right after the freedom of the serfs, and it's one of the best stories I've ever read. And I finished that and I said, well if he did all that in thirty pages, then he must have used compressed action. So I reread it immediately. I said, by God, it is all scenes. And each scene dramatizes more of his theme. He has a wonderful scene with two little girls, maybe five, six, seven years old, showing their innocence and their beauty and showing the effect of the sordid, not intentionally sordid, but sordid by circumstance, environment. They are told by their old granny, who has to keep the family going on nothing, you get a fish, you make a soup out of it, you save the heads. They're told by Granny to keep the goose out of the cabbage. The girls are lying on the slope of a hill and doing Charlie Brown and his friends, looking at cloud formations. One of the girls is the daughter of a woman who has and maintains her faith throughout the story. And she's telling the other little girl about God and angels, and then they start rolling down the hill and playing. And all of a sudden the grandmother comes out and beats them because the goose got in the cabbage. Now the grandmother's reacting violently and unwisely, but she's also reacting that way because it's food. The little girls come in, and it's a particular Russian religious day. I forget what season and what day, for the Russian Orthodox Church, but they were not allowed to drink milk that day. And the girl who doesn't have religion says to everyone, "If Granny drinks milk, will she go to hell?" "Yes, she'll burn." So they put some drops of milk in her bread and water and go back to the stove—they're always sitting on stoves in Chekhov—and watch her. And it's done. And that is part of a story. I mean, I, and many writers, would have written that story. So I finished reading "Peasants" for the second time, I said, "Andre, you're thirty-something years old. I think it's time to learn how to write. I'm going to learn to compress. I'm going to learn to make transitions. I'm gonna restudy Chekhov, and I'm gonna really study him rather than just have read him for pleasure." And that's what I did. I started working on compressing, and that is why I'm here. Yeah, yeah,

yeah, he's had a—he's one of my gods, and my two living ones are Gina Berriault and Nadine Gordimer, who I think write better short stories than anybody alive in the world. And they are beautiful at compressing, Berriault is incredible.

BONETTI: How did you come to the Hank and Edith stories?

DUBUS: I'm glad you mention those stories because I said something earlier which I realize was a mistake—when you said that Luke Ripley is an example of the unreliable narrator, I said oh good, I've always wanted to write one of those. I realized that's not what I meant. I'd like to write one of those stories that Chekhov and Cheever were so good at, and Ford Madox Ford and *The Good Soldier*? The narrator who does not understand the story he's telling. Because "We Don't Live Here Anymore," the first of those novellas, is first-person, but he's not reliable. A friend of mine said to me, you know, the only good person in that novella is Terry. He said, let's face it—she's a good cook, she has trouble at the house, but gets by on little money, and she's the only one who really loves. And I said, old Jack Lindhart tells the story. He hates lies, and he lies all through there. Says he, "I'm going to the Shell station, honey" and he's off with his, with Edith. I started "We Don't Live Here Anymore," and I should've stuck with that. The narrator was a bartender. Anyway I started it because I was at a party long ago, and there was an unhappily married man who was drunk. And he gestured to his wife and said, "You want her? You can have her." And meant, you know, sexually, and I thought, that's not the first time I've come across that. And I saw Mark Costello some time after that, and I told him the story. Mark Costello is my oldest friend in the world. We met on the rifle range in Quantico, Virginia, in 1958, where we were second-lieutenants at the officer's Basin School. We're stationed together for his three years in the Marine Corps, and I stayed in, and he got me into Iowa.

BONETTI: He's the author . . .

DUBUS: We've been close, loving friends, and he wrote this beautiful book, *The Murphy Stories*, and I said I think a lot of what lies behind husbands and wives who are tolerant, or let their spouses have lovers, is a need to get rid of them. And I also see that in Costello's great story "Murphy Agonistes," where Costello's character masturbates to an image of his wife with somebody, and I remember when I taught that story, I told students that I believe what we're supposed to be seeing is a man who does not have the courage to leave his wife because he can't bear the guilt, so what he hopes is somebody will take her. Then he'll be free of her and free of guilt. So I decided to write a story about a man who was doing that, and I gave him the job of a teacher simply because I wanted him to have some resolve to get into trouble.

BONETTI: You're talking about "We Don't Live Here Anymore."
DUBUS: Right, which was the first one I wrote. And so that's why I make him a teacher. What I was really lazy about was I wanted his friend to have a profession which so preoccupied him that he didn't really care what was going on. And I took the simplest route, and I very lazily made him a writer. Because I never wanted to write about a writer. So I think about had I been a little bit older when I started it, I would've given them different jobs. Also, I think I was in a trap that I won't say people can get into, but I got into. By being educated, by being an officer in the Marine Corps, then by going to graduate school, then by going to college, I lost touch with the majority of people. And I got that touch back when I was very broke one year, I think in 1972, and I tended bar at the local bar, which I use in my stories on Friday and Saturday nights. I relearned something I should not have forgotten. That everybody, nearly everybody, if they're born with the right set of nuts and bolts, is articulate. And I'd forgotten that. I'd made my two male characters a writer and a teacher so they could think, and that was a very elitist notion that I had. It's something that we used to talk about at Iowa, my friends and I. What do you give your—what do you have your people do for a living? You know? We used to talk about examples, and they get, they get really weird—you look at Hemingway's characters, a lot of them are writers. Robert Jordan is a writer. Jake Barnes is a journalist. And you know it's a problem you have to deal with. You have to give your characters a job, and if you're hung up as I was and you're thinking well the only people who can really talk are lawyers, and I see [William] Styron use lawyers, *Set This House on Fire*, and *A Long March*, and *Lie Down in Darkness*. Lawyers or teachers or actresses or something like that, I think you lose a lot. Matter of fact, those so-called common people who go to that working man's bar are too smart to watch television. I got a theory—I'm gonna get back to "We Don't Live Here Anymore"—but I got a theory that, or a hunch, that the reason there's so much crap on television and in magazines is because there are few people who dictate what goes on there, and they are snobbish. That is based on the fact that I've gotten many rejections from commercial magazines saying this is too tough for our readers, especially *Women's Magazine*. I've also talked to editors at *Playboy*, say, well you know, this is a little subtle. We don't have really mainstream short-story readers. I think that is really a lot of

crap. You think people who read *Redbook* have not been divorced, have had a child killed or a Down's-syndrome child? That their world is something sweet and Midwestern? I mean it's a New York provincial idea. Styron said in *Lie Down in Darkness*, Peyton Loftis says, "New Yorkers are the most provincial people there are because they think nothing exists outside of it." And those people whom I drink with now at the bar are men and women who work at normal jobs, many of them menial. But too smart to watch the crap on TV. I think if they had something good, they would watch it. That's what I'm trying to get to. I never wanted to be a writer who writes about teachers and writers. I don't want to read about teachers and writers either. So, but anyway—so I simply start off: "We Don't Live Here Anymore" is gonna be told by a guy who is trying to get rid of his wife. So the story developed and that was that. And I finished it in 1970. Then I started worrying about Edith, or I should say, she started talking to me, and I wondered, how is she doing?

BONETTI: She's the center.

DUBUS: Yeah. So, and I felt bad for that. She's married to a terrible guy. I hated Hank all through the first and second novellas. People have said, that's you, right, because he writes, and I said, not me. He's based loosely on somebody I know, but very loosely. The person I know, I like, but Hank I don't like. He's terrible. I never liked him. Anyway, I started worrying about Edith, and so it took—what'd I say?—seven drafts, four hundred typed pages, during one of those drafts I was reading about Little May and I was thinking about the connections between Love and Death—at that time I was also very lonely, so I thought a lot about love and death and the connection between loneliness and death. But anyway I was thinking about all these things, and we've talked enough about the process, so I guess you started with a kind of a "what if." Give her a lover who is a dying man which will intensify their relationship and make everything special, or what I call a secular sacrament. There's a scene in there where she's vacuuming, I think a room.

BONETTI: She cleans his apartment.

DUBUS: She cleans it, and I wanted to use the word *dance*, but I said that's too obvious. I said maybe I can write it in such a way that a reader will feel that this is not a simple pushing of a vacuum cleaner. This is a—what's the word I'm looking for?—metaphysical act. This is the sacrament. This is a gift she's giving. And I'm sure I didn't succeed in the prose. But that's what I wanted to show. And that everything, because he was dying, everything she did for him was like a sacrament, bringing him shrimp. Making love with him. Because of that relationship with him she sees what—understands, sees more clearly—what she and Hank have lost and decides. I thought she was heroic. I loved her because I didn't know, of course, how it was going to end. She decides that it's worth the pain to get what she knows can be gotten from a human being, and to be able to give that to a human being.

BONETTI: The triumph, though, in "Finding a Girl in America," is that character has just about everything that I can find to hate about a male character, and you end up liking him, although I think the question is left open at the end of whether or not he's just stepping out of one delusion into a new delusion.
DUBUS: Well, I felt the same as you. I ended up liking him, too. The notes for the novella, "Finding a Girl in America" were very simple: write a story of about twenty pages about a man who learns that a woman aborted his child, or whatever you're comfortable calling it, at whatever stage. And since I disliked Hank so much, I said hell, I think I'll make it happen to Hank. It's about time something happens to that bastard. And I really thought of a very short beginning with his current lover telling him this, and as Luke Ripley did in "A Father's Story," it took off, and it wouldn't stop, and all these things kept coming and I started liking him more, and I thought, by God, that's interesting. I asked a young student of mine, a wonderful, wonderful woman, I was troubled and I asked her about somebody I know: "What changes selfish people?" And she said, "Pain." And I realized that's what happened to Hank, that he went through pain and he got better. A wonderful friend of mine, the same one who says Jack Lindhart tells lies all through "We Don't Live Here Anymore," wrote to me when he read it, and he said, "Hank has finally learned that it takes as much discipline and commitment as it does to write, and he's finally become human." And I thought, yeah, okay.

BONETTI: I couldn't help but wonder—I guess I did fall into the autobiographical trap, since Hank is a writer—if in fact Hank's progression was in any way parallel to any kind of moral and ethical progression you yourself have gone through in your life, and I guess your answer would be no.
DUBUS: No, and he writes novels, too. And he quit smoking. No, actually the business of abortion did happen to me, and that's why I was going to write it, and I learned from that, that it's happened to a lot of men. So that's what I was going to write about. And I don't mean the political statement either: "Men feel too." I mean, you know, I wouldn't write a story about that. But I just simply wanted to explore the man going through this, and then

it became longer with flashbacks to other women and God. He makes this long speech about the sexual revolution, by which I believe, too, that women got shafted again. I noticed NBC just had a program on that this week. And you know, a lot of women said, wait a minute. We made it too easy. And nobody's getting committed and we're getting into our thirties and we want babies.

BONETTI: It's just another way of women living on men's terms. I mean that's the point that he comes to there.
DUBUS: Oh yeah.

BONETTI: That sexual liberation . . .
DUBUS: I thought that sexual revolution was a terrible mistake from the beginning. I get frightened. I said you know, when the pill came out, I was still in the Marine Corps, when the pill started getting used, I don't know when it came out. And I was too young to reach many conclusions, but I began to wonder then with fear, what's going to happen to women? And I thought of a John O'Hara novel, where the woman says, "Do you have something?" That's a big shift in responsibility. I remember a woman friend of mine, a close friend whose hair was falling out—and that's tragic, she wrote a beautiful poem about it—because of the sequential birth control pill. And the IUD didn't work with her. And she said whatever happened to the rubber generation? And I said yeah, exactly. What kind of men are we raising now? You know when you write something, at least when I write something, it comes out of so many experiences, and especially with students, that I'll write something and realize I've been talking about that for two years in classes. And that's what I was doing when I was getting ready to write this. I want to add one thing, too. I implied that I sort of cavalierly made Jack Lindhart happy, but it came from something deeper than that. I think that since I'm forty-seven, I guess when I turned forty, maybe forty-two, forty-three . . . not only needing my wife, Peggy, around, but—who's also a writer—not only needed her, but also observing my friends, my own life, but I began to write fiction which I think is more affirmative. I think, one, is for the first time in my life, I was absolutely happy in the true sense of the word with Peggy. I even wrote to Thomas Williams and said I've never been happy my whole life. I didn't think this happened. Does this mean I'm getting ready to die? I thought this might happen at the end. He wrote back. He said relax and enjoy it. And I'm a very lucky man, I have a lovely daughter. I have a publisher who publishes four books of stories and doesn't put pressure out in front of it all. But also I noticed that so many of us, like Mark Costello, who

married in the fifties, because Mark Costello said once to a class of mine here at Bradford, he said in the fifties, a young man wanted three things: a bachelor's degree, a commission in the armed forces, and a wedding—preferably all in the same week. Well, many of us got divorced. And you and I could talk three hours if we had the time in comparing sexual morality of the fifties and the seventies and eighties, and I still don't know which was right. I know both were wrong.

BONETTI: And many of them got married because they had to. Your stories are full of shotgun weddings.
DUBUS: Oh yeah. I—it was incredible how many people got married because they had to. Anyway, a lot of us in our thirties were divorced, and I saw the world as a very bleak place because the women and the men were not doing very well. People got into our forties, and we looked around and people were alright. They had survived. So I think growing older has also made my work more affirmative, as well as having Peggy, and I see a lot of my children, always have, despite the divorce. So the children and Peggy and the new baby, and also seeing that Mark and I are still going, amidst a lot of pain, and most of my friends from that period were divorced, and what sort of pyramid, thinking, that feeling more sorry for the women than I should have. I had this notion that I guess many people have this notion, and it's absolutely false, that marriage is for women. Louise said, "All marriage is for women." And then I find out that a lot of the women have not remarried, and they're doing very well, okay? Then I read a book on it, which isn't worth citing by name and author, but showing that the single man in middle age has more accidents, more deaths, more illnesses, makes less money, drinks more; we are the ones who needed . . .

BONETTI: Marriage exists for the convenience of men.
DUBUS: Oh that reminds me. That's what I was rambling on about.

BONETTI: In your analysis . . .
DUBUS: I think that the reason Jack in "Finding a Girl in America" ten years later is getting plumper and happier is that I think that like many people I know, he and Terry survive. Something that happened in their twenties.

BONETTI: They became friends.
DUBUS: They stuck with their marriage and became friends, yeah. And I have a feeling in a better sense that in Tolstoy's sad novella, *Family Happiness*, in which the marriage—the intimacy of the marriage—is destroyed

and they become friends, it's an interesting novella to talk to people about because you can tell what they think about love by how they react. Some people say it's wonderful. And those of us who are romantics say it's awful. They talk to each other through the children. They can't be in the same room together; they feel uncomfortable. But they reconcile themselves to that. But I had a teacher I taught with, and his wife taught high school, and she said, I have sixteen-year-old girls who can take care of any man I know, I mean my sons, I'd love them to hear this tape, I know they will laugh. I tell them, little Cadence at two puts away the food when she doesn't want to eat it. She puts it on the counter. You guys walk around and bump into things. But males are clumsy; we are a strange animal. My wife, Peggy, says none of you should marry until you're thirty. You're little boys. And the truth is, at least in my case and I think in a lot of other cases, it's not the physical nature of the younger woman; it is that they are often at a stage in their lives where they have not compromised their souls and their hearts. And they're already intellectually in the true sense at your level. They might not have read enough, but their perceptions are there. I mean they're full-grown women, which I guess is what nature wanted anyway.

BONETTI: Now I have—
DUBUS: Men are really kind of . . . I keep thinking the whole problem is we were supposed to get a lot of girls pregnant and get killed by a sabertooth tiger at the age of sixteen. And now that we live longer, we find out that there's really not much that a man is good for in this world. They tried to make us feel part of it—the moms—and that just made me feel more the distance.

BONETTI: There's one question that I think is central in asking any writer, and a writer like yourself who comes so down on the traditional side you know, the Conradian side of Realism in terms of what you're doing, and with Chekhov. And as you know there are contrary trends in fiction. You know, that "language is all," that "characters are nothing but linguistic centers." You know, I'm drawing quotes from various writers that come in the school. Where do you stand in that debate?
DUBUS: Well, I admire anybody who continually turns out work or just turns out one good piece of work, but I can't read them, because I can't read something unless my soul is engaged, and unless I forget I'm me. I can't read somebody who is conscious—

BONETTI: They are, in fact, doing—

DUBUS: —of writing, and letting me know the person is there. I love, and I strive to do what Chekhov does, and I'm not successful at it—you can't find him in his stories. One of my favorite novellas of his is called, "A Dull Story," or "A Dreary Story," depending on the translation, and what he wrote to his editor about that story is absolutely true: it is full of arguments and philosophical debates, and Chekhov said, "But you will not find me in there." And that's what I like. And let me quote a friend of mine. Gabriel Márquez doesn't need our praise, so I'll go ahead and we'll attack him a little bit. He's a big man, and he's a wonderful writer too, okay? But I had trouble reading one of his books, *The Autumn of the Patriarch*, and halfway through I stopped and called a poet friend of mine Kenneth Rosen. I called him on the phone, he's up there in Maine, and I said, it's surreal and I said I don't mind surrealism, but after half the book, I realized there were no characters. And I understood the political statement and philosophical statement the novel was making, and so there was no reason to finish it because I wasn't concerned with any human being in there because there weren't any. They were fleshed ideas.

BONETTI: The artist and what he's doing—that is how I'm understanding you? That it is so obvious that the act of writing is taking place in that kind of work?

DUBUS: Yes. Yes. You're always aware you're reading something.

BONETTI: Many readers of yours have said that you consider yourself a short-story writer, but that all the stories you have written add up to a novel. And that they add up to the same kind of a world as a novel. Do you think so?

DUBUS: Well, I'm very happy that people say that. Yes, I think so, but again I wouldn't call it a novel. I think that we clarified that one earlier. But I would hope that the experience of reading those stories gives you the depth of feeling and of change that a novel would, yeah.

BONETTI: One thing we haven't covered is like, at what point in your life, I mean, have you always written? Have you always—is this what you've always wanted to do?

DUBUS: I did, but I didn't know it, though Nadine Gordimer says that the strange thing about writing is—this is from her great introduction to her selected stories—she said the writer himself often doesn't know when he's working. So I'm saying I was always writing because I was always telling myself stories, but they weren't about me.

BONETTI: When you were a little boy, you mean.
DUBUS: Right. I made up stories, which seemed to me normal, but I have a feeling other boys weren't doing that. And once a year in the Christian Brothers Catholic School—I went from third grade to the twelfth—every year everybody wrote a story, third grade on. And I used to love when that came around. And I'd write a story. Any way to get me out of the class. Again I didn't read much. I wasn't an intellectual kid. I don't like that word. I didn't read much. I read, but I didn't read literature, and I read baseball novels, football novels, anything I could find. And around the junior or senior year in high school, I started to get a little interested then, but I didn't know anything about writing. And I didn't know what I was gonna be. And then after graduation from high school, my father was driving back to Lake Charles. We moved while I was a senior in high school, but I stayed with friends so I could graduate with them, and he came to get me. He stopped at the brothers' house, Christian Brothers. He went to speak to my teachers and came back to the car. He said I asked them what you're good for, and they said English and writing. Well in the fifties, we used to say "Big deal. So what." I said, "Big deal." He said it's a good living. And my heart leaped. And that's when I knew that I wanted to write, and I went home and started writing stories. Because I always wanted his approval. And as soon as he said alright, it was alright. I started writing stories and I majored in journalism the first year, and I realized I was learning how to write backwards. I switched to English my second year. That got him worried. What are you going to do with that? But by that time I was enrolled in this Marine Corps officers' program, and I settled for being in the Marine Corps, so he was happy.

BONETTI: And you saw a life where you could combine the military with writing?
DUBUS: Right.

BONETTI: What changed your mind?
DUBUS: Well he died. My father died in July of '63 . . .

BONETTI: I know.
DUBUS: I had just been promoted to captain. But it didn't hit me that I was free. Because I believed that I was doing what I wanted to do. I had

a wonderful first wife. We saw what was happening to the barracks, and over a beer in Bellingham, Washington, we decided that's it. We're getting out. And it's "we" in the military; it is "we." She was in the Marine Corps, too. Our marriage didn't make it because we were nineteen and twenty-one in the fifties. She was pregnant; we got married. You will notice if you look closely that the ex-wives in my stories are wonderful because they're all based on her because we had a splendid divorce. And she was a strong woman. I mean, she had a child in '58, at nineteen, '59, '60, and then went to sea duty in '63. She had four kids, and that was it. And well what can I do now? I don't know. And she said, call Mark Costello. And I said ah, no, I'm not going to teach. And I didn't know what teaching was like. I thought you become dry and abstract. I had an image of a tweed coat. I called him. He said I'll get you to Iowa because I had a story in the *Salon Review* by then. And about a year later in Iowa I'm walking down this street, and I said, yes, your father set you free. You would not have left the Marine Corps with four children to go to graduate school if your father were alive. When he finally died of cancer at home, I said thank God. I thought it meant because finally the pain is over. It did. It also meant now I'm no longer the sissy he's ashamed of. I'm me, but I didn't digest all of this. I went back as a Marine, expecting to do twenty years, only to resign in two months. But a year later I realized, sure there were the immediate causes, as they used to say in the history courses I took, and then there were the long-range causes. And this is the man who told you at ten you're not good for anything. This is the man who never said don't become this or that, but you always felt that you weren't worthy of him. This is the man you joined the Marine Corps for because you weren't good at sports.

BONETTI: I was going to say in light of everything you've said about male games and female wisdom, what on earth was your attraction to the Marine Corps?
DUBUS: I weighed 105 lbs. when I got my driver's license, ninety pounds ago. I was little, and I wasn't a good athlete. And in the fifties that meant you don't get a girl. Alright? It's not just my father either. It's my image of myself and because of that history I really believe the sixties and seventies might have distorted things a bit between girls and boys. I'm talking about high school and college. But I still think there's some truth in this because I see it in my sons. That a little boy, growing into adolescence, has to—I don't know, I won't even start with adolescence—has to, in his childhood, feel accepted by his male friends before he feels that he has something to present to a girl when he's fifteen. Maybe that's been changing. I'm not even sure it

should be changing. But I know that it wasn't simply my father but my rela-tion with all boys, and all males that made me feel I was not worthy of a girl, had nothing to offer. Because if I could throw footballs, I'd have something. So I did that for myself, too. It's simple to say, well, why didn't you just write? Because writing is not isolated. I still had to live in the world, and I needed the Marine Corps, and the Marine Corps was very good for me. I'm sure it contributed to the discipline I had. And I needed to be able to go in it and outgrow it.

BONETTI: What about your Catholicism? What kind of a Catholic are you?
DUBUS: I'm very lucky with that. I'm a believing Catholic. I believe in the Eucharist. But I always had. I'm just lucky. I'm glad I never lost—matter of fact, when I was writing "Adultery," when I got to the passage about the priest and the Eucharist, I was afraid because I thought I might discover that I'd been fooling myself and I don't really believe that the Eucharist is the body and blood of Christ. And I thought if I—if it turns out that I don't, then I have to find a new philosophy because I'm not gonna live like these many people I know with no philosophy. Just get up and react. And I was very happy. When that section was over, I realized, I do. I do believe in it. I'm not fooling myself. That's not just a fiction writer who goes through that. You must have written letters, and you start thinking you believe this, and if it's an intimate letter, by the time you finish, you've found out that you believe something else so that it's not a change so much as going more deeply.

BONETTI: How are you able to receive Communion? Have the rules changed in the church? You're divorced and remarried.
DUBUS: They haven't, but I'm sort of living in a little existential foxhole. In other words, I think I have a tacit agreement with my parish priest. I've been in the same parish for years. I think they don't ask, and I don't volunteer. I think what people are telling me is what I feel. Matter of fact the priest said it when I was in high school. He said there's no one who can tell you you can't receive because there's no one who's qualified to know. I do believe in Christ and Christianity. I agree with what Faulkner said, "It's a nice religion. Somebody should try it someday."

BONETTI: Thanks very much for this.
DUBUS: Thank you.

A Redneck Intellectual
at Home in New England

Mimi Read / 1984

Dixie Roto Magazine (of the *Sunday Times Picayune*) 15 July 1984: 30–31. Reprinted in *Leap of the Heart: Andre Dubus Talking.* Ed. Ross Gresham. New Orleans: Xavier Review Press, 2003. 68–71. © 2011 The Times-Picayune Publishing co. All rights reserved. Used with permission of *The Times Picayune.*

Andre Dubus doesn't buy the one about Southern-born writers being bur-
dened with the job of understanding the South. His novellas and short stories are about men, women, and children who could be anywhere as the
subtle currents of emotion pass between them.

As it happens, they usually are in generic New England, chain-smoking
cigarettes or committing adulteries or having good days at the beach, but
with minor adjustments of geographical details they could just as easily be
inhabitants of some small town in, say, modern Nebraska.

Among the novelists, poets, and critics of New England, Dubus is famous
for writing realistic stories that instruct the heart, though perhaps his fame
should transcend mere literary circles. Perhaps his name should be added
to medical annals as the first Southern writer to be born lacking whatever
gland it is that secretes nostalgia.

Born in Lake Charles and reared in Lafayette, Dubus has for the past sixteen years lived, taught, and written in the unremarkable town of Haverhill,
Massachusetts.

Critics in sacrosanct places have been good to him. Some of them rave.
In 1976 in the *Atlantic Monthly*, critic Richard Todd nominated Dubus as
a candidate for the most underrated writer of 1975, unfortunately an imaginary award.

David R. Godine, one of the most prestigious publishers in the country, keeps four of his books in print: *Separate Flights, Adultery and Other Choices, Finding a Girl in America,* and *The Times are Never So Bad.*

Meanwhile Dubus lifts weights, wears cowboy boots, and gleefully refuses to get a credit card. He is in love with New England, his young wife, and their beautiful redheaded daughter who is nearly two. He has a "great divorce" with his first wife, who is the mother of his four grown children.

Dubus's feeling for the South is neither of the garden variety melancholias—blind love or blind hatred—but a critical, amused indifference. As a happy, deracinated redneck intellectual leading a passionate life in the North, he has neither the time nor the inclination to conduct pen-and-paper conversation with the abiding spirit of Robert E. Lee.

It is a rainy day in Haverhill under pewter skies. Outside the sliding glass doors in Dubus's kitchen, redbirds peck at a tubular glass birdfeeder hung from the balcony and swaying in the blustery weather.

Dubus has had a fairly typical day. He's written fiction by hand, in a little black book in his study. He's counted the words. Taken out the trash. Popped the tops off a couple of cans of Australian beer and mixed their contents with V-8 juice. By the time his wife, Peggy Rambach, walks through the front door carrying their daughter, he seems anxious to turn the afternoon into a party.

"Is there anything to eat in the house?" he asks.

Rambach touches her hair and smiles.

"Well, we certainly have some pate and octopus and other useful items. Andre spent $200 on *gourmet*," she explains, in tones intimating that the man should, on occasion, be chaperoned.

He zeroes in. "What about that boudin blanc!"

Rambach arranges the Cajun sausages they made earlier that week on a stoneware platter, along with tiny cooked onions, crackers, and pate. She kneels in front of the open refrigerator, softly chanting, "Smoked cheese, smoked cheese," as if calling the cheese to come forward and reveal itself.

Rambach is twenty-six, a softly pretty woman who dresses in the casual New England fashion of jeans, running shoes, leg warmers. She is also a writer. Born in Manhattan, educated at elite boarding schools, she met Dubus when she was a nineteen-year-old sophomore at Tufts University working part-time at Godine.

"Now she's living with a decrepit short-story writer," Dubus says, "breedin' kids in a dead mill town."

"Andre loves that," says Rambach, wiping pate from the baby's hair. "Jap grows up."

"Parents baffled," Dubus says. "Sisters have no comment for the press."

It's not that Dubus didn't try, at first, to write dutifully about the South. He did. The efforts soured. He realized the root of the problem one day while his first wife was driving and he was riding shotgun reading Camus's *The Plague.*

"Ever read that book?" he asks. "Remember that guy who's trying to get the perfect sentence describing the Champs Elysees, only he's never been there? Well, I was writing about lynchings and Southern Baptists and I knew nothing about them. That's Faulkner's territory."

Dubus was born in 1936, the year DiMaggio broke in with the Yankees. He was educated by Christian Brothers at Cathedral School in Lafayette.

During summers, his friends worked as roughnecks and he worked construction. Graduation night, he and a bunch of friends drove to New Orleans, went to the Famous Door nightclub on Bourbon Street, got in, couldn't afford the drinks, and went home.

Later he attended college at McNeese State in Lake Charles, where he began writing stories. All of his male friends were, like him, in the ROTC. Most of them plugged right into the available systems of marriage, military, and work, he says.

"Men in this country are weird," he says. "You talk to a regular American male at the age of forty and you're talking to death.

"I can't stand the Southern men I know who are middle class," he says. "I don't like their irony. I don't like the way they treat women. I was in the New Orleans airport once, on a layover, and a three-piece white man was giving a hard time to the black clerk, who was a woman.

"So I said, 'Oh come on. Ease up. Everybody's had a first day on the job.' He turned to the woman and said (and here Dubus's voice goes into lavish mimicry), 'Oh, was I givin' you a *haaaawd taaaaam*? Well I certainly didn't mean to.'

"I said to myself, Jesus, I gotta go home to New England," Dubus says, "where they either shut up or say go to hell back to you. I go crazy when they get their goddamn smirk and that effeminate thing in their voice. I can't help it. Middle-class white men, with that irony and that false position they maintain, have created women who are clandestine and mischievous but who maintain obeisance."

In his stories, Dubus imagines his way into the minds of women as well as men, and does so with startling tenderness and credibility. In "Bless Me

Father," for instance, he imagines the point of view of a daughter who discovers her father's infidelity and writes him an angry, self-righteous letter from college. In "Miranda Over the Valley," he explores the heart of a young woman who has gotten pregnant by her boyfriend, and whose parents urge her to have an abortion instead of marrying and becoming a "dumb little housewife." She has the abortion, and it breaks her heart, changes her.

All of his people are ordinary, and he charts their progress through a highly recognizable world, trailing them closely from one hour to the next, recording their banal dialogue as well as their moments of insight. They buy packaged meat at the supermarket. They take laundry out of the dryer and heave in on the sofa. They stop for gas.

In short, Dubus doesn't write about the breakdown of regional affiliation or the mutterings of a land with a complex, dark history and an uncertain future. Instead, he writes about what happens afterward: when the man leaves the South and doesn't look back as he struggles to create his own unit of warmth and meaning, his own family.

He leans over and tenderly kisses his daughter, Cadence. She is dressed in overalls and her uncut hair falls wildly around her shoulders. Happy and beautiful, she climbs into her daddy's lap and begins pointing at all the dazzling objects she would like to hold or put into her mouth.

Cadence is named after one of Dubus's short stories. "It's a nice word, a musical word," he shrugs. "It also means pattern of life."

Interview with Andre Dubus

Robert Dahlin / 1984

Publishers Weekly 12 October 1984: 56–57. Reprinted in *Leap of the Heart: Andre Dubus Talk-ing*. Ed. Ross Gresham. New Orleans: Xavier Review Press, 2003. 72–78. Reprinted with the permission of *Publishers Weekly*.

When Andre Dubus laughs, the sound comes from the back of his mouth, not from his bearded throat or his rounded belly. A self-consciousness sounds in this rather shallow bark of amusement, and an edge of wariness shows in his eyes. It's not that Dubus is shy, far from it. He is happily loqua-cious and confidently tosses writers' names from Cyril Connelly to Tolstoy into the conversation, stirring them into a verbal bouillabaisse of literary allusions. It's simply that Dubus seems more at ease with talking than listen-ing, and sometimes he'd rather not be interrupted.

He teaches four classes in writing and literature at Bradford College in Bradford, Massachusetts, and his own accomplishments are a string of short stories and novellas lauded, sometimes lionized, in a growing number of publications—the *New Yorker, Harper's, Playboy*, and more.

In these stories, Dubus writes of the everyday folks with whom most of us are acquainted. Sometimes they even seem to have parts of ourselves within them. His characters are frequently undone by the complexities and pitfalls that can put satisfactory male-female relationships out of reach, and the pursuit of these unions sometimes leads his people down twisting paths that offer sidetrips into adultery and violence.

The two latest books treading into this sensitive territory under Dubus's name are *We Don't Live Here Anymore*, published in July by Crown, four novellas previously contained within other collections of his work by David R. Godine; and *Voices from the Moon*, a longish novella (or a shortish novel) published this month by Godine.

In writing and in speech, Dubus has a flavorful vocabulary, and some of the words he uses don't ordinarily find their way into the pages of such mag-

63

azines as *Publishers Weekly*. He dresses in an assertively masculine fashion: jeans and a Western-inspired blue shirt, white snaps down the shirt front and on pocket flaps, its sleeves rolled up. He is rarely without a cigarette. Dubus is that sort of manly figure that baldly emphasizes a tough gender, but he confounds expectations by using salty language to muse on the troubling puzzles in the man-woman bonds that he portrays so movingly in his stories.

Born in 1936, Dubus grew up in Louisiana and attended McNeese State in Lake Charles, studying journalism until he realized that he was writing backward, starting with the most dramatic aspect of a story and then shoring that up with background. He switched to English, where he learned vital facts like "Lord Byron had a club foot and all that kind of crap."

Matter-of-factly Dubus says, "I'd been a sissy all my life. I never played any sports. and I didn't have any self-confidence." He joined ROTC and after college went into the Marines. "Man, in those days, it was the normal thing to do, and a lot of people in my generation did it. I wanted to feel like a man, and they do make a man out of you. They make you confident. You meet a lot of English majors in the Marines wanting the same thing."

To Dubus, the marine experience is translatable to the young civilians in his charge today. There's something in the acquisition of self-esteem that he is impelled to pass on to his students. "You've got to unteach them many things," he says. "I think a lot of English teachers don't teach well. They teach literature as if it's a thing to acquire. They go a little crazy symbol hunting. I don't let my students say symbol. I tell them, 'Say dramatic statement of theme.'

"Maybe it's because English teachers sometimes feel that their work is not enough, that they have to put their personal stamp on what they're teaching, like a jazz musician playing with a melody. To me, the most important task is to get students confident enough to follow their own instincts. Their instincts are usually right. They're usually afraid to articulate what they think, so they tell you what they think you want and give you a lot of bullshit."

The last noun is one fundament of life that Dubus claims to have nothing to do with, and this goes in his writing too. A reader may not agree or approve of Dubus's vision of life, but there are no hedged bets in the stories. They are hard and blunt, and he's been at them for many years. He doesn't glamorize what he does.

"It was never a decision I made, to write short stories," he says. "It's just my natural bent. Whenever I'm asked why I write short stories, I always end up demeaning myself, I say I work with one idea and with two or three characters. And, as Thomas Williams says, a novelist creates a whole world."

For a time Dubus did work on a novel, and Dial even published one that is now out of print. "But then I read a short story by Chekhov," he says, "one called 'Peasants.' I finished it and I said, 'Wait a minute.' Chekhov created an entire microcosm of Russian society in thirty pages. I knew I had some learning to do, and I've never written anything longer than a short story or a long short story since.

"I've been happiest with short stories. I wrote one called 'The Fat Girl.' I had a fat girl in one of my classes, and I wondered what it would be like to be a fat girl. How did other people view her? Thomas Merton said, 'If you live the life other people expect you to live, you live only in their imaginations.' To which I added, 'And if they don't think about you, you don't exist at all.'"

Dubus's conversation is difficult to direct. He isn't so much obstinate as he is likely to chase after his own thoughts. He is a man with whom it would be entertaining and enlightening to hang out on evenings in a neighborhood bar with a cold bottle of beer at hand. But it would be advisable to have the empties removed on occasion, because otherwise the accumulation would probably reach unseemly proportions. When the talk touches upon the thick thread in his fiction, however, the man-woman thing, he quickly picks it up, explaining what he sees in contemporary life that conspires to keep men and women from ever really getting to know each other.

"One of the first reasons is all the stuff a boy goes through to feel like a man, and for a girl to feel like a woman. Everything that goes into this process only increases the isolation between them. I think that's why we're all essentially lonely. People don't know about other people. Boys and girls grow up in a strained society, one that drives them apart. It's a solipsist society, and then when we get older, we have problems.

"Add to that that we have mostly meaningless jobs today. The only thing to be gotten out of them is money. There's no satisfaction, and it's hard for a young couple, especially when both work as most have to today, to have a working life and then come home and have anything to do with the family.

"This country is really screwed up. So how can people not be screwed up? When I grew up, I learned that the most important thing you can do is to get married and have children, and if you are one of maybe 10 percent of the country, you'll get a job you like. I think somehow that people can do something at work that serves no purpose and then come home at night and expect to be a whole person. But it's hard to do. When I got married for the first time, my wife and I had no knowledge that things could go wrong. We thought there was a set of rules and happiness followed."

It didn't follow Dubus and his first wife, whom he married in 1958. He feels they were victims of the great American myth promising fulfillment of unrealistic expectations. He says theirs was a friendly divorce, however, and he sees his four children frequently. He is now married to his third wife, and this time it is a marriage of equals. She is a writer too, and they share both affection and expenses. They don't share a religion: she is Jewish and Dubus is Catholic, a faith that is a significant force in his life, despite his divorce, and one that forms a critical underpinning to many of his stories.

"My third marriage is my last," says Dubus and adds, "You know, I was happy to leave home when I was twenty-one. The marriage between my father and mother wasn't what I thought a marriage should be. I didn't think they were happy, but now I realize that nobody knows anything about anyone else's marriage. Unless maybe you live under the bed for a year."

As for knowing the marriages he writes about in his stories, Dubus is quick to say, "Oh, I just make them up. And it's like *Voices from the Moon*, none of the characters is me." After a brief pause, he admits, "Although my wife says she does see some of me in the father there."

Voices from the Moon is a mellower Dubus than his readers have come to know. Its small roster of characters includes a long-divorced father and mother, their three grown children, and the divorced wife of the eldest son. The father and his one-time daughter-in-law fall in love and plan to marry, and the book is made up of reactions to this, most particularly of responses from the youngest son, who hopes one day to become a priest. There is an unusual amount of compassion and forgiveness within this Dubus story as a priest counsels the teenaged son to help ease his shock and shame and as the mother offers loving advice to the older son, urging him to come to terms with the romantic relationship between his father and his former wife. It is perhaps the most tender plot Dubus has devised.

Dubus looks surprised and pleased when the explicit benevolence of *Voices from the Moon* is mentioned to him. "Yes," he acknowledges, "but I didn't even realize this until I read the galleys a month ago. It wasn't something that I'd intended to do. I said to my wife, 'Isn't it wonderful? Everybody comes through for everybody else.' It just goes to show that you never know what you're doing as you write. And the chapter about the father and the daughter. Isn't that wonderful? But that's also partly why this book isn't a novel. It's some moments in a day. It's a glimpse of people and what they can overcome. It's not the length that makes a book a novel. It's instinct. Like

Joan Didion's *Play It as It Lays*. I don't think it takes much longer to read that than it does *Voices from the Moon*, but her book feels like a novel and mine doesn't. Well, maybe mine's a short novel."

He says, "I never know where I'm going with a story. When you write with an outline, your story is dead. That's the excitement for the writer. In one of my stories, 'The Pretty Girl,' I knew that at the end I would have a man and a woman and a pistol together in a room. And I knew the woman would have the flu. I have the flu a lot. But I didn't know what would happen. Would the man shoot the woman? Would the woman shoot the man? Or would nobody shoot anybody at all? My job is only to form the words on the paper as they are performing their acts."

In fact, the acts in "The Pretty Girl" do lead to the shooting of one of the characters, but, as told, there is an inevitability about the brutality because other brutalities precede it. Discovering the conclusion took time, however, because as he writes, Dubus polishes and repolishes his prose. He polishes less today. "That's because I write more slowly now," he says. "I used to need to write a thousand words a day; now if I write a hundred I'm happy. I guess it has to do with being calmer these days. I used to think, 'What if I died leaving a story unfinished?' Now I realize that if you die with one unfinished, you're not going to care."

A number of his stories have appeared in big and little magazines, but when it came to publishing them in book form, nobody had any use for them. "The rejections really didn't hurt so much," Dubus says. "When they said they didn't like them, that was all right, but some publishers said, 'When you have a novel, then come back to us.' That hurt, and I was very discouraged. I remember crying. I remember crying frequently. I said to a woman I knew, 'Now I know what it means to be told to be something you're not.'"

Then agent Philip Spitzer entered his life. "I'll get them published," he told Dubus. "No, you won't," countered Dubus. As *Books in Print* proves, he did. Godine was the one to flout the negative reputation of short-story collections. And now one of the big guys has stepped in, as Crown has pulled together four of the novellas.

Perhaps this is one cause for Dubus's optimism. He believes that the prospects for shorter forms are artistically assured. "I think that short stories have a great future," he says. "There used to be more magazines to publish them. But who can say there's no place to publish stories today? That's bullshit, with all the literary quarterlies around. True, you won't get rich, but I'm convinced, too, that book publishers today are realizing that short stories are not necessarily a losing proposition."

As for himself, he comments, "I'm a very lucky short-story writer. How many writers have four collections published in a row? And Crown paid $15,000 for the novellas, and for *Voices from the Moon*, too. I must confess I don't really understand. I have about five thousand readers, and they've already read the novellas when they were first published. Crown says not to worry, they'll find more readers. I said to Betty Prashker, 'You've paid $30,000 and you're not going to make a buffalo nickel.' She said to me, 'We'll see.' Maybe they know something I don't."

The Outrageous Andre Dubus

Jesse Kornbluth / 1985

Horizon 28 (April 1985): 16–20. Reprinted with the permission of the author.

"I don't know how I feel till I hold that steel."

O Lord, I think at the end of that first sentence of "The Pretty Girl," the novella which opens Andre Dubus's *We Don't Live Here Anymore*, what's more unpromising than a weight lifter with a penchant for interior rhyme? A paragraph of this and I will abandon the book.

Only I don't. Because what follows in that paragraph is as precise a description of the pleasures of pumping iron as I have ever read—and not just emotionally and physically accurate, but something else, something that, in modern fiction, is actually astonishing. For though Ray Yarborough is a bartender—a man who doesn't have much of a future in a white-collar world—he's not stupid. He can't be patronized. He knows what he feels and why. And he can tell us, directly and without artifice.

Indeed, by the second page, I find I'm agreeing with him. Life in New England is good, what with the Celtics and Patriots and Red Sox and Bruins to watch, and the ocean, and the pretty country, and the hunting and fishing and skiing. And it's better not to have a credit card if you're the sort who doesn't have a line on ready cash.

But this isn't Ray's recitation of blessings. Although he's treated his wife well, helping out with the cooking and cleaning and such, Polly has left him for Vinnie DeLuca. "Never marry a woman who doesn't know what she wants and knows she doesn't," Ray concludes. Or wishes he could conclude. For earlier this summer, he has raped Polly. And now he's about to stomp Vinnie DeLuca in a parking lot. Which will only propel him deeper into his obsession with his wife—an obsession that will end in a cabin overlooking a lake in New Hampshire with a question, a gun, and a tragedy.

In sixty-five pages, "The Pretty Girl" tells a more complete story than most novels. Considerably impressed, I turn the page and begin the title story, the first of three about the Linharts and the Allisons, two couples living outside Boston. Both husbands teach at a small college on the New Hampshire border, where they make too little money, smoke too much, drink just enough beer to make their five-mile runs necessary, and, because they married too young, are adulterous—mostly with the other's wife.

Halfway through "Finding a Girl in America," the last of these three novellas, I must leave my home. Yet I can't leave without knowing whether Hank Allison (divorced and consorting with students) will marry Lori (who loves and understands him but is, after all, nineteen). So I read as I walk, circling my destination twice to get to the finale.

No writers since James Salter and Peter Handke have taken me over this way. But Andre Dubus is different from those novelists—he comes unannounced. No one I talk to knows him. Of my literary friends, only two have read him.

In the next few weeks, I read everything he's written: four collections of stories and one short novel, *Voices from the Moon*—all published by David Godine of Boston. All hold up. Hold up so well that it's impossible to understand why the mass market was denied Dubus until Crown issued *We Don't Live Here Anymore* as a $7.95 paperback last year. Hold up so well that it soon becomes imperative, in the name of justice, to discover why, if Andre Dubus is so good, so few of us have ever heard of him.

The campus of Bradford College reminds a visitor of more-celebrated New England institutions. But Bradford is set in Haverhill, an hour outside of Boston, and many of its 360 students come from the neighboring community. When I visited Andre Dubus there, he had resigned his job and was packing his books and preparing to move. He suggested that I arrive around eleven. He'd be back from morning mass by then, he said, so when I reached the faculty houses, all I had to do was look for the yellow Subaru.

In his book-jacket pictures, Dubus is a kindly, round-faced man with a salt-and-pepper beard. In person, he's something else. He wears a large gold cross around his neck, a maroon corduroy shirt, blue jeans with a wide leather belt, and cowboy boots. His manner is hearty in the extreme, as is his candor—as he lets me in at the appointed hour, he announces that he tied one on last night, has missed mass, and is just contemplating breakfast.

I am immensely disappointed. Who would have guessed that the man who knows women's inner lives better than most contemporary women writers seems like nothing more than a barrel-chested neo-Hemingway?

Dubus leads me into the kitchen, where Peggy Rambach (his third wife) plays with Cadence, their two-year-old daughter. Peggy, who also writes and teaches, is only twenty-six. As Dubus shuts off a Waylon Jennings tape and makes his eggs, I do some math. It doesn't take a graduate degree to wonder if Peggy's the model for "Finding a Girl in America"—and, if so, how many more dazzling turns of fiction will be reduced to modified autobiography. Then Dubus begins to tell his story. "I was raised in bayou country—Lafayette, Louisiana. My father was a civil engineer who got an A in a short-story course from John Crowe Ransom and really wanted to be a golfer. My mother read a lot, wrote letters in the morning, and always listened to the Metropolitan Opera on Saturday afternoon. I have two older sisters. I was small and a sissy—couldn't get a girl till I got out of high school."

He studied journalism and English at McNeese State in Lake Charles, Louisiana. When his father asked him what kind of man's work that led to, he joined the Marines. "The Marines are full of small guys. I guarded a nuclear-ammo dump, ran security, and led trainings. I stayed in for six years, but I'm not patriotic in the traditional sense—my death wish is to die at eighty-five, ambushing fascists who are taking over the country.

In 1964, as a twenty-eight-year-old Marine captain, he had a story accepted in the *Sewanee Review*. Emboldened by that $125 check, he resigned from the corps and signed up at the Iowa Writers' Workshop. He studied with Richard Yates and watched "Batman" with Kurt Vonnegut. He wrote many stories and one novel, which was so widely rejected he held a drunken funeral-mit-pyre for it. ("Well, if it had been published, I'd have had a publication party.") And, over the next five years, Dubus and his wife produced two daughters and two sons.

In 1966, when Oregon offered him $9,000 a year to teach English and Bradford offered him $7,200, he remembered a friend's description of Bradford—"near Boston *and* the sea"—and moved his family to Haverhill. Two years later, Burt Lancaster optioned his novel *The Lieutenant*. But even with that infusion of capital, the marriage was in trouble, the result of marrying too young and with too many expectations. By 1970, he was divorced.

Although Dubus had other offers, he chose to stay at Bradford. "We tried for a good divorce," he explains. "I'd have dinner with one child each Wednesday and spend weekends and holidays with my kids. And by then I'd fallen in love with the area and my students. The school had changed from a junior college for girls to a four-year school that draws some local kids. I preferred teaching some of the sons and daughters of factory workers. They're not as articulate, but they're educated in other ways."

Dubus taught twenty classes weekly, wrote his stories, lifted weights, ran three miles a day, quaffed a six-pack every day, smoked a carton a week—

and, on top of that frenzy, had a complicated emotional life. It took its toll. On January 1, 1975, he woke up with a woman he didn't know and hadn't slept with. "I thought, You're in trouble, and went home to visit my mother. In New Orleans, I called the widow of a college friend, and before the week was out, I'd asked her to marry me. I knew why I proposed—I was crazy— but it never occurred to me to wonder why *she* dropped everything." That disastrous marriage lasted two years.

Peggy Rambach was a sophomore at Tufts with a part-time job at David Godine when she was assigned to oversee Andre Dubus in his editor's absence. During their first phone conversation, she told Dubus, "It's hard to read you without falling in love with you." After that, how could they not meet? Peggy was, Dubus discovered, the first woman he'd been with who didn't need to be entertained. And, of course, the first woman he'd love whose involvement with him was unsettling to his mother. "I was forty-one, she was nineteen—and I wasn't a mother's dream," says Dubus.

In the fall of 1983, having embarked on what he insists is his final marriage and his fifth go-round with infant feeding schedules, Dubus collapsed. Peggy taught most of his classes for him while he rested. His blood pressure was still high last spring, so he took that term off, too. And when it still didn't drop to normal by the end of the term, he called the dean and said he'd be taking the fall off. With that, his blood pressure "dropped like the '29 crash." Taking the hint. Dubus retired.

With the money Crown paid him for the paperback rights to his novellas and *Voices from the Moon*, Dubus bought a wooded acre north of Haverhill and set a $50,000 prefab house on it. Though small—it is, he learned recently, really a vacation home, so his library has been renamed the "book closet"—it costs only $400 a winter to heat. Which isn't an inconsiderable factor when, at forty-eight, you cut yourself off from a regular income and what you have to show for twenty years of writing and teaching are small royalty checks and a monthly pension of $658.

It doesn't have to be this way. Dubus was recently invited to apply for Raymond Carver's $40,000-a-year job at Syracuse. "What the hell would I do with $40,000 in Syracuse?" Dubus says dismissing the possibility. "Anyway, I refuse to live in any state where George Steinbrenner lives."

More to the point, Dubus could do writing that's considerably more commercial. But although he loves movies, he rejects all screenwriting opportunities. And in a world that can be very good to novelists but which is known to be inhospitable to short-story writers, he could write longer fiction.

His refusal to turn writing into a business—even for reasons of survival—suggests both Dubus's pride and commitment. His rules are only two: "Not one line for money" and "No alcohol before writing." He always thought, he says, that he'd publish fifty stories in literary quarterlies and die with dignity. (This attitude recently paid off: Dubus has just been awarded a $20,000 National Endowment for the Arts grant.)

The struggle to maintain dignity is not just Dubus's, but the animating idea of his fiction. "I'm a 'cradle Catholic' who never went through metaphysical doubts. If I didn't believe Communion was the literal blood and body, I'd have to look for something fast. I couldn't live in a world where Reagan as president is the absolute reality."

His characters don't enjoy much spiritual certainty. Nor, for their pains, do they make do with worldly prosperity. Instead, a father whose son has been murdered finds himself unable to endure the period before the trial, when his son's killer walks the streets; with a friend, he revenges his son's death. A college girl decides to break up with her townie boyfriend; he kills her. A fat girl loses seventy pounds and gains a husband and a nice life, only to choose to balloon up again. And, over and over, couples in their late twenties find themselves worrying about such unglamorous and unfashionable problems as insurance premiums.

Life isn't all glum in Dubusland—in one story, a girl with a checkered reputation discovers how to regain her virginity; in another, a weekend father scraping ice from the inside of his windshield realizes this is the frozen breath of his children—but it is always serious and it's never about people who are well-off. And there is always passion and a great desire to be free and no real way to escape; as a woman remarks in *Voices from the Moon*, "We don't live great lives, we just have to understand and survive the ones we've got."

"I'm tired of reading about people with money," Dubus says. "Most of the people I know don't have any and don't have the luxury of having a nervous breakdown in Rome." But it's more than economics that grates on Dubus; it's the literary myth that people without money are unworthy of our interest. "At Ronnie D's, the bar in Bradford that's the model for Timmy's in my stories, I relearned something important. It's widely thought that people who work with their hands aren't very deep. In fact, they're no different from my friends. They don't like TV. They know what the truth is—they just don't say *angst*. It's magazines and TV producers who think these people are dumb."

In all this, Dubus reminds one less of other writers than of Bruce Springsteen, the first rock musician to make art from the lives of the forgotten. And like Springsteen, Dubus has a tonic effect on his devotees. Betty Prashker, editor in chief at Crown, recalls the day she scheduled Dubus's book—only to realize that the catalog for the coming season was closed. Still, she asked the young woman in charge of the catalog if one more book could be slipped in.

"Impossible," the woman said. "Whose book?"

"Andre Dubus."

"O my God!" the woman cried. "He's the greatest writer I've ever read."

And she not only got Dubus's *We Don't Live Here Anymore* into the catalog, but, at Prashker's suggestion, represented the book at the next sales conference.

Dubus applauds this anecdote less because it adds to his cult than because it is active; of all the facts of life he hates, passivity strikes him as about the lowest—"more evil than a passionate act." That is why he carries a small, licensed pistol in his pants when he and Peggy go to Boston ("I'd never use it to defend property, but I've resolved that no woman walking with me is going to be harmed while I look on") and keeps an ax handle in the trunk of his car.

The gun has never been fired. He *has* had occasion to use the axe handle. This past October, Dubus was driving from his favorite bar when he saw a crowd in front of a pizzeria. He slowed and saw a tall man beating a young girl against the wall as his friends watched. "I was alone, wishing my sons were with me," he recalls. "But I got out, got the ax handle, and stood in front of the car. Why an ax handle? Well, an ax handle is not, say, a baseball bat, but it's heavy enough to make a man test his commitment. And it gets a man's attention."

One of the teenagers moved in on Dubus, unaware that the short, bearded man was once a Marine trained to move toward trouble—and fight with sticks. Just then, a police car pulled up. And Dubus found himself the only objective witness.

Dubus was proud of the girl's mother for pressing charges. And, on the day of the trial, he put on one of his two jackets and went off to testify. But the judge dismissed the charges before Dubus was called to the stand.

Outraged, Dubus stood up and challenged the judge. He was declared out of order and hustled from the courtroom. It was just as well—his services were more useful in the corridor, comforting a girl who had been beaten twice.

As Dubus tells this story, playing all the parts and cursing eloquently where editorializing is suggested, there might as well be no inquisitive child, no wife, no dog in the room. I see the pizzeria, the girl, the confrontation, the anger before trial, the mockery of justice—I see this story as clearly as if it's been printed.

And I see also that this storytelling not only transforms the butt ends of sad lives into something fine and enduring, it also transforms Dubus. This is, I realize, no campus cowboy, no macho mythmaker. On the contrary, this is a writer who looks at his life and the lives around him without idealizing anything and then, at whatever cost to health and wallet, sets it down. Which is why, when we want to find out what our lives are really like, Andre Dubus seems more and more like the most reliable witness we have.

Our Dinners with Andre

Amy Schildhouse / 1986

Indiana Review 10.1/2 (1987): 9–20. Reprinted with the permission of the author.

Andre Dubus was driving home late one humid night last July on U.S. Route 93 to Haverhill, the small, blue-collar town north of Boston where he lives. Dubus was coming off a string of summer writers' conferences, workshops, and readings. He was tired, but he felt good. David R. Godine, publisher, would bring out his seventh collection of short stories and novellas, *The Last Worthless Evening*, in November. His wife, short-story writer Peggy Rambach, was pregnant with their second child. He'd retired from full-time teaching at Bradford College, had just won a Guggenheim, and he planned to spend the year writing. That evening, in fact, he'd been to a dangerous Boston neighborhood called "The Combat Zone" to research a new story.

Then Dubus saw a motorcycle, riderless, lying in the middle of Route 93. He noticed a Pinto stopped near it in the fast lane. Automatically, he slowed down, pulled up ahead of the car, flicked on his hazard lights, and rushed out of his car to offer assistance.

"*Señor*, please help. *No hablo ingles*," said a young Hispanic man, coming around the back of the car. The man and his sister, the driver, had just hit the motorcycle, and feared they'd hit a person. Dubus tried to soothe them and led them down the highway toward his car. Just then, a Honda Prelude neared the trio. Its driver, a woman, saw the Pinto and swerved left to avoid hitting it. Instead, she hit Dubus and the man. The man's sister was unscathed because, she later claimed, Dubus pushed her out of the way to safety.

Andre Dubus ended up on the trunk of the woman's car: his right hip fractured, a broken bone in his right hand, broken ribs, two compressed fractures of the vertebrae, a compound fracture of the femur in his right leg, a compound fracture of the tibia in the same leg, a gaping hole in his left thigh, and his left tibia nearly decimated. The force of the impact tore off his cowboy boots, and a quarter that was in his right pants pocket was bent neatly in half. Yet miraculously, his spine, vital organs, and head were largely uninjured. He was alive.

Dubus and the young man were rushed to the emergency room of Wilmington Regional Health Center. Three hours later, the young man died. Dubus was treated at the Center for shock and transferred to Massachusetts General Hospital to undergo the first in a series of ten operations. The surgery cleared his left leg of much contaminated tissue, but the damage to the tibia was too severe. On September 4, the leg was amputated mid-knee. Dubus left the hospital on September 17, more than seven weeks after he'd entered it. His right leg was in a cast, and he would have to endure a painful bone graft on it in November. The slow, torturous, frustrating journey to recovery began.

Sunday in Bloomington, Indiana, June 1986 at the Indiana University Writers' Conference, a few minutes before 5:00 p.m. We are gathered in the Distinguished Alumni Room at the Indiana Memorial Union. We are sixteen writers, many from the Midwest, but some from as far away as California and New York City. The workshop leader, Andre Dubus, is late.

What have we to go on? Some of us have read his latest work, a short novel called *Voices from the Moon*. One workshop member, a housewife from suburban Chicago, wonders aloud how Dubus coaxed a believable ending of hope from his story's seemingly hopeless domestic tangle. A tall, greying, retired cemetery owner tells us that he read Dubus's "A Father's Story" a few days earlier, and it made him cry. Another participant, a deceptively young-looking father who lives in the area, recalls picking up Dubus at the airport on Saturday. "Wait'll you meet this guy," he shakes his head. "He's crazy."

At 5:40 p.m., Dubus announces his arrival from twenty feet down the hall.

"Where is this goddamned Distinguished Alumni Room?" he bellows. "I've been lost for thirty minutes. Where's the bar? Anybody else need a drink?"

Dubus bursts into the room, a stout, bearded, sunburnt man dressed in white chinos and a white short-sleeved shirt, a stack of manuscripts and a pack of Pall Malls in his hands. He spies one member of the group, a woman publicist he knows from New York. He runs up and envelops her in a bear hug. Then he turns to the group.

"Now don't get all worked up," he admonishes them. "We don't know each other that well, and besides, there are no grades."

Dubus takes a seat at the head of the long, wide conference table and proceeds to tell us what we can expect from the workshop.

"Don't plan to get out of here before five any afternoon," he warns, a faint Southern drawl softening his threat. "We have sixteen writers and at least sixteen stories. I'm not leaving here Friday until we've discussed every one of them."

"Anybody seen an ashtray?" He looks at us. "Jesus, don't tell me I'm the only smoker." He lights a cigarette.

"I hope that you will learn some things here," Dubus says, "but please, don't any of you call yourselves students. You are writers. And you should remember: the apprenticeship of a writer is long." He gazes around the table, inspecting our faces.

"I'm going to be fifty in August; I've been writing since I was nineteen. I still consider myself an apprentice. I learned two new things about writing last year from reading Gina Berriault and Nadine Gordimer, so I guess I'm no journeyman."

"We all write to find out what we're thinking. The ones who are going to learn the most this week are not the writers whose stories we're discussing. The process of figuring out why you like someone *else's* manuscript is how you will learn. It's much more valuable to look at a manuscript with mistakes," he adds. "If you can say, 'I see that those two sentences ruin that paragraph. I won't do that in my story,' you've learned more than you could have from a perfect work."

We exchange manuscripts. Dubus is incensed when he finds out that tonight is the first time we are receiving each others' stories. He swears.

"I hope some of you caught a good look at Bloomington on the way in, 'cause I imagine that'll be the only chance you get to see it. We'll have to spend every free minute reading manuscripts." A thought strikes him and he bursts into laughter.

"I feel sorry for myself," he says, "but you poor suckers . . . At least I'm getting paid for it!"

Dubus proceeds to relate a few stories about Faulkner, Hemingway, and his favorite writer, Chekhov. ("When I write, Chekhov is my imaginary audience," Dubus says. "He reads my finished stories and he is always very kind. He says, 'Someday, Andre . . . someday.'") He tosses off writing advice as casually as if he were listing spelling rules: "Always stop in mid-sentence when you're writing well." "A writer should touch on each of the five senses in every paragraph." "Pay close attention to proportion in your stories." "Read your final drafts aloud into a tape recorder and hear how they sound. Only then can you rewrite them properly."

We are growing accustomed to Dubus's method. He heaps anecdote upon story, bandies about names like Tobias Wolff, Kurt Vonnegut, Jr., Richard Yates, John Yount (writers he knows and admires), and quotes from countless memorized stories—all the while interrupting his patter to tell more stories of his own. This is a man who censors nothing. All stimuli are fodder for his fire. So that depending on how much one knows about his homelife, his friendships, his stories, a newspaper account he read that morning, or what he ate ten minutes ago, one understands more and more his field of reference. Dubus's thinking follows a wild rhythm. He moves in the present tense.

Tonight's "introductory" half-hour meeting has stretched into two hours. En masse, we hurry into the hallway, wondering if we'll find any food left at the Welcome Buffet that started at 5:30 p.m. Two thin, bespectacled female workshop members leave the conference room together.

"I have a feeling this week we'll be running on Dubus Time," the one in the headscarf comments dryly.

"Where's this goddamned dinner?" asks Dubus, sweeping ahead of us into the hall.

Monday, 1:45 p.m., the Distinguished Alumni Room. Dubus spent fifteen minutes trying to find our meeting place. We will grow used to it, or else try to draw him a map. My story is up first today. I think about how Dubus said you learn less when your own manuscript is critiqued, yet I scribble in my notebook and the margins of my story.

Dubus reads aloud a line from my work, a sentence about a young boy riding in the "mesmerizing" cocoon of an older neighbor's Buick.

"Mesmerizing?" asks Dubus. "Are you sure that's the word you want? Is there some witchcraft going on in this story?"

He seizes the opportunity to make one of his favorite points.

"Don't use a word that is almost right," counsels Dubus. "As Flaubert said, we must search for *le mot juste*—the precise word."

"Avoid cliches," he instructs. "They make your reader turn from the story to his own memories instead. In fiction, action is time," he says. "You can compress a whole childhood into two paragraphs. Just use a few lines of very characteristic details."

Suddenly, in the midst of the critique, I'm hit with a solution to my story's central flaw. Dubus, who's been watching my face throughout his discourse, raises his finger to his lips.

"Ssh," he tells the others. "I think the writer knows what she needs to do. Let's all shut up now. This is where the magic begins."

Someone asks Dubus where his stories come from.

"I start with an idea or a situation, never a character," he says. "I write a story to understand my concerns. *Voices from the Moon* came from a newspaper story about a marriage, "Killings" was one of my 'what—if' stories. What if the father of a murdered child was offered the chance for revenge? In the novella *Rose*, I wanted to understand child abuse."

"Don't y'all love to just sit in bars and listen to people?" Dubus asks. "Everybody tells each other stories all the time. But why listen, why eavesdrop?" He thinks for a minute, then answers his own question. "I guess it's fucking curiosity. I love for people to tell me about their lives. The human heart is my main interest."

"I don't know about you folks," he looks at us, "but I told myself stories as far back as I can remember. Then when my Daddy said writing was a good, honest profession, my heart leapt. 'Cause telling stories was all I ever really wanted to do."

After nearly five hours, we are ready to adjourn.

"I'm starved," proclaims Dubus. "Who's up for some chow?"

Six or seven of us pile into cars and head down the highway to Pancho's Villa, a Mexican restaurant owned by a friend of one of the workshop members. Pancho's is crowded, loud, down—at—the—heels. The salsa dip is spicy, though, and the Margaritas, cold. We push three tables together and hunker down on benches. Dubus summons the waitress.

"How 'bout a pitcher of Margaritas, darlin'?"

He glances around our table. At one end, he spies an ex-Marine, ex-schoolteacher from Michigan.

"The lieutenant here will have a tequila, straight up, with a Dos Equis beer chaser. And this lady," he point to a mousey young woman across from him, "looks like she's craving a Kahlua and cream."

Drink orders given, Dubus reaches into the bowl of taco chips. He chomps on a handful, then lights a cigarette. We all begin to talk at once. The enchiladas and chimichangos disappear from the plates. Pitchers of frothy Margaritas are filled and refilled. Beyond Pancho's streaked windows, a glorious Midwestern sunset erupts and fades into night, and still we are gathered around the table, talking far into the night about everything that matters.

Tuesday, 1:45 p.m. We kill time waiting for Dubus to locate us by examining the portraits of Distinguished Indiana University Alumni hanging on every available wall space in the room. The only one anybody recognizes is Hoagy Carmichael. Dubus comes in, carrying a copy of his collection, *The Times Are Never So Bad.* He is muttering to himself.

"What's wrong, Andre?" asks a pretty blonde writer from California. "Bad karma?"

"I packed my own suitcase before coming out here," says Dubus. "I forgot to throw in any of my books. I've got to give a reading in a couple of nights, and goddamn if I didn't have to go to the college bookstore and buy my own book."

"Fifteen fucking dollars!" he groans, shaking the book in the air, and then to himself, as he settles into his chair. "Why do I only get a dollar-and-a-half?"

Today we examine three members' stories and again, Dubus teaches with a captivating mixture of suggestions, illustrations from stories, anecdotes, and spur-of-the-moment insights.

"Do you know what I wrote in the margin of this fucking story?" he asks, donning his glasses to read his handwriting.

"'Holy shit.' That's what I wrote. I can't remember the last time I wrote 'Holy shit' in the margin of a story. But this is such a powerful, fucking scary story. I don't recognize the author's name. Who wrote this?"

A very pale woman at the foot of the table raises her hand timidly.

"Wow," he says. "Who are you?"

The woman's voice shakes as she tells Dubus her name. Then she says she's afraid she cannot write. She'd turned the same story in to an earlier workshop, and the members told her it wasn't a story.

"They said, 'The responsibility of fiction is to answer the questions it raises,'" she recalls. "Maybe they were right. Maybe I should just go home."

"Which eggheads said that?" Dubus roars. "That's a bunch of bull— 'answer the questions it raises!' Don't they know we have philosophers for that?"

Then he tunes out the rest of us and focuses on her slight figure at the end of the table.

"Listen, sweetheart," he says softly, "you are a writer. My job as a teacher is to give you the confidence to voice your own instincts. You've got great instincts. Trust yourself. If I can't get you to do that, I'm the one who should pack up his bags and go home."

In hushed voices, the two of them converse. Everyone listens in on their public/private conversation. Slowly, the shy frightened woman opens up to Dubus. He coaxes her confessions by confessing himself; he erases her fears by praising her talent.

"Your story is different, but it is not wrong," he says to the woman. "Writing a story is like being in love with someone. You can't structure it. When it's over, it's over. It will take you where it wants to go. Trust your instincts. Trust yourself."

Trust and instinct. These two words surface frequently in our discussions. Dubus teaches us that emotional input is more important than technique. We talk about having compassion for our characters.

"When you're writing, you love somebody as God does," says Dubus. "In Chekhov and especially in Cheever, you can love a character yet never want him in your house."

"Don't set out to make moral points in your stories," he cautions.

"People ask me if I think Luke Ripley did the right thing," he says, referring to the protagonist of his work, "A Father's Story." The character is a father who shields his daughter from the law when she accidentally hits a man with her car and kills him.

"I don't know if he was right," Dubus shrugs. "But he is my character. I know that I love him."

We move on to examine another member's story, and enter into an argument about the actions of a character.

"Listen to us," says Dubus with glee. "We're all worked up about someone who doesn't even exist."

Dubus encourages dissension in his workshop. He urges us to speak out if we disagree with his, or anyone else's assessment of a story.

"Don't be a bunch of wimps," he exhorts. "Say what you think. No one's opinion is worth more than anyone else's, mine included."

He dispenses tips throughout the discussion: "Physically act out every movement in your story to see if it works, and exactly how." "Be like Chekhov: don't tell me there was a moon in the sky. *Show* me a piece of glass on the road reflecting the moonlight." "Do not editorialize when writing about violence. Let the action speak for itself." On tone, he quotes R. V. Cassill, his mentor at Iowa Writers' Workshop: "Tone comes from diction and subject matter." "Be like Hemingway: let action truly happen on the page. Don't merely tell us what occurred." And: "Writing a story should be like cunnilingus, in which you see, touch, taste, smell, and hear your lover's orgasm. If you can't do all the above in your story—as gently and with as much love—then don't write it."

It's nearing six o'clock, and as we wrap up for the day, someone comments that a lot of our characters in today's stories are struggling to overcome hardships.

"It's rare to see so much honest affirmation in contemporary fiction," muses Dubus. He grins. "We're going to call this workshop *Rocky V*."

Then he crushes out his cigarette in the ashtray, stands, and stretches.

"*Mis amigos*," he asks, in a better than passable Spanish accent, "*Vamos a* Pancho's Villa?"

Wednesday, 1:50 p.m. Dubus enters the Distinguished Alumni Room in grey gym shorts, a red t-shirt and Etonic running shoes.

"My work-out duds," he tells us, flexing his muscles. "All this reading is tiring me out. Perhaps we can finish on time today, and then I'll go exercise before the sun sets."

In this session, we find out more about Dubus. His Southern accent comes from growing up in Lake Charles, Louisiana, where he attended Catholic schools, and majored in English at McNeese State University. "I switched to English from journalism when I found out journalism was teaching me to write ass-backwards."

"Then I joined the Marine Corps," he says. "Five years in the company of other small guys and sensitive writers who wanted to show their girlfriends and daddies that they were men," he jokes.

He emerged a captain, and at the age of twenty-six, published his first short story in the *Sewanee Review*. Emboldened by success, he quit the military and enrolled in the Iowa Writers' Workshop. Dubus says Iowa taught literature for writers: "When the writing was good, they showed us how the writer achieved the effect. It was like disassembling cars for people who want to become mechanics."

Dubus tells us that he's been married three times ("This time is the last," he swears) and has fathered five children. His son, Andre III, he proudly reveals, is also a writer.

Dubus starts to describe his nearly twenty-year-long teaching career, and interrupts himself to exclaim, "I love teaching. A room filled with apprentice writers is a collection of souls trying to make language. To me that's very exciting, and beautiful."

Today we critique four stories: the ex-Marine's, two by an energetic student from a graduate writing program, and a third story by another woman graduate student. This last is a simple, eloquent tale of an extramarital affair. When we come to it, Dubus falls silent. He clears his throat. And then he says:

"I'm just going to read what I wrote on your manuscript. 'This is a beautiful, moving story filled with the human heart. When I read it, you made me cry, deep in my heart. This is a hymn to love. There's nothing shabby about it. Submit it, submit it, submit it.'"

Dubus stands up. He walks halfway the length of the table and hands the manuscript to its author.

"Thank you," he tells her. "That's all I have to say."

Before we leave the room, an announcement is made of tonight's Open Mike Reading.

"Oh, I could never get up and read in front of people," a woman murmurs. "I'll go watch the rest of you, but I can't read myself."

"I want to tell you a story," Dubus says.

Familiar now with that line, we settle back in our seats.

"You wouldn't have recognized me when I was in high school," he says. "I was a one-hundred-and-five-pound weakling who couldn't get a girl. I was scared of a lot of things and innocent of others. And no way in hell could I get a girl to look at me." He lights up a cigarette.

"In fact," he recalls, "I was in college before I convinced a girl to kiss me. You know how I did it?" He stares at the shy woman who spoke before. "I showed her some of my stories."

"But I was still a little runt. So my Daddy got me a job working construction for the summer. I made good wages, could afford to go for beers with the guys, and, this is very important, I developed some muscles. At the end of the season, I was up to one-hundred-and-twenty-five pounds.

"That wasn't enough. I still had to prove myself. So I finished up college and, as I told you before, joined the Marines. 'Good,' said my Daddy. 'They'll make a man out of you.' Next thing I knew, I was shipped off to Quantico."

He drags hard on his cigarette. "I didn't tell you my sissy history so that you'd feel sorry for me. I'm telling it to you to say: we are all the same. Inside of every one of us is a scared, skinny kid." He stands up and heads for the door.

"See you at the Open Mike Reading," he tosses back over his shoulder.

◆ ◆ ◆

Thursday, 1:30 p.m. Dubus strides to the head of the table, neither greeting or smiling. He sits down stiffly.

"There is something I have to say to one of you," he begins. "I found out something last night after class, and I am deeply hurt and deeply angry. I'm angry on behalf of all of you," his arm sweeps the room, "because—with one and only one exception—everyone here has given and given and given generously of himself."

"Our workshops have been long, I know. The time we've spent outside class reading each others' manuscripts has probably been even longer. You people have blessed each other with your time, your care, your hearts. This sort of special exchange cannot happen unless everyone gives equally and freely."

He turns to a woman on the left side of the table. She is a handsome older woman, tanned, lean, dressed in tennis clothes, her reading glasses dangling from a gold chain around her neck. She has told us that she's taking two workshops at the Conference, and she leaves our group early every day to meet with her other instructor.

Dubus says to her, "I found out that your 'conferences' with your other workshop leader are taking place on the tennis court."

There is pain in his voice. Everyone is silent.

"I asked the instructor why he would do this, and he was surprised. He didn't know you were leaving this group early."

The woman blushes, but she gazes back at Dubus levelly. It is the rest of us at the table who shift in our seats uncomfortably.

"You walked out on this woman's story yesterday," Dubus points to one of Wednesday's authors. "I believe you owe her an apology."

Without flinching, the older woman turns to the younger and offers an apology that's readily accepted.

"I could not have lived with myself if I didn't say something about this. Not for myself, but for everybody in this room," Dubus says. "I believe in fairness. Now let's get back to work."

In today's lesson, we learn to sharpen our techniques. Dubus advises us to lay out pages of our stories on the floor before us.

"Look at how much weight you've given to particular incidents," he instructs. "If they've received a disproportionate amount, then re-weigh your stories. Don't provide unnecessary details that you think might better explain your characters. They'll detract from the real story and screw up its balance."

"Art is pragmatic," says Dubus. "You needn't use something because it's true, but if it's true and it works, use it. I agree with Isaac Babel, who said, 'A well-chosen word is stronger than a spike driven through the heart.'"

He illustrates points with examples from our own stories, quoting passages without error. Among the farrago of stories, poems, and books he recommends today are Anton Chekhov's "My Life," "Fun with a Stranger" and *Eleven Kinds of Loneliness* by Richard Yates, "Protocols" by Randall Jarrell, *The Savage God* by A. L. Alvarez, Thomas Williams's "A High New House," and Lewis Hyde's *The Gift*. Our discussion touches upon the Catholic religion, raising a family, racism in America, heartbreak.

We turn to a story by a workshop member. The story is a nearly flawless one about a dedicated rural schoolteacher. Its author is a studious-looking, attractive young man.

"How old are you, kid?" Dubus asks the man.

"Twenty-four."

"Twenty-four? *Twenty-four?* Shit, man!" Dubus hollers. "You're a fucking child prodigy. Do you know how old I was before I could write a story half this good?"

Dubus holds his hand up like a gun, and sights at the writer down the length of his index finger.

"I'm going to have to kill you," he tells him. "No one that young should be allowed to write so well."

That evening more than one hundred writers assemble in the Whittenberger Auditorium. Dubus is there, showered, shaved, out of his work-out clothes and into white slacks and a vivid gold shirt. He winks at us, his workshop group, as we take seats together in the front of the room.

A poet reads first, then comes Dubus's introduction. He climbs the stage to the podium and begins to read from "A Father's Story":

> My name is Luke Ripley, and here is what I call my life: I own a stable of thirty horses, and I have young people who teach riding, and we board some horses, too. This is in northeastern Massachusetts. I have a barn with an indoor ring, and outside I've got two fenced-in rings and a pasture that ends at a woods with trails. I call it my life because it looks like it is . . .

Dubus interrupts his own reading twice to tell two stories. One is about how much like his image of Fitzgerald's Daisy Buchanan did a woman in our workshop appear, one night at Pancho's, her chiseled face silhouetted against the window and the setting sun. "Visions like that are why we write," he says. The other story, a convoluted tale, takes place at a conference cocktail party and ends with a woman saying to him, "Andre, you'll die young." "Robley Wilson was standing there," Dubus says, "and he told her: 'He can't. He's already forty-nine." Dubus roars with laughter. Save his own disruptions, his reading continues without incident. The packed auditorium is quiet, listening. Forty-five minutes pass like a single moment, and Dubus reaches his tale's end. Luke Ripley, a father, is talking to God:

> But You never had a daughter, and if You had, You could not have borne her passion.
> So, He says, you love her more than you love Me.
> I love her more than I love truth.
> Then you Love in weakness, He says.
> As You love me, I say, and I go with an apple or carrot out to the barn.

1:50 p.m., Friday. The last day of the workshop.

"How am I going to leave you people?" asks Dubus. "Goddamn it. It happens to me this way a lot. Before I come out here, I'm grumbling. I don't like to leave home and I don't like to leave writing, but I like to be around people who like to write."

"So then I arrive," he says, "and I start to love you." He reaches out and squeezes the arm of the retired cemetery owner. "And I don't want to say goodbye."

"So, let's talk about writing." He shakes his head. "Shit, today that may start me blubbering, too. I want to look at 'Valley of the Angels.'"

He names a manuscript by a woman from Ohio in our group. It is a sad, beautiful story about a child whose friend has just died, and whose parents are going to separate.

"This conference has been wonderful, but Lord, it's made me tired. So after making it through five days as demanding as these past five have been, to suddenly come upon a story that, in my numb state, has the power to move me so much . . ." Dubus's voice trails off.

He looks at the author. "I read your story this morning before our meeting. I was sitting out under a tree, in a big field on the side of the Indiana Memorial Union. About halfway through it, I started crying. Now what do you think people thought of this sight: A big, old hulk sitting under a tree in work-out clothes, reading a manuscript, and bawling like a baby?"

"But I couldn't help myself," he tells the author, his voice cracking. "Your story was so sad and so honest. It was so beautiful." Dubus wipes his eyes. "It's a pity we all had to wait until the last day to read this and know you through your lovely story."

To end the session, we gather at Pancho's, drinking and laughing, as night falls on Bloomington. Then Dubus has to leave us; he's got a staff dinner to attend in town. A cab is called, and it waits in the parking lot while Dubus says his goodbyes. He hugs the lieutenant, the former cemetery owner, the pretty woman from California, the publicist from New York. When he comes to the young-looking father who met him at the airport, he embraces him, too. Then he steps back, shakes the man's hand, and looks up into his face.

"You are a writer," he tells him.

No embellishments, no further explanation, just that simple statement of fact.

We watch Dubus walk out of the door of the restaurant and approach the cab driver, who stands leaning against his cab. He shakes the cabbie's hand, and through Pancho's open windows, we hear him say, "Hey, my man, how's it going?" The man's reply is lost to us, but we can hear Dubus's laughter as he walks around the car and gets into the front seat. We watch the cab pull out onto the highway.

Andre Dubus was confined to a wheelchair, a hip-to-toe cast on his right leg, for eight months following the accident. On January 10, 1987, Dubus's wife gave birth to Madeleine Elise, their second daughter. After a depressing, frightening period of writer's block—the first in his life—Dubus got his tip-off sign, insomnia, and started to write again in January. He titled his first effort since the hiatus "The Curse."

In February and March, John Irving, Kurt Vonnegut, Jr., John Updike, and several other writers combined forces to present the "Friends of Andre Dubus Literary Series," a string of benefit readings given to help pay off Dubus's $100,000-plus medical bills.

Late last winter, Dubus graduated to crutches, and in the spring, was given a smaller, more flexible cast for his right leg. His left leg was fitted with a prosthesis ("my falsie," Dubus calls it), and with the aid of a physical therapist and the Willie Nelson tapes blaring from his cassette player, he began to learn to walk again.

Interview with Andre Dubus

Patrick Samway, S.J. / 1986

Xavier Review 8.1–2 (Spring–Fall 1998): 1–15. Reprinted in *Leap of the Heart: Andre Dubus Talking*. Ed. Ross Gresham. New Orleans: Xavier Review Press, 2003. 131–47. Reprinted with the permission of the author.

Q. If you had to look at your life, what key events do you think were important in your career as a writer?

A. I have to think a long time about that. The word "events" already has me thrown off. I've written for so long that I don't even remember a time when my main life was not interior. I've always told myself stories, even as a boy; I wasn't in the stories, but I always assumed everybody thought I was. I never thought of writing books, though I read a good deal. I guess the key event for me was when I started thinking in my junior or senior year in high school that I wanted to write; back then, I wrote Mickey Spillane parodies with my friends, which we shared with others. (A few years back, a woman sent me one she still had.) I was editor of the school newspaper and in my senior year, because of that experience, I thought about a career in journalism, and so in preparation I read a little Hemingway—that was about it. But the day after graduation, my father drove to the Christian Brothers' house (not rectory) and said, "I'm going to ask your teacher what you are good for." I always felt that he didn't feel I was good for anything, so I was worried about the answer. And when he came out, he said, "You are good in English and writing," and I said, "Oh, big deal," and he said, "That's enough to make a good living." And my heart leapt.

So my heart knew I wanted to write, but I had so many masks that I myself didn't know where to begin. That's when I decided; within a week or two, I started writing a story. We lived in Lake Charles, Louisiana, then, although the Christian Brothers' school was in Lafayette. I went back to it for my last year. My father was transferred, and so I moved in January from Lafayette to Lake Charles and made the principal of the school promise I could go back and graduate with my original class. When I took my first aptitude test, I found out that such tests always tell you what you feel you want to do at the time anyway. Once it said I should be a lawyer; sometimes I think I should have been one. Another time, it indicated I should be a career military officer, and that's what I planned on becoming.

I was writing a monthly editorial as editor-in-chief of the newspaper at Cathedral High School in Lafayette, and because of that, I entered McNeese State College as a journalism major and found out I was learning how to write backwards. I won the first prize in the Louisiana College Writers' Society contest in my freshman, junior, and senior years, and third prize my sophomore year. That helped. I didn't really have anybody to show manuscripts to, even though I had a fair number of literature teachers. They didn't know a hell of a lot about writing and would just say whether or not they liked my stories and then proceed to lecture me on split infinitives. So I changed to English during the second year, which worried my father. I remembered him saying to me, "How are you going to make a living?" By that time, however, I was in the Marine Corps Officer program, and so I said to him, "I'll just stay in the Marines." That was fine with him.

After entering the Marines, I started writing seriously. That was a good experience; it got me out of Louisiana and away from my parents. Somebody asked me once if it gave me discipline. I said, "I don't think so because I have that." But I think it got rid of some of my self-consciousness and fears, so that later on I could tell editors to shove it. That's when I learned about courage. As a Marine, I got to see some of the world, and my wife and I had four children for five dollars apiece, and I never have had a bigger income since I left in January 1964 as a captain. Never. Never made it from one pay day to the next. So it was a pretty good life; it was fun. But my father died, and I had a quarrel with the commanding officer, and I resigned. A year later in Iowa City, I realized that I quit because my father had died; if he hadn't died, I would still be there and I would have gone to Vietnam.

I guess the time in Iowa was an important period for me as a writer because I wrote all the time. That's always important. I learned to write while working 7:30 a.m. to 4:30 p.m. most days—or sometimes spending two to three weeks working in the field and not writing, and coming home and raising a family and finding time to write. I always knew I had to make a living somehow. Iowa was the best time of my life, as far as having time to write. Had a $2,400-a-year assistantship, a wife without an income and four children. I picked up $100 a month teaching a correspondence course and $100 a semester teaching an adult education course. I sold blood at $25 a pint every three months. But everybody was poor, so life wasn't expensive. When you wanted to see your friends, you brought over a plate of food and your six pack and your kids and you didn't pay a sitter and you put all the kids down out in one room to sleep. The evening cost at most five dollars per couple. Then I went to Bradford College in Massachusetts and had energy and was able to write every morning, work out, then teach five afternoons a week. I planned to go on to another college, but I fell in love with that one and with the region. My wife and I divorced in the 1970s, and I wouldn't leave because we agreed to stay in the same town while the kids grew up so I could be with them always. I stayed as promised, and by the time they were grown up I was pretty well dug in. I had offers to go to the Midwest and other places—terrible places with more money and half the teaching load, but I wouldn't go since I feel geography and friends are terribly important. So I stayed. I think I got burned out and collapsed and then retired. And then I had it nice from May 1983 until September 1985, just writing and working out. No money, but my blood pressure was down, and I could relax at night. Then I went to the University of Alabama and my health got screwed up again. So I'm feeling very futile about things. It used to be writing could get you a good job, but the only job it could get me was the one my body would no longer do. But I know myself well enough to know that the reason to write is the reason I've always written: I cannot be happy unless I write. But there is not a nickel in it for most writers, and I have a family. If I could bear not having a family, I could live on $300 a month, in some dump. Eat beans. Write. But I need my family. I guess that fills you in about some of the events in my life.

Q. You mentioned your Catholic high school education and your desire to be educated by the Christian Brothers. I note that Joe Ritchie in "Adultery" is much different from some of the stereotypical priests in contemporary drama, say in *Mass Appeal*. How do you regard Joe Ritchie? What's going on in his character?
A. I tried to write Edith's story so many times that finally I can't remember the process, but I know Joe Ritchie's function. I initially wanted Edith to have an affair with a dying man. I thought if that happened, it might give her character a focus, and also allow the secular sacraments of erotic love to come into play. Joe, for his part, simply left the priesthood and brought to Edith something pure. She says that all adultery is symptomatic, and realizes that while she is with Joe Ritchie she is seeing his love for her as something spiritual and something moral in the face of mortality—either in defiance or

in harmony with it, I don't know. I don't know if he knows. Yet, they do not procreate.

She had such a different experience with him than with her husband; the symptomatic adultery she's been committing with Joe brings her back full circle to the reasons she was first drawn to Hank. This second relationship gives her a new perspective not only on lovemaking itself, but on love. In those passages when she serves him, I tried, without directly using the words, to show that her acts of bringing shrimp and vacuuming are sacred dances, sacraments of a sort. I did use at one point, however, the rather heavy-handed image of anointing. Because of his fervor and his belief in the sacraments and especially the Eucharist as an important way that God shows himself to people (in its own way, a sacrament is a sensual experience that takes into account our fleshly nature) Joe's belief parallels his priesthood and the act of lovemaking with someone he genuinely loves. Edith becomes purified by this screwing around and, as a result, begins to see Hank for what he is. Thus Edith is able to say to Hank in her own mind, "Joe is dying and you're dying and I'm dying. We forget this; we have to remember it every moment we are together. We are dying and when Joe and I are together, we receive a holy sacrament to help us through that knowledge."

What I like about Joe Ritchie is that he knows he is committing a sin, but he doesn't know whose sin it is. It might be Hank's or it might be Edith's or it might be his. He won't confess this sin because that would unduly complicate any relationship he might have with one of his fellow priests. Father Joe Ritchie is a thinking Catholic, and I love that about him. He doesn't believe that merely because his flesh is with another woman's flesh, they automatically sin, even though as a married woman she should not be with him, in his mind, she is *not* married. There is no sacrilege in their acts. When I think of Joe and Edith, I think of Jesus's words: "Take and eat. This is my body." Don't write or think too much about these words or the implied action; you will never probe their significance. Just believe in them. I think that's what sacraments are. After having lived with sheep on a rented property for one year, I know why Jesus called his followers sheep. They are the dumbest animals I have ever had contact with in my life. That picture of Jesus carrying a lamb is a romanticization. Sheep are dumb. They have to be protected from themselves; they really need shepherds and dogs to keep them alive. Edith and Joe imitate in their own way a salvific act that they themselves could never comprehend.

Q. In a number of your works, you deal with a young boy growing up and having to confront the church, his family, sexuality, grace, and so on. In particular I think of "If They Knew Yvonne" and *Voices from the Moon*. Do you see any resemblance between *Voices from the Moon* and James Joyce's *A Portrait of the Artist as a Young Man*?

A. God, I hope there's none. The last time I was teaching *Dubliners*, I threw the book against the ceiling and said I would never teach that book again. You see, Joyce likes only a few people, the little boy in "Araby" and then two or three sisters in various stories. The rest of the book is written with scorn, even though it is probably the most beautifully crafted book of stories in the world. There is no love, no heart. As I recall, he wrote to his brother from Trieste, "I'm getting back at them for what they did to me." So he writes about Irish clerks made spiritually impotent by poverty, Catholicism, overbearing clergy, and dominating women. I said to Richard Yates once, "You know, you once said in a interview that the two problems of fictional autobiography were self-pity and self-aggrandizement. What do you think about a book that starts with a boy in bed and ends with him becoming the conscience of the cosmos?" He said, "I think Joyce violated both of those rules." As you see, I can't stand Joyce. I have not read anything of his for a long time. I think he was a self-absorbed son of a bitch. And Richard Yates and I are the co-chairman of the "We Hate James Joyce Club." We are also its only members, but we predict that in the year 2000 people are going to realize Joyce wasn't a very good writer anyway, and all those guys making a lot of money reproducing and critiquing his works are going to be out of jobs. So I hope there are no parallels between our approaches to writing and the sacred.

There is nothing autobiographical in *Voices from the Moon*. I was never an altar boy. As a Catholic and a daily communicant, I have thought about becoming a priest as thousands of others have done before me. But those moments were fleeting. What I think I have done is to give my characters burdens that are genuinely and humanely spiritual. "If They Knew Yvonne" was much more autobiographical. It came out of some conversations; one was with a priest named Father Clarence Stanghor, who was a chaplain at the University of Iowa. He would say, "Come over tonight to talk." I have always considered him a wonderful priest. He had formerly been a Lutheran and a soldier in World War II. He has been around a lot, and I was in my twenties and was just getting very angry at the sexual upbringing I had been given. I used to tell him about my problems. I told him the theme of "If

They Knew Yvonne," which I hadn't yet written. I wrote it much later. I said it just occurred to me that all this focus on masturbation by the Christian Brothers was crazy; nobody ever talked then about how you can hurt *other people* with sex. I told Father Stanghor, "I think it was their problem. That is why they were so maddened by it; they never related sexuality to human growth and love." As long as nobody ejaculated, everything was all right. Boys should let nature—nocturnal emissions—solve their sexual inclinations. And, of course, plenty of cold showers and no candy. We should have been learning about the difference between loving other people and using them as objects, as pieces of meat. Nobody talked about that. Father Stanghor agreed. He was the one who said, "In my moral theology book in the seminary, masturbation was worse than rape, because rape was a natural act and it approved *caveat emptor*. When I got out of the seminary, I burned the book." I said, "When my sons get older, I am going to tell them those organs are yours, and if you want to masturbate, that is your decision. It does not hurt anybody. I am also going to tell them that when you become involved with another human being, then you have to start thinking morally." Good God, from fourteen to nineteen it's terrible; at nineteen, somebody told me I had reached my sexual peak as a male. That was a year of agony. It's like having a migraine headache in the southern end of yourself instead of the northern end. This thing just takes over. Yes, "If They Knew Yvonne" came from a ten-year delayed fuse—all that guilt my friends and I went through for doing something that no teenage boy can resist doing.

Q. Is that why you included the rather open confession with Father Grassi?
A. Yes. That's right. I went to confession to Father Stanghor—a very complex, complicated confession. I sat down next to him on his couch and told him this story with various degrees of evil (sometimes I thought it wasn't evil and sometimes I thought it was) for a couple of hours. After we had talked, I said, "I want to go to confession." He said, "You just did." I said, "No, I want the real one thing—the stole and absolution." He said, "O.K." So he sat at his desk and put his stole and I said, "Bless me, father. I want to confess what I just talked with you about for the last two hours." He said, "For your penance, say 'alleluia' three times. And wherever you go, I want you to be a Catholic, which is to say I want you to be who you are." I said, "O.K."

Q. Was it good advice?
A. It was great advice. What the young man finds out in "If They Knew Yvonne" is that by using a girl and making love to her, he has committed

a sin he never heard of. And it was worse than any sexual sin he had ever committed, and that had made him feel worse, even to the point of wanting to mutilate himself. He realized that he simply used her for an elegant form of masturbation that felt so good that he didn't confess it. Kind of a complicated story, isn't it? As a matter of fact, that is the only story I've ever had a character who explained what he did. I was going to do without the confession scene because I thought I was copping out. But I decided that if he doesn't go to confession and explain what is going on, no reader will understand this story just with the concluding image of the two boys killing crabs and saying, "Goodbye, poor crab," and taking their part in nature and every once in a while staring off and playing with their penises. The young man hopes that Lee and Paul will grow and know that sometimes in nature you kill living creatures and you eat and you must do it with compassion (in much the same way that you should handle with compassion your genitals and those of another.) I didn't think that concluding image would make it without the confession scene.

Q. It's a very striking ending. Very optimistic, I think.
A. I think so. I think the boy has learned a lot and he learned a lot from his sister, too, who is smarter than he is.

Q. She has been through a very rough time.
A. Well, as I tell people, everything in that story is true but the good parts; there was no Father Grassi and there was no sister and there was no Yvonne!

Q. Let me move on to one of my favorites, *We Don't Live Here Anymore*. Could you tell me why you have no family histories in this collection? Everything seems to deal with the present.
A. Since I don't know, I guess it didn't seem important to me. Edith comes from money and Hank never mentions his parents. They are all living away from where they grew up. They have mothers and fathers, but their parents are not big influences. It could be because I compress. I never have thought of their families. That's funny. I never thought about whether or not their parents reacted to the divorces or not. I don't know.

Q. One aspect of your fiction I enjoy is the manner in which relationships seem to constantly change. In *We Don't Live Here Anymore*, I think, particularly, of Ray and Polly, Jack and Edith, Joe and Edith, and Hank and Lori.

Those relationships keep on shifting back and forth. Do you see that as being a pattern in your work?

A. Is it a pattern? I don't think about my work much. It's certainly a pattern in many of the marriages I write about. I assume it's a pattern in most marriages in general. No, I don't know if I do. I guess I don't know the answer to that.

Q. You have some relationships that are fairly stable, as in "Blessings," for example.

A. Yes, that relationship is stable. There I wrote about a man and a woman who love each other and have for thirty-five years. They have a family who loves each other; they take vacations together when the children are grown. I guess in "A Father's Story," too, Luke's relationship with Jennifer doesn't shift. In fact, it deepens. He showed his love for her by violating what he thought he believed in, but the relationship didn't shift; it got deeper. His relationship with his priest-friend shifted, because he couldn't reveal to his priest-friend what he did. He didn't think it would be fair to confess to his friend what he did, and put his friend on the spot of possibly reporting the situation to the police. He also thought it wouldn't be fair to wait until the statute of limitations ran out and then confess it. That would be cheating. Hank does shift. I had made notes in my notebook—a story about twenty pages long, no sex, in which he learns a year later that a woman has aborted his child. I've always hated that son-of-a-gun. He is selfish; he is mean; he is a manipulator. It's about time he suffers some pain and, as soon as he got on stage he just took off. I couldn't stop him. I had no idea he was going to end up with this woman, Lori, whom some reviewer put down because she made Cs. She made Cs because she wasn't ambitious in the American way. He loves her because she's a good human being and he hadn't met many of them. A friend of mine wrote that Hank learned that writing takes the same amount of work and discipline as loving takes. He had to go through the pain of a separation, of losing some of the women in his life.

Q. Hank teaches at Bradford College. Why such an autobiographical fact?

A. Yes, I had him teaching literature at Bradford, a coeducational, four-year college. Julian Moynahan of the *New York Times* chose to say that he taught creative writing at a girls' college. That angered me; I'd like to meet Mr. Moynahan once and throw a drink in his face. He made a few more mistakes in his review, but that's all right. I don't mind bad reviews; I just hate bad reviews that make mistakes. I don't mind if somebody says, "I just don't like this," but when they make mistakes that you would give a student a D for, then you know that they made up their mind very early, and they didn't read the story very well. The one story he did like, he completely misunderstood. I hope he reads what I'm saying. I wrote a story called "Waiting," which he thought was about a woman coping well as a Korean War widow. Actually, it is a story about a woman who is considering suicide for the first time and is going to do it, and she is waiting for the appropriate night.

But back to your point. Yes, Hank and I had the same geographical problem. I think I used a line from a friend of mine, who also got divorced while teaching at Bradford. Bradford is part of Haverhill, which is a dead mill town. My friend said, "You get divorced in Haverhill and there is no one to date but mill workers, secretaries, and students. It's very lonely for *men* and women. I've warned men *and* women who are coming to work in this area that if they are single, it is not a good place to be to meet people. It's a very small town and the odds are against pairs being hired or couples being hired. It's not a good situation if you are alone, unless you are desperate enough to join a group. I know an ex-seminarian teaching in a town nearby who, imagine this, even went to a singles' group meeting. I took him aside and said, "Look, girls are mature now; go after one of your senior students in high school." He was the basketball coach, a very young guy. He said, "I couldn't do that. I would get fired." I said, "It beats loneliness." I think St. Paul said something like that it is better to marry than to burn. I told this fellow, "You know you might get a wife out of this. Your age difference isn't that much—perhaps eight or nine years." He was in the same situation as Hank. Bradford is a small New England town surrounded by rural communities, and you find that most men or women, depending on their situations, are married. Loneliness is not good.

Q. Hank does start again, though, with Lori. Will their particular relationship continue to grow?
A. Yes. She says, "We are going to have babies." I think she even said they are going to have a religion, didn't she? I know that the woman she is based on said, "We are going to get married. We are going to have children and have them go to parochial schools and we not going to raise them like goddam Americans." Yes, I tried to write a story about them buying a house, but it was difficult. I was too personal about the themes, so the story never could work right. I had too many preconceived ideas, so the story couldn't grow. I'm hoping to get back to them, and I might put him through a course on natural childbirth. He is about due for that.

Q. One of the most moving sections is where he becomes extremely distraught because Lori has aborted his child. "Miranda Over the Valley" also contains an abortion. If Miranda has one, then she can go to Acapulco and enjoy herself and not be tied down. Would your literary examples of abortion reflect your own moral standards? Any comments?

A. Absolutely. That's why "Miranda Over the Valley" was so hard to write. I started every fall for years and couldn't finish it, I had to try to get myself out of it and not preach. And Miranda finally took over very well. As a matter of fact, I wrote the ending over several times because she was so hard at the end and I didn't want her to be so hard. I kept writing that last scene over and over, but Miranda remained hard. At key points in this story, people say "Christ" or "Jesus"—and why they do that is my own little secret. To me, these words are prayers. She finds out that she's pregnant on Halloween, I believe, and flies home immediately. So later, on either All Saints Day or All Souls Day, she is convinced to get the abortion which she doesn't want. I am angry at American parents who want to save other people from suffering, and offer to buy them out of very human experiences. Her boyfriend's name is Michaelis because that is the name of Lady Chatterly's first love, who also copped out. It was quite intentional on my part to have Miranda read "Antigone" by Anouilh because in the play Antigone tells Creon that she doesn't know why she is going to die; he just knows that his pragmatic world is not the one she wants. A poet friend of mine said the story is about reason defeating instinct, and her instincts are all good. Once she gives up her virginity, she begins a process in which everyone lets her down. Something very valuable in her is destroyed because she is eighteen; had she been twenty-nine, she might have simply had the child. But she's eighteen, and she also loves her father. That's what the rattlesnake scene is all about. There was a woman teaching at Bradford (a Catholic), who didn't understand the religious significance of the story. She said the rattlesnake was a phallic symbol. This woman said I couldn't put a snake in a story without it being a phallic symbol. I said well it's not; it's simply a snake. Miranda does not want to make love to her father; she looks up to her father. Like many young women, she respects him and is deeply attached to him. It is Michaelis who lets her down and she can't fight all the people she loves.

Q. One story I found very unusual is "Land Where My Fathers Died." It has Greeks and Turks and multiple points of view and everything. It seems to me there that one of the themes that comes through is the defense of those who have been victimized. At the end, there is a sense that justice will be done, and as I was reading this story, I thought of John Dos Passos and his becoming involved in the plight of the underdog, especially in his concern for Sacco and Vanzetti. Do you think this story is typical of your writing?

A. No, not really. I was trying to write a detective story, just to pay homage to the form and to challenge myself to see if I could do it in a short length. I had to do some research. I don't know a lot about police work and found out from a lawyer-friend that if he is broke like the lawyer in "The Verdict" with Paul Newman, he will have to do his own footwork. I decided to make him a Greek based on a Greek and a Greek family I know. Once Nionakis got into the story, then really the Greek took over, the immigrant without a country because he doesn't remember his father. He's a lawyer but he doesn't make money and doesn't want it and doesn't go to work much. He realizes why he doesn't fit in society is because the values of it keep getting disclosed in front of him. Throughout the first part of the story he notices women's weight and everything about them. As he does the research into these women victimized by Madison Avenue, he begins to change and finally Paula, I think, says, "*You* look at women that way," and he says "You couldn't let it go, could you?" So the story takes on a different theme than murder. He begins to understand why he's not a Greek and why he can't be an American; he despises the values that his uncle and brothers have embraced. They laugh as their hair falls out; they take their children to church; he doesn't know whether they believe in God or not. They believe they should take their children to the Greek church every Sunday, and make a lot of money and play the stock market. He doesn't want those either. Suddenly he is confronted with the murders, which happen because as he notices none of the women involved is fat, they only believe they are. I remember noticing a July 1963 *Saturday Evening Post* about Faulkner's funeral. I went first through the advertisements and there was not one with anything for low-cal people—not a soft-drink ad, none for puddings, custards, or bread. The cover story was "The Daring New Look in Swimsuits" (I didn't read it so I don't know what was daring) and it had to do with the material, I think. There were simple two-piece bathing suits. The women had broad, athletic-looking waists, solid arms and legs. They look like the kind of women you would expect to see hiking or jogging today. They didn't look like they were going to be anorexic. So this all happened in one generation. Vanity is not new though in human society. So the only thing new, I think, is the detective story structure.

Q. Do you mind talking about an early work, *The Lieutenant*? Is this story related to "Over the Hill"?

A. Both incidents happened while I was aboard *The Ranger.* Also, "The Dark Men" story happened while I was aboard that ship. Some people I have talked with have commented on the homosexuality in these stories. The only homosexual was the commander in "The Dark Men," and his men should have left him alone, since his men knew he was homosexual. He had been an ace in World War II and Korea, and was the commander of the *Andrew.* He committed suicide by shooting himself. But I found out years later from a friend who came to visit that they had kept him aboard because they were afraid that if he went ashore and he would fly his plane and deliberately crash it. So I thought, now I've got a story. I'm going to let him do it. I don't really think there are any homosexuals in *The Lieutenant.* The service is absolutely hypocritical about that; they just don't want any homosexuals in the service. They say that homosexuals are security risks, but we know from international news that even heterosexuals are security risks.

Q. In terms of what you've written so far, where does *The Lieutenant* fit into the scheme of things?
A. I don't know. I told that story so often in Iowa that someone said I should write it down and I did just that in two-and-a-half months. Then it got published and it got only one bad review—in the *New York Times.* I like the story fine. Then I outgrew it. Mr. Greenstreet said he would publish it. I asked what I should cut. He said, "No, there is nothing to cut. The writing is different, but it's you. The moral complexity is there and I want to publish the book." So I said, "All right, I'm not going to touch it anymore," though it is a novel written by a short-story writer and it should have been a hundred pages long. But this guy said it couldn't be a hundred pages long. So I just let it alone. It's an early work; I'm glad I wrote it and I've never forgotten the characters. A lot of people misunderstood the ending, but I changed my mind about the ending away.

Q. What do you mean?
A. Well when I wrote it, I was hoping that he would resign, that he would go all the way. But when Freeman got killed, then he chose his career, and he broke my heart. I remember being very sad and telling my wife, "Tierney just copped out." He has the courage to fight all the way for an ideal. He is treating Freeman like a dead horse and he is becoming an organization man. I saw him at the end as the guy who would press the button. But after reading *Goodbye Darkness* by William Manchester, I realized that actually millions of Americans would have died assaulting the beaches of Japan. I

still think the bomb should have been dropped offshore. But I've read other stuff that makes me think that wouldn't have worked because even after two bombs there were many influential Japanese who did not want to surrender. So I don't know. It's a terrible moral question, but I don't mind having a different view.

Q. In this story there is something about if you want to be a Marine you have to learn to live to lie.
A. That was from that first mess night I remember. There was a wonderful speech by a Marine lieutenant general named Merrill Twining. I couldn't remember most of the speech because of what we had drunk; he did say, I do remember, that being a Marine officer is living the lie and making the lie come true, and I thought that was a wonderful line. His brother was General Nathan Twining of the Air Force who was the Chairman of the Joint Chiefs of Staff.

Q. Was it part of your experience do you think?
A. Absolutely, I think it has been part of the experience in my life ever since. In a book on the Korean War I was reading about a year ago, a young officer in San Diego went into General Twining's office and said that the First Marine Division had been surrounded by the Chinese Army and Twining looked up and said, "Young man, I feel sorry for those Chinamen," and went back to his desk. Now I think he was living a lie and making a lie come true. I think beneath all of that he thought, "Oh shit, it could be 20,000 dead." But there wasn't. It works. I don't think it's a bad way for some to live.

Q. Do you think some of your characters live lies?
A. I would have to think about a specific character. You know, the game's not over until it is over. O.K., we've got to get five runs in the ninth and we are going to get it. Well that works sometimes. I think that's what Twining meant; the lie is that you are the best in the world. Well, make it come true; you are not the best in the world. You are just normal.

Q. Where would the notion of truth come into play here?
A. I suppose truth would fit into the commitment to accomplish the lie. How is that? I say, "I can save you, but I'm a bad swimmer." Let me fill in this picture. Supposing a child is in the middle of a swollen river. If the child believed I could save him or her, and I intend to pull it off, that's the truth, even though we both drown.

Q. Do you think Hank is living a lie or trying to find the truth?

A. Towards the end of "Finding a Girl in America," he is not living a lie, though I think he thinks his life is pretty lousy. He is trying to find the truth and I think his friend Jack helps him. Hank sees in Lori a good woman and he no longer sees a woman as something you come home to after work. He is looking for the truth. He probably is living a lie in the early novellas, and trying to make it come true.

Q. One final question. What do you think is your best work and what would you recommend that people read first?

A. I usually judge the success of a story by how hard I had to work on it. Using that criterion, I would suggest "Adultery" and "Molly," because they took so much out of me that I didn't even know I had. Maybe I would recommend "The Pretty Girl" too, but I can't be sure about that because I was writing that while I was teaching a seminar on *War and Peace* and *Anna Karenina* and teaching three other courses at the same time. I remember sitting one Thursday evening with my wife Peggy at dinner (I was so tired I could barely lift my fork) and I said that "The Pretty Girl" wasn't worth it. It took so much energy to write that story, though really it was the teaching rather than the writing that was exhausting. What I liked about "Adultery" and "Molly" is that I told these stories from a feminine perspective. Not bad for an old man, eh?

Accident Robbed Author
of Desire to Write

Stacey Chase / 1986

The [Lowell, Massachusetts] Sunday Sun 11 January 1987: A2. Reprinted in *Leap of the Heart: Andre Dubus Talking*. Ed. Ross Gresham. New Orleans: Xavier Review Press, 2003. 148–53. Reprinted with the permission of the *The Sun* of Lowell.

Author Andre Dubus doesn't remember the moment of the car's impact. A hospital nurse told him no one ever does.

He remembers feeling calm, waving at the car to stop; believing that it would. He remembers the last words of the young man beside him who was killed.

Now, he's trying to remember how to write.

Dubus, forty-nine, of Haverhill, spoke recently of the accident that robber him twice: of a left leg and the energy to write.

"I imagine myself writing and walking, but I don't have much confidence in that anymore," Dubus said. "I don't have much confidence in much anymore."

The author of seven books, Dubus gained a reputation as a fine fiction writer following in the tradition of native son Jack Kerouac, some said.

In 1975, a collection of short stories, *Separate Flights*, won the Boston Globe Laurence L. Winship Award for best book of New England origin.

"I assumed it (writing) would come back," Dubus said. "They say I'm just concentrating on getting well and have no energy left to write. I don't know why I can't write."

"I'm waiting for it to start coming," he said. "I just can't get that feeling of opening myself to some images."

It was the search for some images that led Dubus to Boston's Combat Zone the night of July 22. Dubus wanted to write about the Zone. To write about it meant he'd have to see it.

103

"I can't write about a place unless I've smelled it," Dubus explained. "I thought it was some jungle, I didn't have to go—that's the stupid thing."

Returning home shortly after midnight, Dubus passed an accident on Route 93 in Wilmington. A woman, Luz Santiago of Lowell, had driven over a motorcycle that had been abandoned in the roadway. Dubus got out to help her.

A Marine Corps officer from 1958 to 1964, Dubus said he never thought twice about lending help.

"Because of the Marine Corps, you're trained to move toward a situation, even when you don't know what you're doing," Dubus said.

"That's been a pattern in my life; it's not surprising I'd end up losing a leg."

Ms. Santiago's brother, Luis Santiago, twenty-three, came around from the side of their car and said "probably his last words on earth." Dubus recalled: "Por favor, señor, please help. No habla ingles."

The three, walking abreast, began to cross the highway when a car driven by Nancy Anthony of Woburn struck Luis Santiago, police said. In that instant, Dubus threw Luz Santiago to the right side of the road and out of the car's path. But he was hit.

Dubus's doctor later told him he saved Luz Santiago's life.

"I needed to hear that so I don't get angry at myself," Dubus said. "I'm thankful I wasn't doing something crazy. I wouldn't be able to handle that on top of everything else."

He added, "I hope with a wooden leg I would stop (and help) again."

By May, Dubus hopes to be able to walk several hundred feet on crutches before having to submit to the wheelchair.

"Missing a leg isn't bad," Dubus says, laying flat out on a bed at his home. "It's waiting for the right leg to heal."

Dubus's right leg was so badly crushed in the accident that he cannot even use a prosthesis—which he calls his "falsie"—on the amputated leg in order to walk.

The writer's two adult sons, Jeb and Andre, built a maze of ramps leading to the dining room and kitchen of his home for easy wheelchair access. A ramp also covers the step between the dining room and den of the modern wood home.

"I'd be walking if it (right leg) had healed," Dubus said.

"I wouldn't have had to get someone else to cut down the Christmas tree," he added, finally allowing tears that had been rising in his eyes to break over the bottom lid.

Dubus said friends send him letters saying they are inspired by his courage. But courage, he pointed out, is to face danger with bravery.

"What courage?" Dubus said. "I can't change it. I can't just decide to get up and walk."

Dubus said the physical pain of his injuries is mild now, "thought I used to chorus for pain killers in the hospital."

"It's the kind of pain if I was healthy it wouldn't bother me," Dubus said. "I didn't build up an endurance to pain."

He said, at times, he is afraid the physical agony will again become as unbearable as it was in the hospital.

"I think I've become a sissy to pain," Dubus said, deprecatingly.

"I get some of that phantom pain," he continued. "If it's going to be a phantom feeling, why can't it be a good feeling?" he said his wife, Peggy Rambach, had wondered.

Rambach, also a writer, and Dubus are expecting their second child in less than a week. The due date is January 17. They are also the parents of a four-year-old daughter, Cadence. Dubus is the father of four adult children from a previous marriage.

On a recent December day, Rambach stood trimming her husband's beard in the middle of their dining room. From his wheelchair Dubus joked good-naturedly with friends who filled the house; one doing dishes in the kitchen after fixing a meal; another, vacuuming rooms down a corridor.

"Nothing ever happens quickly around this house," Rambach said.

"I hate asking people to do things for me," said her husband. "If I had writing energy, I'd be in good spirits all the time.

"Writing kept me going; writing, and working out."

Dubus, broad-chested with muscular arms, used a cross-country ski machine and participated in light weight-training before his accident. He fast-walked for exercise when his legs were able to carry him.

He also went to mass daily at 9:00 a.m.

Dubus confessed he was "depressed," then rejected the word.

"I get the blues a lot," the Louisiana native said. "I get sad, I cry. I'm crying because I can't walk and I can't work."

Has he thought of writing about the accident?

"No," Dubus says sternly, then laughs. "I don't want to relive it."

"I had some energy and was writing an essay about vignettes of bed-ridden life, but I lost it," he continued.

"I can't even get excited about French professors inviting me to France. That's a pretty low level of emotion."

Dubus was invited to read in France by a group of professors there but turned the offer down.

"I don't want to go to France in a wheelchair," he said. "I don't want to go anywhere in a wheelchair, to tell you the truth."

Other writers have rallied to help Dubus and are planning a series of benefit readings to help defray his enormous medical costs. Leading the impressive roster of writers is John Irving, author of *The World According to Garp*. The Friends of Andre Dubus Literary Series will be held in February–March at the Charles Hotel in Cambridge.

"It's kind of like a long flu," Dubus said, describing the way the accident has left his health.

"When I got home (from the hospital), I saw myself in the mirror and I looked like my father the day before he died of cancer.

"I had three vocations: family, writing, and teaching. One had to go," the writer explained.

Dubus had been planning to resume his teaching career though the prospects of that have now been extinguished.

"When I retired, I had all this time to write," Dubus said. "I asked my wife, 'How did I find time to write before?'"

The answer, he said, is a basic one: even when he didn't feel like writing, he'd put on tea and get pumped up to write again.

Discipline is what has been stolen from him as a result of his injuries, Dubus said. Though he is trying to woo it back by reading a great deal.

"There's no energy. That's it," Dubus said. "I can't get into it. In the Marines, I got up at 4:00 a.m. and wrote." When teaching, Dubus used the "nights to write and mornings to sleep."

And while he still dreams of writing and walking as robustly as he did before, Dubus hopes the two aren't inextricable.

"If they are, I'm a doomed man," he said. "This is my permanent head."

An Interview with Andre Dubus

Stacey Chase / 1989

Puerto Del Sol 25 (Summer 1990): 108–19. Reprinted in *Leap of the Heart: Andre Dubus Talk-ing.* Ed. Ross Gresham. New Orleans: Xavier Review Press, 2003. 154–65. Reprinted with the permission of *Puerto Del Sol.*

When Andre Dubus and I first met, he gave me three words of advice: *Piss on it.*

The "it" was anything that prevented me from writing—bills, errands, my job; all the annoyances of daily living I complained got in my way. Piss on it—that was Dubus's encouragement to me.

Or, rather, *Piss on it* was Dubus venting his own frustrations in the form of counsel to a younger writer.

We met in December 1986—only five months after Dubus's left leg was amputated at the knee, and his right leg crushed into uselessness, when he was accidentally run down by a car while assisting two motorists stranded on Massachusetts Interstate-93. (One of the motorists was killed by the car.) Daily living was all Dubus could manage then. And even that was difficult.

Two years later, in January 1989, Dubus was missing his family more than his legs. He seemed, in fact, to have traded one tragedy for another or to have combined them into a conglomerate tragedy. But, this time, the thick-chested, salty-tongued Southerner and his hard luck looked to be an even match.

"If it weren't for prayer, I'd be fucked," Dubus said when we met the sec-ond time, after his third marriage broke up. "Sometimes I can get the focus that, actually, I've got things better than most people in the world. I mean, how many million people would swap places with me, right now, to have this house, with their children and medical care and food and all that?

"When you grow up with the Passion of Christ as an example, I mean, you know at least there's a membership of suffering. And you can get the focus that you're not the only one in the world who's got things tough."

But sometimes Dubus (pronounced to rhyme with abuse) loses that focus.

"Life's hard when you've got two legs, when things are normally bad," Dubus also said. "Take away the legs and the kids and there are some days I need to talk to myself a lot to make myself eat."

But the important thing is, the talk works. The talks Dubus has with himself and the ones he has with his God, as was taught him in Christian Brothers Catholic and schools in his native Louisiana. Prayer, and the discipline he learned as a Marine more than twenty-five years ago, have helped Dubus stave off the misery still threatening to consume him.

Two recent literary awards have also helped by allaying Dubus's financial woes. In May 1988, the fifty-two-year-old author received the Jean Stein Award, and its accompanying $5,000 stipend, from the American Academy and Institute of Arts and Letters. Two months later, he was the recipient of the grandest of grants: a MacArthur Foundation Fellowship. "I had insomnia and loose bowels for about three days [after notification]," Dubus said. "I just felt incredibly blessed."

Dubus used the first $1,900 of the $310,000 MacArthur money he'll receive over five years to buy a state-of-the-art wheelchair, with the brand name *Quickie*. "All my gimp friends said, 'You gotta get a *Quickie*,'" said Dubus, darting his eyes to see if I caught the sexual innuendo.

Ironically, Dubus's injury set off an avalanche of attention that was never his when he was a writer with, what he's now fond of calling, the "biped advantage." In February and March 1987, a group of fellow writers led by John Irving teamed up for a series of benefit readings in Cambridge, Massachusetts, to help defray Dubus's mounting medical bills. They raised $86,000.

They also raised public interest in Dubus, already then the author of seven original short-story collections or novellas, six of them brought out by David R. Godine Publisher, Inc. of Boston. *Selected Stories*, a compilation of twenty stories from Dubus's six other Godine books, plus two stories never published in book form, made its debut in November 1988.

"We wanted to keep him in the public eye while he's writing slower," explained Godine publicity director Clare McKeown.

Dubus, himself, admits his writing ability has slowed to one-third the rate it was before the accident. "Sometimes," he added, "I get afraid it's gone, as recently as last week."

"But if everything I do is harder . . . why shouldn't the hardest thing be harder?" Dubus reasoned. "If it's harder to get cereal in a bowl, why wouldn't it be harder to write a page?"

The energy to concentrate on fictive lives, rather than his own, started coming to Dubus in May 1987, nearly a year after his mishap. Much of the new writing—in all: two stories, five essays, and fifty-three words of a novella—is about being disabled or bed-ridden, new discoveries to a man who spent fifty years counting on legs he never thought about.

A collection of seventeen essays, tentatively titled *Broken Vessels*, is scheduled for publication by Godine in the spring of 1990. Four of the pieces deal with Dubus's injury and recuperation. The novella is for Harper & Row. In addition, *Andre Dubus: Studies in Short Fiction* by Thomas B. Kennedy, is one of the first releases in a new critical series by Twayne Publishers of Boston.

Dubus credits National Book Award–winning author Tim O'Brien (*Going after Cacciato*, 1979) with encouraging him to write again.

O'Brien, one of the readers in the Friends of Andre Dubus Literary Series in Cambridge, didn't meet Dubus until the night he read but knew Dubus's stories and knew he wanted to lend a literary hand.

"It seemed like the right thing to do," said O'Brien. "I think if it'd been some lousy writer I would've said 'one more casualty,' but you want to salvage the good ones."

O'Brien, who lives not far from Dubus in Boxford, Massachusetts, visited the convalescing author six or seven times after they met, often playing poker, but always asking Dubus if he'd written that day.

"He'd come out," Dubus remembered. "We'd talk and then he'd say, 'I'm going to go write.' Shit, I thought. I've got to write, too. He's *driven*."

O'Brien is modest about his role in Dubus's writing recovery.

"I just said I liked his writing and hoped he'd get back to it as soon as possible," O'Brien said. "Human contact is all it was. I really didn't do that much."

Six months after Dubus began to write again, his wife Peggy Rambach (also a short-fiction author), moved out of their Haverhill, Massachusetts, home, taking with her the couple's two young daughters—Cadence, six and Madeleine, two.

"I don't mind being dumped by a woman, but there are some mitigating circumstances," Dubus said. "I can't walk. I get lonely a lot. I think, shit, a lot of nights, just general human loneliness comes. And, on nights like that, I normally would say, 'Well, shit,' and I'd just hop in the car and go down to McMino's [a local bar], have a couple, sit with the bartender, everything's fine. The whole world does that. But I don't have that option."

"My paraplegic friend said, 'I got it bad and my wife *stayed* with me,'" said Dubus, telling of another man's misfortunes to better gauge his own. "He said, 'Show me a disabled person that never thought about suicide and I'll show you a liar.'"

Dubus went on, the thought of suicide coming around to love. He mocked Romeo and Juliet's star-crossed love, displacing his own pain into a literary context he could talk about under the guise of objectivity. For a few moments I saw in Dubus the professor who taught at Bradford College for eighteen years before exhaustion forced him to retire in 1984. I saw the violence of his pain.

"Romeo and Juliet were neurotic," Dubus said. "What, there weren't any other fifteen-year-olds in Italy to love? Everyone is replaceable. Somebody can love again. Somebody can die or lose a leg. If you gave me a choice: You can lose your woman or be a cripple; I'd say, 'Well, I guess I could look in the phone book for a wife.'"

It was a treacherous question, but I knew I had to ask it: If the accident hadn't happened would the break up have?

Dubus went silent for a long time. I didn't think he was going to answer. Worse, I thought I'd asked something he would not forgive me for. Finally, he said, "I don't think I'll ever know."

After Rambach moved out, Jack Herlihy moved in to "help with mortgage and save my ass," Dubus said. Herlihy, thirty-six, manages a local bookstore and lives in a basement apartment Dubus refers to as "the love dungeon." Herlihy's girlfriend let me in the house when I arrived to talk to Dubus, and then let herself out.

Later, in a quick phone call to the bookstore—to ask Herlihy to bring home an issue of *Esquire* that carried a Tim O'Brien story—Dubus gave his housemate a bad time about the "good time" he feigned he was having.

"I just lay there like bait," Dubus said, stroking his beard and inflecting his best clipped Cajun. "But I fucked *your* woman before she left, when she brought me my coffee."

"Nah," he added, "I'm being *interviewed*, not *screwed*."

Dubus was sleeping when I arrived, a few minutes early, to interview him. Herlihy's girlfriend woke him before she left and Dubus, trying to prove his earnestness, told me he'd showered ("Sniff!" he said) and laid out his clothes (they were in a heap on the bed beside him) in preparation of our meeting. Then he said he needed more sleep (he'd take another nap later), ate half a cookie I'd brought, and covered up with a blanket, offering me anything in the house.

"As kooky as you are," Dubus said as he settled into sleep, "it's good to hear a woman's voice in the house."

The house, a ranch with ramps added after the accident, is writer-sloppy. There are newspapers, letters, literary journals, broadsides, and books strewn all over. Dubus's own books are among the clutter.

There's also a long-haired hamster in a cage on the floor, a bib with a Santa Claus face laying over the kitchen chair, a bowlful of oranges and grapefruit on the table, a plastic poker chip rack, a brass ceiling fan, and a hammock wedged against a wall of more books in the den.

In the hall leading to the rear bedroom where Dubus sleeps, there is a painting actually *on* the wall. It's a child's painting of an apple tree, several suns, flowers and birds. Dubus's daughter signed the artwork, drawing a heart between "Cadence" and "Dubus."

A picture of "The Wall," the Vietnam Veterans Memorial, hangs above Dubus's stereo. It shows a vet in camouflage and a fishing hat fingering the engraved shiny black names, a little boy hoisted on his shoulders. The child is kissing the wall.

When I stop concentrating on the details of his house, I hear Dubus and his old golden retriever, "Luke," snoring in sync, so I know I haven't made too much noise, waiting.

Dubus awoke, dressed, lifted himself into his *Quickie* and rolled at me toward the stereo beneath The Wall. He put on a Benny Goodman tape so I couldn't hear him maneuvering in the bathroom.

"Shit," Dubus said when we sat to talk. "I miss being outside. I miss exercise. I miss standing up at the stove. I miss getting up to take a leak. I don't like to go piss.

"When I think about [the accident], it's with wonder and gratitude that it wasn't worse," Dubus continued. "I mean, she was going fifty-something miles an hour, man, when she hit me. The other guy lasted two hours. I mean, he *had* a chance. Why didn't I get killed? Or some brain damaged shit? Then I'd be in good shape with Peggy leaving, huh? If I was a fuckin' vegetable, and she would've left.

"'You've been kept alive for something,' my friend told me,'" Dubus relayed. "But I don't know what it is. Maybe for something worse."

But Dubus doesn't really believe he was spared to endure an even more brutal fate. Sometimes he makes you believe he wasn't spared at all, but that he willed his comeback.

Dubus attributes part of his resilience to the lessons he learned in the Marine Corps.

"They do exactly what they say they'll do," said Dubus, who served from 1958 to 1964, leaving service with the rank of captain. "They take a boy and they make him a man by showing him that he never needed to quit, that he can do all kinds of things he never thought he could do, and that it was always in him to begin with. Like any good teacher does. Same approach. Just bring it right out of him and say, 'See, that was you all the time. Look at you now. Now, nobody can get you down.'"

Part of Dubus is still that Marine, needing to prove himself over and over in the face of adversity. Misfortune has complied by giving Dubus the testing material. Beyond what he calls his "broken heart and broken body," Dubus suffered a mild heart attack on October 30, 1988.

"Jack was in the basement and I was up here practicing denial [when it happened]," Dubus said. But, finally, Dubus couldn't ignore the symptoms and he was hospitalized for a week.

Hospitalization took the place of a deer hunting trip Dubus was planning with David Mix, a man he called "my one-legged Marine friend." "It was just an excuse to get away," Dubus admitted. "I mean, we weren't going to get a deer. He wasn't even going to hunt. I was going to be in a wheelchair; no fuckin' deer's going to walk up to *that*. But I had a heart attack instead."

Dubus has made a full recovery, but the heart attack compelled him to take the advice he'd once given me: *Piss on it*.

"I didn't have time to write," Dubus said. "I was doing too much shit and I stopped. I stopped editing manuscripts. I stopped having a workshop here. I don't answer my mail or phone [he screens calls with an answering machine]." And, Dubus told me, he won't be doing another interview for a long time.

"I'm trying to slow down everything and get infinitely patient," Dubus said. "I'm not patient enough. I mean, I got to get real patient."

"I don't remember being not tired. I feel I went through all the eighties on adrenaline. I was really burned out making a living. So, if I got any time left, I mean, I'd like to use it peacefully. I'd like to learn how to be patient." Dubus continued, holding an imaginary conversation with himself. "You know, 'Fifty-three words.' OK. 'Worked out for ten minutes.' All right. 'Cook a meal.' That's enough."

"I'm trying," he added, "to get in touch with what my body wants to do."

"I'm trying to see when it wants to [write], 'cause I don't want to wake it up with coffee, do this and that, and play games with it. I'm trying to find out when's the best time. I mean, I really don't have to write first thing in the morning," said Dubus, who got up and wrote at 4:00 a.m. when he was a Marine. "I'm not going anywhere. I don't have a job."

But not having a job doesn't mean Dubus doesn't work, or work out.

Thirty or forty minutes of shadowboxing in his wheelchair, mostly to the elegant voice of Ella Fitzgerald (but sometimes Frank Sinatra) everyday is what Dubus encourages his body to do, want to or not. There's equestrian therapy once a week. And, before the heart attack, there was also weight lifting.

"This country's so afraid of dying, so narcissistic," Dubus said, relishing a Sherman's Slims cigarette. "Health is a god. I've always worked out, but not for those reasons. It gives me peace of soul."

A man Dubus calls his "new leg-maker" may also give the author something else: the ability to stand on two legs. Dubus remembers the exact date—June 11, 1988—he first stood free of his wheelchair. "I was so fuckin' happy," he said, but the leg didn't lock correctly at the knee and Dubus is now awaiting a new prosthesis. "They're making me a more old-fashioned one with male and female parts that lock when you put weight on it," Dubus explained.

After he learns how to move on his new leg, Dubus wants to relearn how to get around in a car. He's already purchased a Toyota Celica and adapted it with hand controls. "I couldn't even *think* of buying a car until the MacArthur grant," Dubus said. "I mean, the only car we had, Peggy left with. It was a Saab her mother gave her."

"I'm just not in a hurry," Dubus said. "I mean, I want to *walk*. I want to get my leg, and it's too icy out there and so, fuck it, I'm going to wait until spring. I mean there's no reason to drive if it's a pain in the ass; if it's an *ordeal* to get to and from the car.

"The other day, Jack was taking me down the front steps, backwards, after dinner. And they were very steep and I could feel him straining. It was so steep that I was kind of, almost, upside down, like I was sliding out. I got terrified. I said, 'This is just like that stretcher on that highway.' Just absolutely helpless."

"I'm not going to fuckin' drive that car until I'm good," Dubus asserted. "There's a friend of mine that's going to take me to an abandoned airstrip and, I mean, I'm going to practice all kinds of situations. I don't want to kill anybody. I don't want to get killed because I use my hand instead of my foot."

Right now, Dubus is content to "work out, write and read—and be with the girls," he says.

"Losing the girls was a lot worse than losing my legs, fuckin'-A," Dubus said. "I don't know what they're wearing today. What they had for lunch. Or why Madeleine was crying on the phone the other day. This isn't fatherhood. It's some other bullshit. The first time, I saw the kids whenever I wanted to—not by appointment."

Dubus's first and second marriages also failed. But unlike the split with Rambach, he termed those break-ups "amicable" and "mutual." Dubus and his first wife are the parents of four grown children: Suzanne, Andre, Jeb, and Nicole.

"My father's idea of fatherhood has definitely changed," said Dubus's oldest child, thirty-year-old Suzanne. "My parents divorced when I was eleven, so maybe I remember it differently, but it seemed like he was able to go on with his life. But when Peggy left, I think it was a real vulnerable time in his physical recovery. He was just starting to become a physical human being again . . . and then he was an emotional cripple."

"You wanted to cheer him up," Suzanne Dubus continued, "but it was like he forgot the other four kids. While I wanted to be there for him, there was this little kid in me that says, 'You're my dad. I'm supposed to be able to call *you* when *I'm* down.'"

Dubus's namesake son, Andre Dubus III, twenty-nine, is also a writer. His book, *The Cage Keeper and Other Stories*, was published by E. P. Dutton in January 1989. But while Andre Dubus III said he couldn't help his father write, he knew he could help him regain his physical strength.

Andre Dubus III put his father on the weight training program he used before the heart attack. He accompanies his father to equestrian therapy, walking beside the horse Dubus is riding, in case of a fall. He and his brother, Jeb, are also building a pool in the Dubus's backyard and plan to add aquatic therapy to their father's recovery repertoire.

"I've been at a loss of how to be there for him," said Dubus's son. "But I think he's getting to the point where he doesn't need as many people around. He's definitely on the upswing. It's the picture of independence—whether that's a walking picture or a rolling picture. I think he knows now it's probably a rolling picture."

Andre Dubus III, like his father, tells stories. His father, he says, knows a neighbor, "John Miller, another gimp, a carpenter, paralyzed from the waist down when he fell off a roof.

"His life's work is gone," said Dubus's son. "There is no work for a crippled carpenter. My old man would hang around people like that and he'd say, 'I'm lucky. I still can write.' He still has his head, his heart, and his sexuality."

His father, Andre Dubus III said, embodies a remark once made by novelist Thomas Williams. Williams said: "I write so I don't die before I'm dead."

"It's that passion to write," Dubus's son said. "There are a lot of things to keep him in despair, but he walks a fine line between self-pity and being a courageous, triumphant man. Here's a man who, for the past thirty-five years, has written every day, or five days a week. I think it is harder for him to be a cripple and not writing, than it is to be a cripple and writing."

His body and body of work are becoming robust again, but Dubus hasn't forgotten that he also needs to fortify his soul. He has taken God as his confidant.

"I do pray a lot and that's some form of talking to someone who, for me, is named Christ," Dubus said. "And it's very much like having a monologue with a person you love when they're not there. I can get angry with Him, sad, I can beg for help, and I think it's good for me to be able to lie in bed saying, 'Please, help me,' rather than having nothing to say that to, except myself. And usually the help comes.

"I mean, yesterday, I was blue. The local priest called and said, 'Can I come by to see you?' He came by. I told him about feeling like a piece of meat. . . . And he kind of said a little liturgy, gave me communion, and you know, the sadness was still there, but I wasn't alone."

"And there seemed a history to it," Dubus said. "A history to the pain. It wasn't just happening to me in 1989. It'd been happening ever since people walked around."

In an almost unbelievable set of circumstances, Dubus's tragedy began with a motorcycle left in the roadway by a man whose wife just left him. It was July 22, 1986. The man was Stephen Bailey of Andover, Massachusetts.

Luz Santiago of Lowell, Massachusetts, crashed into the bike Bailey abandoned on I-93 in neighboring Wilmington. Shortly after midnight, Dubus passed the accident scene and left his car to assist Santiago and her twenty-three-year-old brother, Luis Santiago, a passenger. The three were crossing the highway to safety when a car struck and killed Luis Santiago and hit Dubus. (Luz Santiago was treated for minor injuries and doctors told Dubus he saved her life by shoving her out of the car's path.)

Nancy Anthony of Woburn, Massachusetts, was driving the car that collided into Dubus and the Santiagos. She was not prosecuted, while Bailey served a year in jail.

"I blamed the woman driving for a long time," Dubus said. "Until May 1987. But I prayed for her a lot and, finally, it worked. I had to get rid of that for myself. She didn't send a card or flowers. It wasn't so much that she hit us, it was the way she was afterwards.

"I had a lot of pain and every time I'd walk on that leg with a physical therapist, I'd curse and use her name," Dubus continued. "Not every time. But often. And you can't carry around that kind of hatred. It destroys you."

At Bailey's trial, Dubus requested that the court be lenient and access only the most minimal punishment under the law. He further asked that Bailey be allowed to serve his sentence in a nearby prison, so that his children could visit him.

At the time he testified, Dubus couldn't know the pain Bailey felt when his wife walked out. But he knew the joy of being a father, and he didn't want Bailey to miss that.

Dubus doesn't want to miss that now.

"The main reason I want to stay alive is those two little girls," Dubus said. "I've got a lot to teach them. I've got to try to hang around. If it weren't for them, I don't know if I'd give a fuck whether . . . ," Dubus drew a deep breath. "I love them."

Short-Story Writer's Words Flow on the Page—and Off

Regina Hackett / 1990

Seattle Post Intelligencer. 10 March 1990, C1+. Seattlepi.com/ReginaHackett. Reprinted with the permission of Hearst Communications, Inc.

Watching TV one night, short-story writer Andre Dubus saw squid mating in warm water. The spasms of their tentacles attracted sharks they failed to see in time.

"There's a lesson here," Dubus said. "Naked love is dangerous."

Like the late poet Delmore Schwartz, whom Saul Bellow once called the "Mozart of conversation," Dubus talks almost as well as he writes. Talking to him, even long-distance by telephone, is like being held in the paws of a benign but enormous bear. The listener is not the leader.

Dubus will preside over the lucky Seattleites who come to hear him Wednesday night at the First United Methodist Church, as part of the Seattle Arts and Lectures writers series.

When he rolls on stage, one leg sticking straight out in front of him and the other amputated above the knee, nobody will be able to say getting there was easy. The fifty-two-year-old writer is traveling by tram from his home in Haverhill, Massachusetts, because he says airplane design makes it impossible for those in wheelchairs to use the toilet.

Three years ago, Dubus stopped to assist at the scene of an accident and was run down. After twelve operations and arduous physical therapy, his remaining leg is probably as good as it's going to get, he says, and he has adjusted his sights accordingly.

"All I want to do is write, exercise, and be with my little girls," he said. "Next year maybe I'll want to be in the rodeo."

Widespread coverage of the accident helped Dubus begin to achieve the attention his work has always deserved. With seven volumes of fiction al-

117

ready in print, his *Selected Stories of Andre Dubus*, published by Vintage Books in 1988, earned ecstatic praise from critics and other writers and drew the attention of the MacArthur Foundation, which awarded him a fellowship that year.

Dubus remembers Seattle as unrelentingly gray. He was stationed at Whidbey Island while in the Marines in the early 1960s, during the Cuban missile crisis, and remembers watching KING-TV.

"The announcer would say in a cheerful, excited voice, like he was announcing the World Series, 'This is KING, your crisis network station.'"

Dubus also remembers James Meredith was barricaded in the University of Mississippi at the same time, surrounded by thousands of menacing white people who deeply resented this young black man's attempt to get a college education.

"I thought, those silly rednecks are going to get nuked."

There's an old-fashioned sweep in Dubus's stories, with weather and history, a sense of place, moral choices, and strong family ties.

None of his characters are wealthy. They live in ratty houses, drinking and dreaming of getting even. They are Catholics who break the rules and are full of remorse. They have violent, tender marriages. They argue with God. Sometimes they allow themselves to be moved by His grace and sometimes they pass it up, conscious of what they are doing.

In "The Winter Father," a divorced man scraping ice off the inside of his windshield realizes the gray film falling in curls from the glass is the frozen breath of his children.

Dubus's favorite writers include Faulkner and Chekhov; Faulkner for his passion and Chekhov because he's the best.

"Faulkner's characters go down in flames," Dubus said. "Between grief and nothing they choose grief. Love doesn't die, says Faulkner, it leaves us when we're no longer worthy of it.

"In Chekhov," he continued, sounding like the inspired teacher he was for two decades, "nearly every opening paragraph shows you where the light is, what time of day it is. The scene, you can see it right away."

Dubus blames Sputnik for the decline of literacy in the United States. He thinks that respect for high technology science, hard facts, replaced respect for the humanities, thanks to the "space race."

"People used to read in this country, and they could write too, ordinary people," he said.

"I knew a woman poet in D.C. when I had legs who taught poetry to Marine officers," he said, his voice dreamy. "They knew the language. Do they now?"

Andre Dubus's Knuckler Keeps
Him in the Game

Tim McCarthy / 1990

National Catholic Reporter 13 July 1990: 1, 16–17. Reprinted in *Leap of the Heart: Andre Dubus Talking*. Ed. Ross Gresham. New Orleans: Xavier Review Press, 189–99. Reprinted with the permission of the *National Catholic Reporter*, 115 E. Armour Blvd, Kansas City, MO 64111. www.ncronline.org.

In the darkest hours of a July morning in 1986, writer Andre Dubus stopped to help some accident victims on a Massachusetts interstate north of Boston. Fearing the worst and looking for more hands to deal with it, Dubus tried to flag another car down. The driver bashed into him, nearly cut him in half.

Dubus came out of the ordeal with one leg a stump and the other a moribund appendage that he has to keep elevated so it will not turn black with clotting blood. That physical mutilation of a boisterous man was more than enough, but his art, his marriage, his way of life—all of it came a cropper on that black highway and Dubus has spent the last four years trying to mend, fighting to find his way, to realize that he cannot go back and at the age of fifty-four has to begin most of it all over again.

Apart from some faithful friends, three things have kept him going: his children, his faith, and the struggle to reconstruct his art. With half a dozen collections of short fiction under his belt, Dubus has been hailed as one of the best writers in the country. He has no compunction about declaring himself a Catholic writer. Schooled by the Christian Brothers in the Cajun country of his native Louisiana, he grew into an abiding love for the Eucharist, for ritual, for sacraments of every kind. Most of his characters are secular as sour mash, but it is through that Catholic sensibility that he conceives them and bears them to life.

In *Voices from the Moon*, a story long enough to have been published separately as a short novel, an aging man named Greg announces that he is about to marry his son's ex-wife. Brenda is a dancer. She tells Greg of her need to dance every day, whether she is working professionally or not.

"Some people have things like that," Greg replies, "and they don't have to make money at it. It's something they have to do, or they're not themselves anymore. If you take it away from them, they'll still walk around, and you can touch them and talk to them. They'll even answer. But they're not there anymore."

That is how it is with Dubus and his writing, the reason why the loss of his art would be far more devastating than the loss of his legs, why healing has been such an anguished process for him, why he is fighting so hard for the patience to wait it out, to let his mind and spirit heal along with his body.

"Without the children and stripped of writing, I don't really have a reason to get up," he said one morning last spring. "So that's why I'm trying to get (the writing) back. I know the world doesn't need it. I need it to be happy."

Children's Hour

Dubus was resting on his bed that morning, black satin sheets, the dead leg propped on pillows, in the room where he works at a drawing table in one corner. "Best desk I ever had," he said. The desk looks out onto a high deck, over the front yard with its homemade swing set, swimming pool, and playhouse, across the country road to the greening ridge beyond.

It is a hillside house outside Haverhill, one of the old and ailing mill towns along the Merrimack River just north of Boston. Dubus's two youngest children, ages three and eight, have turned the walls of the long hallway down to the bedroom into a rollicking mural. More children's drawings decorate the dining room beyond. Love messages to their father are chalked on a table there. A wheelchair ramp angles down to the living room below, where the girls' art materials are stored along the windowed wall.

The girls stay with their mother, who left Dubus after the accident, but the house is still very much a place where young children live, their presence echoing even in their absence, among the shelves of books and stacks of papers.

There are six children from three marriages. Five of them still live in the area and for that Dubus counts himself lucky. He is never more animated than when he talks about them, any of them. His oldest, Suzanne, is thirty-one. He pays her to come and keep house, shop for groceries. His oldest son, Andre, is a year younger than Suzanne and had just sold his first novel.

"It changes your life forever to have children," Dubus said out on the deck one afternoon, his ruddy face aglow with sun and a surge of conviction. Bearded, burly, pink shirt open to the spring warmth, gold chain plying the tangle of gray chest hair, he spoke with some heat on certain women writers who had complained in print about how husbands and having children had kept them from becoming the great artists they could have been. "The real women writers I know say that's bullshit," he said.

"The thing about art is it's so tempting to quit and not do it and, boy, if you can blame it on something sacred and that you're fated to do, like getting pregnant, it can be an awfully easy out." He was talking about the women writers, but he could have been talking about crippling accidents as well. His voice boomed, clipped words into the remnants of a Cajun accent, with an anger that seemed to rage against something far larger than the self-pity of a few literary women.

In some ways, Dubus is as macho as they come. He loves tough talk, baseball, and a night out with the boys. Nothing better than a bunch of buddies, a few beers, Canary Island cigars, and the Celtics on TV. Although it has been more than thirty years since he was in the Marine Corps, he still carries a cigarette lighter adorned with the Marine emblem and has a "MARINES" bumper sticker on his red Toyota. Feminists might dismiss him as a male chauvinist par excellence. But they would not have read his work. Most of the women in his fiction are realized so completely, with such passion and precision, that they might be the envy of many a woman writer.

Why? Dubus is not sure. He has spent a lot of time listening to women and observing them, more closely than a lot of men do, he thinks. Does it have anything to do with Jungian psychology, with daring to expose your feminine side? He has never read Jung, so he cannot say. He does not read psychology because he does not want psychology to come into a character because the author read it in a book. "I'd rather discover things through the mysteries of art and religion," he said. "It's dangerous to read anything that demystifies, analyzes, or explains."

"I usually feel worse for women than I do men," he said. The remark echoed the kind of gut-grounded approach that characterizes so much of his fiction. Some would call the comment compassionate, others patronizing. Dubus would call it natural.

In a tale called "A Father's Story," the idea goes downright metaphysical, or as close to metaphysical as Dubus's earthy fiction ever gets. Luke Ripley, "a big-gutted grey-haired guy" in his fifties, owns a riding stable in north-eastern Massachusetts. His wife has left him; his closest friend is "another old buck" who happens to be the parish priest. Luke's daughter Jennifer is there for her summer visit. Driving back to her father's house one night, she hits and kills a man who has darted onto the highway. She panics and drives on. Conscientious churchgoer though he is, Luke covers for her. She drives back to Florida undetected. In the end, Luke is locked in an inner dialogue with the God he worships in the Eucharist every morning. He tells God that if one of his sons had come to him that night, instead of Jennifer, he would have "phoned the police and told them to meet us with an ambulance at the top of the hill.

"Why? Do you love them less?

"I tell Him no, it is not that I love them less, but that I could bear the pain of watching and knowing my sons' pain, could bear it with pride as they took the whip and nails. But You never had a daughter and, if You had, You could not have borne her passion.

"So, He says, you love her more than you love Me.

"I love her more than I love truth.

"Then you love in weakness, He says.

"As you love me, I say, and go with an apple or carrot out to the barn."

"It changes your life forever to have children." Yea. Or accidents on the road at night.

Rites of Spring

One morning Dubus was having a breakfast of waffles and molasses with Jack Herlihy, a friend and fellow writer who rents an apartment downstairs. ("He saved my butt after my wife left," Dubus said at one point. There was no money for the mortgage. Dubus was down in more ways than one. Herlihy, who does painting and wallpapering to earn a living, helped him back up.) Gazing out onto the bright morning, toward the far ridge that seemed to be getting greener by the minute, Dubus said, "A day like today would have been a snap. I'd do some writing, take a five-mile walk, take a shower, have some lunch."

"I used to have all these rituals," he had said earlier. Before the accident, he would get up early, pray, go to Mass, eat breakfast, write, work out. He still works out, still starts his day with prayer, still struggles to write. But much of the rest has changed.

A wheelchair van used to take him to Mass every morning on the way to physical therapy. Then he got the special Toyota with the wheelchair carrier on the roof and found it was too tiring to tackle the trip every day. Loading himself into the car, with his catch-all hunting pouch and plastic urine bottle, is a physical ordeal.

But early last spring, when the writing and a lot of other things were going badly, he convinced himself that if he got the daily Mass back he would get everything back. So he set out one morning and was a little late arriving at the only Catholic church with any kind of wheelchair access. Then he discovered that the double set of doors opened the wrong way and he had trouble getting into the building. "I was brokenhearted," he said. "All during Mass I kept thinking, 'The temple of the Lord and I can't get in here.'"

By the time he got home he was so depressed that he went to bed. But that night he remembered what a Eucharistic minister who comes to his house had told him, that sometimes we have to break so we can be healed, and he realized the Lord had to break his heart that morning to show him again that he should not try to get his old life back, that he should save his physical energy for the writing desk.

That night in July 1986, when Dubus was trying to flag the other car down, there was a woman standing beside him, one of the people he had stopped to help. In the instant he realized the car was not going to stop, he pushed the woman out of the way. Presumably, he could have leapt aside himself if he had not taken the time to do that. Once, when he was saying the sorrowful mysteries of the rosary and got to the crucifixion, he felt grateful. "Not many people in the world get a chance to give up their legs for a stranger," he said. But the gratitude came just once, once in four years.

Beyond that, he can no longer remember a day when he did not have some sort of ache or pain. He has had more than a dozen operations since the accident and still has to take a lot of pills. "I may look happy," he said in a moment of exasperation, "but it's all a pain in the ass."

And in a more reflective moment he said, "I don't enjoy this, but maybe I'm getting closer to God. Maybe I'll become a better person. It would be nice to get old and saintly."

"Saintly" is probably not how most people would describe the younger Dubus. He was the ex-Marine captain who liked to stand at the kind of bar where men could beef and brawl, down a shot and a beer with none of the frills. Former students who knew him at the nearby college where he taught from the time he left the Iowa Writers' Workshop until his accident remember him as something of a ladies' man. He liked horses and guns, baseball and broad-brimmed hats.

But he was also a man who, from the age of ten, had a devotion to the Eucharist, said rosaries and novenas, relied upon rituals of every kind. In *Voices from the Moon*, twelve-year-old Richie Stowe is at morning Mass after overhearing an argument between his father and his brother Larry about Greg's decision to marry Larry's ex-wife: "Now Father Oberti lifted the chalice and Richie imagined being inside of him, feeling what he felt as the wine he held became the Blood of Christ. My Lord and my God, Richie prayed, striking his breast, immersing himself in the longing he felt there in his heart: a longing to consume Christ, to be consumed through Him into the priesthood, to stand some morning purified and adoring in white vestments, and to watch his hands holding bread, then God."

In another story, "Adultery," a forty-year-old man named Joe Ritchie has left the priesthood and is involved with a married woman. Still: "He did not lose his faith in the Eucharist. After leaving the priesthood he had daily gone to Mass and received what he knew was the body and blood of Christ. He knew it, he told Edith, in the simplest and perhaps most profound way: most profound, he said, because he believed that faith had no more to do with intellect than love did; that touching her he knew he loved her and loving her he touched her: and that his flesh knew God through touch as it had to; that there was no other way it could; that bread and wine becoming body and blood was neither miracle nor mystery, but natural, for it happened with the leap of the heart of man toward the heart of God, a leap caused by the awareness of death."

Later, Edith reminds Joe that even if she were divorced they could not be married in the church. "What about your Eucharist?" she asks. "Would you give that up?"

"'I'd receive every day.' he said. 'Who would know? I'd go to Mass and receive the Eucharist like any other man.'

"'I don't think you're a Catholic at all.'

"'If I'm not, then I don't know what I am.'"

Without presuming to confuse Dubus with his characters, there is probably a good deal of the creator in the creation here. Dubus was writing another story about that same priest before the accident. He tried to go back to it during his two months in the hospital, but he has never been able to finish it. None of the material from that time seems to have much relevance anymore. (Dubus said he is going to start keeping himself out of his stories more, that he was "getting excessive" before he got run over "That's probably why I got run over. God thought I needed some editing.")

Edith's comment about Joe not being a Catholic calls up Dubus's attitude toward contraception: "We decided to follow Christ without bowing to that guy in the robes and all the pelf in Rome." Or his rejoinder to a woman who challenged him on his strong stance against abortion: "I'm not following the pope. It's the way I feel about children. It's got nothing to do with that guy."

"Very often I feel separated from the commonweal, in that my difficulties and sorrows are not universal," Dubus said at breakfast that morning. Only the passion of Christ convinces him that is not true.

"I don't know how somebody without a religious or philosophical background could exist in the world without despair. Or at least a great sense of humor," Dubus said.

Later, relaxing on his bed, taking long pauses between answers while he rests and appears to reflect, Dubus said, "I'm glad I believe in Christ and if I end up getting fooled, it would have been worth it. I think he's a good companion to have around."

Learning a Knuckleball

Two years ago last spring, Dubus would sometimes swoon when the Eucharistic minister anointed him at home. He would lie there on the bed with his eyes closed, unable to move. And sometimes he had visions of Mary. In one, he asked her if she had made love with Joseph. She gave him a smile that asked, "What do you think?" Another time she hugged him and he felt really loved. All the visions were tactile, sensual—and so is the vision Dubus brings to bear upon his fiction, the prose he shapes it with.

In a story called "Anna," a young couple robs a drug store. Dubus intended it to be a story about betrayal, after an account he read in a newspaper. But along the way, when the pair went to a bar to celebrate after the holdup, he realized Anna and Wayne were in love and it was not a betrayal story. So he simply followed the characters to see what happened, kept inside Anna, held to the intimate point of view he had worked so hard to achieve, sentence by sentence, as he worried his way inside her, struggled to know everything there was to know about her.

That, said Dubus, was the first time he wrote a story "vertically," pacing himself, going for the *mot juste* instead of sprawling the story over five drafts before getting anything close to what he wanted. He was reduced to fewer than two hundred words a day, but "Anna" was finished with the first draft. "So by writing more slowly, I wrote faster," he said.

That was in 1980. Every story after that was written that way—until the accident. Now he finds himself reverting to the old "horizontal" method and for him it is one more indication that he has to start over, build a new life, as he fights to relearn the discipline he developed with "Anna."

In a baseball story called "The Pitcher" (one of the rare tales set in Louisiana), Dubus writes about that kind of discipline, and the grace it takes to let it happen:

> It was a mystery that frightened him. He threw the first hard one and watched it streak and rise into Lucky's mitt; and the next one; and the next one; then he wasn't watching the ball anymore, as though it had the power to betray him. He wasn't watching anything except Lucky's target, hardly conscious of that either, or of anything else but the rhythm of his high-kicking wind up, and the ball not thrown but released out of all his motion; and now he felt himself approaching that moment he could not achieve alone: a moment that each time was granted to him. Then it came: the ball was part of him, as if his arm stretched sixty feet six inches to Lucky's mitt and slammed the ball into leather and sponge and Lucky's hand. Or he was part of the ball.

For some, it is a moment worth living for.

But that summer the pitcher's wife, widowed to a game, to her young husband's career, leaves him for a dentist. She accuses the pitcher of not being with her even when he is home. He says he doesn't know what that means;

"'It means I'm not what you want.'

"'How can you tell me what I want?'

"'You want to be better than Walter Johnson . . .'

"'Leslie, can't a man try to be the best at what he's got to do and still love his wife?'"

No doubt the question would ring true for many an athlete. For many an artist, as well.

The pitcher appears in another story, "After the Game," a major-leaguer by then. Dubus had hoped to follow him further still, into the time when his fastball would falter and he would have to learn a knuckleball to survive. But so far that has remained yet another voice from the past Dubus cannot return to.

At the risk of stretching the baseball metaphor too far, it may be that Dubus, with a lot of innings and some hard losses behind him, will have to learn a knuckleball. Over breakfast that morning, he said that it was starting to make sense to him. "I wanted everything to resume and nothing did," he said. "So why should the hardest thing (the writing) just—resume?"

While he works and waits, Dubus looks to other writers for stimulation—to his beloved Chekhov, to an occasional story in the *New Yorker*, to the dozen members of the writers' workshop he hosts at his house once a week. And the ideas have started to come again.

The ideas he gets keep his fiction short, he said. "Thomas Williams, whom I think is one of our finest novelists, said a novelist sees a whole world; I never see that." Usually there is a situation and out of the situation comes a character, or characters.

"I would like to be able to write short stories that are like novels—like Chekhov," Dubus said. "I used to tell the students that Chekhov never wrote a novel because he didn't have to; there wasn't anything else left to say."

Still reflecting upon his own work, Dubus said that he has been called a Christian existentialist: "That sounds classy. I don't mind that—but what does it mean?"

It was suggested that being confined to a wheelchair was about as existential as one could get. Living without legs made it much harder to have many illusions about life. ("I have faith in God," Dubus had said earlier, "but no faith in life.")

In a wheelchair, everything takes at least three times longer. Even getting ice cubes from the freezer in a cramped kitchen is a maneuver not without its perils. Dubus uses a fishing lure retriever to turn on overhead lights and ceiling fans.

But at least there are no longer any major money worries. In 1987, well-known writers such as Ann Beattie, John Irving, John Updike, and Kurt Vonnegut gave a public reading and raised $86,000 toward Dubus's medical bills. The next year a MacArthur Foundation grant brought him $310,000 over five years, which paid for the Toyota and the $3,200 switchback ramp leading from the kitchen door down to the driveway.

Given a life where a high curb can kill your day, something like a ramp or a lure retriever can be a godsend, and Dubus calls himself lucky on many counts. One afternoon, on the telephone with one of the writers in his workshop, he was in high excitement over a quotation from Flannery O'Connor that he had come across in the *Boston Globe* that morning. "I suppose the reasons for the use of so much violence in modern fiction will differ with each writer who uses it," she wrote, "but in my own stories I have found that violence is strangely capable of returning my characters to reality and preparing them to accept their moment of grace. Their heads are so hard that almost nothing else will do the work." She went on to say that that idea was "implicit in the Christian view of the world," and Andre Dubus was man enough, and Christian enough, to take it to heart.

While he was resting on those black satin sheets that morning, Dubus recalled how an old priest in the hospital had told him that "Maybe this (accident) will help your writing, but God knows how." Dubus went quiet for a moment, gazed toward the row of broad-brimmed hats hanging on the far wall. Then he said, "I gotta hope for that, right?"

Profile in Courage

Susan Larson / 1991

Times-Picayune 28 July 1991. Reprinted in *Leap of the Heart: Andre Dubus Talking*. Ed. Ross Gresham. New Orleans: Xavier Review Press, 2003. 200–202. © The Times-Picayune Publishing Co. All rights reserved. Used with permission of *The Times-Picayune*.

Until five years ago, Andre Dubus spent his days in perfect writerly fashion—writing, teaching, caring for a growing family, and crafting wonderful short stories that showed how even the simplest everyday decision can be an act of faith. Now he spends his days in an unending personal demonstration that even the smallest real-life act can be an example of incredible courage.

Dubus's life was changed forever in 1986, when he stopped to help two motorists in distress and was struck by an oncoming car. The accident resulted in the loss of one leg above the knee and the use of the other, confining him to a wheelchair. A short time later, after the birth of his youngest daughter, his third marriage ended, partially due to the strain of his post-accident life. His consolation? He saved the life of one of the people he stopped to help.

Dubus, fifty-four, is rebuilding his life with the help of his friends, fellow writers, and admiring readers. Shortly after the accident, writers Ann Beattie, E. L. Doctorow, Gail Godwin, John Irving, Stephen King, Tim O'Brien, Jayne Ann Phillips, John Updike, Kurt Vonnegut, and Richard Yates gave readings, with the proceeds earmarked for Dubus's considerable medical expenses. A MacArthur "genius" grant ($310,000 over five years) awarded in 1989 also has helped to provide financial relief.

Along with fellow writer Frederick Busch, Dubus recently received the fourth annual PEN/Malamud Award, funded by a bequest of Bernard Malamud to the international writers' organization. It says something about the company Dubus is keeping these days to note that previous winners of this award are John Updike, Saul Bellow, and George Garrett.

Selected Stories, a welcome collection of Dubus's previous fiction, was published in 1989. This month marks the appearance of Dubus's ninth book, *Broken Vessels*, his first collection of nonfiction, which, among other things, discusses the accident and its aftermath.

Born in Lake Charles, Dubus grew up in Lafayette and was educated at the Cathedral School, McNeese State University, and the Iowa Writers' Workshop. His family includes a number of well- known writers. His son, Andre Dubus III, recently published his first collection of short fiction; his sister, Elizabeth Nell Dubus, is a novelist; and his cousin, James Lee Burke, has written award-winning mysteries.

Dubus may be a longtime resident of the Northeast, but traces of a Louisiana accent still wander through his speech. "I know," he said of this trait during a phone interview from his home in Haverhill, Massachusetts. "All I have to do is hear one or see a movie set in Louisiana and it comes right back."

Traces of that accent are present in his writing as well. In *Broken Vessels*, he writes about his days chasing baseballs for the Lafayette Brahman Bulls in the Evangeline League; his education at the hands of the Christian Brothers; the Cajun heritage, embodied in silver spoons and forks make of spoons that once belonged to Marie Antoinette, that was his birthright.

Then there is the French Catholicism that is the enduring legacy of his Louisiana upbringing. "I am a Catholic writer," Dubus said, discussing a story in which a father's love is compared to God's, a story in which a father takes the blame for a daughter's hit-and-run accident. "I always look for 'What's the ethical question here?' I had to think about how I'd react to that situation and I had to think about how that character would react. That's just the way it is. Men shouldn't back off."

Dubus, a former Marine, doesn't back off. After the accident, a friend told him it would take five years to recover. Dubus thought this sounded a little excessive at the time, but it has proven, some five years later, to be true. "I spent the winter of '91 learning a new vocation," he said, "and that is how to keep my spirits up. It used to be, if I got depressed, I ran or walked five miles. There's nothing a good workout wouldn't cure."

Now he works out in different ways. Much of his recovery has been aided by the support of friends. It's been a learning process for Dubus, one in which he's come to see the world from a different point of view. "I spend a lot of energy getting through the days without getting the blues or getting angry. A lot of my friends who are in AA told me that all you have to do is just get through the day.

"I realized that I'd been waiting to wake up one morning and be myself again. What I learned from other crippled men is that you're not going to wake up like that. And the best thing to do is to shout and cry and let it out."

Dubus recently resumed writing fiction. "Andre (his son) came over to mow my lawn the other day, and I told him I'd finished the first section of a novella in six years. I almost don't remember what that was like. Now I get cripple thoughts, and I'm afraid I'll go back and stare at the ceiling."

"Cripple thoughts" aside, he sounds strong and optimistic, without a trace of self-pity. During this interview, he watches a baseball game with the sound off, updating the score from time to time. He has a Coke, grumbles over a misplaced fly swatter, excuses himself to "take a pee," and talks about how he'd rather be interviewed by a woman than a man. His earthy good humor is still in place. He talks about his indifference to critical reaction ("can't keep it, can't cherish it, can't show it") and says he'd rather have actress Debra Winger admire his work.

His days are busy. His two girls, the youngest of his six children, are coming for the weekend, and he's made plans, lots of plans.

He talks about how some people in the world treat children like handicapped people. "My daughter Cadence is a beautiful redhead and she's always talking about how people only see that when they look at her. Now when she's out with me, she sees people who talk about my being in the wheelchair, talk about me as if I weren't even there. And I say to Cadence, 'Now see? There's my pretty red hair.'"

He can swear like a sailor, but then he can write like an angel. "I feel better now than ever before," he said, adding quickly, "knock on wood." Then, "I have faith."

Andre Dubus

Eleanor Wachtel / 1991

In *Writers & Company*. San Diego: Harcourt Brace & Company, 1993, 125–37. Interview prepared in collaboration with Lisa Godfrey. Reprinted with the permission of Eleanor Wachtel.

In one of Andre Dubus's short stories, a mother tells her son, "We don't have to live great lives, we just have to understand and survive the ones we've got." Pain, vulnerability, and hard-won strength are the veins that run just below the surface of Dubus's fiction, set in the blue-collar world of waitresses and bartenders, mechanics, and laborers. Infused with compassion, his stories and novellas revolve around relationships between men and women, the Catholic faith, and the loss of permanence.

After eight books of fiction, including *Adultery and Other Choices* (1977), *Voices from the Moon* (1984), and *The Last Worthless Evening* (1986), Andre Dubus published his first work of nonfiction, *Broken Vessels* (1991), a collection of personal essays which is in part about the tragedy that devastated his own life. In the early hours of July 23, 1986, he stopped on the highway to help a stranded motorist, and while flagging down an oncoming car he was hit. Dubus lost one leg and the use of the other, and underwent twelve operations and years of pain and therapy. Then his third wife left him, taking with her their two small daughters.

For a while Dubus couldn't write at all. Finally, he began to write about what had happened, and this became the title piece in *Broken Vessels*. Here is a man determined to be honest, even when overcome with confusion and despair.

Andre Dubus became a MacArthur Fellow (the "genius" award—more than $300,000 over five years, no strings attached) in 1988. He is much admired by other writers and critics. Ellen Lesser, in the *Village Voice*, wrote that Dubus's stories "cut deep enough to leave you weeping or gasping for air." Short-story aficionados always include Dubus in their ten best American writers lists.

Dubus was born in Louisiana in 1936 and still has a slight Cajun accent underneath his New England speech. I spoke to him from his home in Haverhill, Massachusetts, just north of Boston.

WACHTEL: The American writer Tobias Wolff, in his introduction to your book *Broken Vessels*, writes that the real possibility of the personal essay is to catch oneself in the act of being human. What does that mean for you?
DUBUS: In a personal essay you are writing about yourself and trying to find, not the whole truth, but a truth. Then you learn that truth is something that was happening in your own life. Certainly, in some of these things I wrote, I actually caught myself, as he says, in the act of being human.

WACHTEL: Being human seems to me to mean admitting to all sorts of doubts and weaknesses and needs, and not hiding behind the authorial mask of fiction.
DUBUS: That's true. A book of essays, for me, is a very different experience from a book of fiction, because in fiction I've always been able to say, "Oh well, that's what she said in the story, but that has nothing to do with me." In an essay I can't say that because there I am.

WACHTEL: The personal essay by its very nature makes us feel that we know you, that we know about your life and who you are, but of course even the confessional form is a kind of construct. Were you conscious as you were writing of the kind of persona you wanted to create in this book?
DUBUS: No, I wasn't. Writing is a very strange process: everything you're talking about is happening while the act of writing is going on. While I'm writing—that's when I face the exposure, that's when the right word comes, or the temptation to use the wrong word and duck out, the temptation to skip something. That's when I always have to bear down and try to write as closely to what is the truth as I can feel with my senses and with my heart. After that's done and typed up and sent off it begins to feel less like me and more like something I wrote. Does that make sense?

WACHTEL: Yes. You often write about what it means to be a man, about masculine values and image. You grew up in the South, in a small town in southern Louisiana, and you spent more than five years in the Marines. What do you feel shaped your own sense of male identity?

DUBUS: Oh boy! You know, I don't know the answer to that. When I was younger, I was a sissy and small—I mean, I was 105 pounds when I got my driver's licence. In the fifties a 105-pound guy with his mother's car was not really an attractive item on a young woman's agenda—they liked quarterbacks and stuff. Later, when I taught in the sixties, I was very jealous of my students because then girls started liking skinny guys with long hair. Being small and sensitive was certainly partly the reason I became a Marine. The Marine Corps is full of small men! Actually, Tobias Wolff, who was a Green Beret, told me a lot of little guys joined the Green Berets, too.

Also, I respected my father, who stressed honor. He had very high standards about that, and I certainly looked up to that, too. And you can't leave out Gary Cooper; he was a shaping influence. Gary Cooper was a good person to have around: he was kind to women and children and loyal to his friends, and nobody crossed him!

WACHTEL: But he was a quiet man, wasn't he? Wasn't he the strong, silent type?

DUBUS: Yes, I'm not quiet, I've never been cool, and I've never been able to live up to my standards!

WACHTEL: You write about your role as a man in relation to your children and also in relation to the women in your life. You describe an incident in an essay called "Running" concerning one of your sons. You're jogging with your teenage boy and suddenly he turns red, he looks sick and you tell him to stop but he doesn't. And in a remarkably compact sentence you describe your reaction to this: "I believed he should stop, hoped he would not, remembered first aid I had learned years ago." Can you tell me about these complicated feelings?

DUBUS: It's a very strange thing. I think if it had been a daughter I would have said, "That's it, we're stopping." You know, we are animals and men feel differently about their sons. There's something about being the father of a son that makes you allow him to take a risk because you know he needs to. I knew that if he actually made that run—like me, he was a small boy—it would be important to him, and I wasn't really worried that he would die. What I really wanted, of course, was for him to have the courage and the resilience to go on when he really couldn't anymore, because I knew he would need that strength in whatever life he chose. Of course, a woman does too, but I'm a very tenderhearted father towards daughters, much more protective. I think had I been running with a teenage daughter, I would have said,

"Honey, it's hot and, you know, this could kill you, and let's walk, you and Daddy." I'm not saying that's good or bad, I'm just saying that's the way it is.

WACHTEL: In another essay you write about how you feel it's necessary for your sons to prove themselves through fighting, by being neither cowards nor bullies, and you talk about how you too had had to prove yourself to yourself. Is fighting part of being a man?

DUBUS: No, I don't think so. I really think that men and women would be more fulfilled if we all lived according to the ideals of Christ, which are love and tenderness. I actually believe in turning the other cheek. What I've never understood, though, is what you do when it's somebody else's cheek. That's what that essay was about—having to prevent violence against a third party who could not defend herself. For boys in school there's always somebody who challenges you in a physical way, and unfortunately I don't think it works to tell a ten-year-old to turn the other cheek. A boy that age has to learn to swing back. My sons and I didn't learn until we were older. It's a way to prepare yourself for something much more important later on, so that when your boss or your wife or your best friend wants you to sell your soul for a better condominium you have to say, "Wait a minute, I'm being bullied here and I've got some moral integrity I have to keep intact." Does that make any sense? I'm saying it shouldn't be physical, but it turns out that at a certain age among boys there are these physical challenges and it's important for the boy to learn then to do what he is afraid to do.

It is certainly important for girls too, but generally it happens to them in a different way. You know, it's so hard to be an adult human being, and so many people sell out and live lives they don't want, that you've got to decide really early—these are my boundaries, this is where I stand, this is what I stand for. Dietrich Bonhoeffer, the German philosopher executed for trying to assassinate Hitler, had an entire page in his book *Ethics* about what you do to a human being when you slap that person's face—the deep violation of the person. It would be wonderful if human beings never felt the urge to assert themselves physically, or in any way, over other people, but that's not how the species is.

WACHTEL: You also write about manliness in terms of your desire to be a provider and a protector. In one instance you write about wanting to hunt or fish, to be an old-style breadwinner, and you say quite candidly that you know you're not supposed to yearn for these male pleasures but you do anyway, and that leaves you with uncertainty.

DUBUS: That was written maybe a decade after the feminist movement really got strong in the United States—I think a lot of people of both genders are paying for it now. I'm sure there was something good that came out of the sexual revolution, but there are a lot of confused people out there. Anyway, at the time I wrote that, you could not do anything for certain women without angering them; there was a whole new set of rules. The truth is in nature: Take the pheasant. The cock pheasant is the beautiful pheasant. Now, I was raised to believe that that's because he's the male, and most male birds stand out and are more beautiful. But I realize now that it's because the male's expendable; the male attracts the predator away from the nesting female, allowing her to give birth in safety and keep the species going. That's really the male function.

Men are supposed to procreate, we are highly expendable, we die sooner and things just go on without us. If you also take from the male his role as breadwinner, what is he? What is he in the world? So many jobs—I'm thinking 90 percent—are unfulfilling. At least, they're fulfilling only insofar as you know you are putting in that time and doing your best for the people you love. You'd rather be fishing or hunting in order to bring home a paycheck for your offspring and for the woman you've committed your life to. The only thing that makes most jobs meaningful is if the fruits of your labor go to something. It's not a problem I have, but I think it is a difficulty that has to be dealt with.

WACHTEL: One of the moving aspects of your book is a kind of faith and optimism in relationships. You were married three times, but you still believe in marriage, even in its permanence. Why is that?

DUBUS: I believe that marriage is for the good and is the essence of a society. I would like very much somehow to have stayed together with each of my wives and our children. And my not having achieved that doesn't make me like the fox in Aesop's Fable—you know, the one with the sour grapes. I know that it's worth more than most things for people to be able to stay together and love each other through all their changes, and that people without love are not fulfilled. I've never ever written what I would like to write either but I keep trying. So, I write and I date!

WACHTEL: Vivian Gornick, in writing about your fiction, put you, along with Richard Ford and Raymond Carver, in a group of writers whom she called "tenderhearted men," but at the same time she suggested that there is a profound misunderstanding and distance between men and women in your books, and that this is based on a fantasy about what relationships between men and women could be like. Is this something you try to work through in your essays and in writing about your own life?

DUBUS: No, not at all. She made several mistakes in that essay: the biggest one was accusing us of not understanding more than our characters do. I always do, so I thought that was a weird reading. And when she says marriage, romance, monogamy is all passé, that we're longing for the past, well, that's her past, too. This generation of children is going to grow up, date, fall in love, make mistakes, marry, and have babies; it's not going to change.

WACHTEL: What about the distance between the men and women in your fiction and their inability to really know each other?

DUBUS: I do think we have a hard time knowing each other when we're sexually attracted; when we're not, there's just no problem at all. If you have a man and woman, let's say, traveling by train from the east coast of Canada to the west and they're good friends who work together, there'll probably be no trouble. If they're lovers, there's going to be a fight somewhere around Saskatchewan. I mean, I get along so well with my men friends because we're not lovers, and if one of them hurts me or I hurt him it's not really a big problem. We've never been naked in all the truth of that word, physically and spiritually. When you're really deeply involved with somebody it gives a new form to the relationship, a form I obviously have not mastered, nor did my wives in my company! I've never had trouble with a woman because she's a woman, but I've had a lot of trouble with women I loved and who loved me.

WACHTEL: In your essays you write, both directly and indirectly, about your Catholic faith. In one essay, "Out Like a Lamb," you draw parallels between real and metaphorical sheep. What was the experience that prompted that?

DUBUS: My first wife, our four children, and I moved from the University of Iowa to New England. We got a really good deal on a house and seventy acres of land and a swimming pool—a two-storey colonial house, two hundred years old, the whole thing for only $105 because the landlord just wanted someone to live there and take care of the sheep and the roses. I'd always thought of sheep as these mellow, sweet little creatures, but they were really stupid beasts and they kept breaking out of their pen and then trying to get back in. We'd lead them to the entrance and they wouldn't see it and they'd run away again. We finally got very frustrated and we'd tackle 'em and punch 'em and throw 'em over the fence.

Then finally one night one of them was eating the landlady's roses. (She had terminal cancer and her husband had said, "You've got to make sure those roses are there for when we come back for a month next summer.") So I shot the sheep in the rump with some number seven birdshot, which I thought might get through the wool but probably wouldn't. That ewe just looked at me and kept chewing, and I said, I give up, you know, the roses are gone, the sheep are gone. Back in the house one of the kids said, "There's something wrong with that sheep." Her legs were straight up in the air and she was dead. I realized during that year that when Christ called us his lambs, he wasn't thinking of us as cute little things to cuddle, but as really stupid brutes who were trying to get through the gate, but once we were in front of the gate we couldn't even see it, and we just kept running away. Running to exactly where we did not want to go, which reminds me of my marital history, as a matter of fact.

WACHTEL: There are Catholic writers and writers who happen to be Catholics. You've always identified yourself as a Catholic writer. What does that mean in terms of your writing?
DUBUS: I see the world as a Catholic does. I didn't really know that that was a whole lot different from other people. I didn't know that there are people who perceive physical reality as the only reality of their lives. The Catholic Church is filled with sacraments, which are physical transactions with a spiritual meaning. This really helps with my young four- and nine-year-old girls: simply peeling a banana and slicing it into a child's bowl is a spiritual act; it's an act of love between you and the child. I often tell myself that you're not just pouring Raisin Bran here, you're loving your children, and that makes me feel better about things because it's a deeper truth.

WACHTEL: How do you think your beliefs affect what you write, the way you write?
DUBUS: In the title essay in *Broken Vessels*, my beliefs literally led me to whatever affirmation there is in the ending, because that essay does start, I do believe, with a couple of days when I didn't want to be alive. When I'm writing fiction, I'll often put a character in a situation something like one I've lived through. I'll give the character meaningless work and no religious convictions, and then give him some experience I've had—like being a di-

vorced father. And then I put him through the same things I went through and see how he does. Or sometimes I just say, I'm going to write about a Catholic this time.

WACHTEL: Five years ago something terrible happened to you that would test anyone's faith. You had a series of almost Job-like ordeals and losses. It started with an automobile accident that the title essay of *Broken Vessels* describes, along with the aftermath of that. Can you describe what happened?
DUBUS: I was driving home from Boston around one in the morning, and there was a clear stretch of road on Route 93 here; no cars, it was a clear night. There are four lanes on this highway; a speed lane is the fourth one; I was in the third. I noticed a car far ahead stalled in the middle of the road and to the right a woman was at the emergency callbox off the shoulder of the road, calling the state police. I slowed down, went to the end of the speed lane to the driver's side of the car to see if she was injured. She was: she was standing beside the car crying, bleeding. So I pulled over and went to get her out of the road and I was thinking of first aid—bleeding, shock. When I got there, she said, "There's a motorcycle under my car." She pointed down and there was a black pool of liquid, which I took to be blood, so I assumed there was a motorcycle and a crushed human being under there. Then from around the trunk of her car, a man—her brother—came. I had not seen him. They were Puerto Ricans. He said: "*Por favor*, no speak English, please help." So we left the road and I was waving a car down because I wanted someone to go with me to look under the car. I was afraid of what I was going to see. I assumed the person was dead but I'd have to look, right? And if the person wasn't dead I don't know what I would have done; I was really afraid of the horrible body I was going to see. It turned out there was no body. The motorcycle had been crushed and that was motor oil on the highway; no one was under there. The motorcyclist was actually unhurt; he'd abandoned his bike on the road. The woman I flagged down didn't see us. She ran into us and killed Luis Santiago—I guess he died in an hour or so—and I got very badly hurt. I was in the hospital for about seven weeks and had about twelve operations and lost my left leg above the knee. I was in physical therapy for three years and never really got back the use of my right leg, so I'm in a wheelchair.

WACHTEL: You have written that living as a cripple allows you to see more clearly the crippled hearts of some people whose bodies are whole. I'll ask you a very big question, and you answer it however you like, but can you tell me how the accident changed you?

DUBUS: Well, you know, I'm not sure why I wrote that line now. People who knew me before and after the accident say I have changed, and changed positively. I don't know that yet—I'm still dealing with how to get to the ashtray, and longing, on a lovely day like today down in Massachusetts, to be out walking. I'm trying to learn to live in the present, because in a wheelchair you cannot live in the future—you get messed up because you cannot hurry and you just have to try to stay in the moment. I certainly pray more fervently and frequently than ever. And I'm afraid for people I love, ever since I got hit. I really get worried when people I know are on the road.

That perception I wrote about came to me in '88 or '89, and I assume that it must have felt like the truth at the time. Now it sounds arrogant to me, to tell you the truth, and it embarrasses me a little that I wrote it. But it also may be the truth. You see, I just don't know, and that is finally interesting. This is not a boring existence—frustrating sometimes, sad sometimes, angering some times, and depressing sometimes, but it's never dull. I mean, I get excited over little things: finding that I can reach this or knowing where something is, and there are these little challenges and things to learn.

WACHTEL: The image of a broken vessel is a compelling one. How did you come by it?

DUBUS: I have this wonderful physical therapist. A woman who has been through a lot, has been a therapist for a long time and found God in, I guess, her fifties. People like that who have been around and are very worldly are just wonderful to be with. She said to me once: "You have to be flat on your back to look straight up." She was always saying things like that, One day I really just cracked up and wept during the physical therapy, which she never stopped—I mean, I was crying and walking on crutches and she and her two attendants were standing there waiting for me to fall. Then she got me up on her table to start working on my leg and she said, "It's in Jeremiah. The potter is making a vessel and he breaks it, so he has to make a new one." She said, "You can't. You can't make a new vessel out of a broken one; you have to make a new you." She said, "Now it's time to find the real you." Maybe she was just being encouraging, but the truth is, if you've been an active man for fifty years, trying to be Gary Cooper, Cary Grant, and Sean Connery all at the same time, and a father too, and then you're in a wheelchair, you certainly do have to find a new you.

Now there's nowhere to go. There are no boardwalks on the beaches and no boardwalks in the woods. I mean, I can get in the car and drive and 90 percent of the places I drive by have curbs. I take pleasure in taking a drive and sometimes just stop in the parking lot watching people walk by, but it's an inaccessible world. The world is not built architecturally or spiritually for people in wheelchairs.

WACHTEL: Why do you like to use the word *cripple*? There are other words to describe your condition, even neutral expressions such as "differently abled," but you reject them.

DUBUS: My crippled buddies call themselves "disabled," but I don't think of *cripple* as pejorative. I think it's because I'm a writer; I don't like euphemisms; I don't like words designed to cheer me up. One of my children, my oldest son, came to visit me when I was in the hospital and he said, "Pop, you're not handicapped, you're physically challenged. It's a new phrase." I said, "*You're* physically challenged: you're breathing hard from walking the stairs. I'm crippled." I think it's a word I would have used before. I've never liked euphemisms.

WACHTEL: In this book you give us an angle of observation, literally, that we rarely get in writing, in fiction, a view of the world from a man in a wheelchair. You describe a kind of fringe society that you're now part of made up of very different people, like your "crippled buddies," who got there, like you, by accident. What's that world like for you?

DUBUS: Encouraging. It makes me feel so good to speak to my paraplegic friend because as soon as I speak to him I already feel better, because I *am* better off: I can feel the lower part of my body. Also, when you speak to someone in a chair you don't have to explain anything. You just get this litany of response: I hear you, I know, I know, I've been there, yes. You don't have to explain the fatigue, you don't have to explain the humiliation. A lot of bipeds do not understand what it feels like for a person in a wheelchair to be carried upstairs: you feel like a piece of meat in somebody else's hands, It's an incredible surrender of integrity, of yourself; it's also dangerous and scary; and guys get into "Hey, we can get him up, c'mon Andre!" It makes you miss your legs.

People in wheelchairs have all been through this, and instantly they know what I'm talking about, and they feel the same as I feel about it. They're the ones I turned to after meeting with a psychologist in '89, when I was really in trouble. I mean, every morning when I woke up, I woke up crying, and one morning I couldn't stop. So I called my doctor and he sent me to a therapist, and when I left the therapist I called my paraplegic buddy. And I said, you know, this is near the end of my third year, and I keep waiting every morning to wake up happy, like I've had the flu and it's over. (None of us that I know of dreams of being in a chair; you know, I always have legs in my dreams; I walk. But when you wake up, there's your wheelchair beside you and there's your crippled body. You have to dress lying down or sitting down and then make the bed under you while sitting down and all this.) And he said to me, "Every morning, the first thing I do when I wake up is cuss for about five minutes about having to get my chair into the car," which is a very difficult, intricate thing and enough to keep a sane person inside of the house for a long time.

I called him this year and I said, "You know, John, this is my fifth year and for the first time I'm starting to feel pretty good. I'm not as tired, I don't hurt as much, I feel some energy coming back." I said, "How was your sixth year?" He said, "My sixth year was my worst." So, I'm waiting to see what's going to happen in the sixth year. And no one else could tell you this.

"Into the Melody":
A Conversation with Andre Dubus

Olivia Carr Edenfield / 1993

Resources for American Literary Study 33 (2010): 219–75. Reprinted with the permission of *Resources for American Literary Study*, © 2010 AMS Press, Inc. All rights reserved.

Edenfield: I'll start with some general questions and then move through *Selected Stories*, story by story, if that's all right.
Dubus: There'll be some I won't remember specific things about.

Edenfield: Thomas Kennedy [in his book on your stories] says that there is an existential Christian vision at the core of your fiction. Would you talk about that?
Dubus: That's hard for me to do because I never understood what that meant. [Laughs] That's the truth. I said this year at some reading, "I never have known what Existentialism meant. Every time someone defined it, I didn't understand it." Jack [Herlihy, Dubus's personal assistant] told me "Here's a definition you can use: 'The existentialist believes that he is doomed to choice." I said, "What the hell did people ever think that they were doomed to?" So I guess that's my answer to that. This was a revelation when I heard that from Jack. He said some people believed that they didn't have any choices. That's kind of weird.

Edenfield: Your characters have a choice, but they don't deny the existence of God.
Dubus: That's true.

Edenfield: You said to Kennedy [in the 1987 interview, included in the Twayne's Studies in Short Fiction], "If I cannot become the character in the book that I am reading, I quickly lose interest" (92–93). In which of your characters do you most see yourself?

Dubus: I have some autobiographical stories about my boyhood, but I'm not about my boyhood anymore. When I wrote the stories about a boy named Clement, I used actual events. I realized this year working on an essay that I have never known what it feels like to be anybody else. I know what it feels like to be a character in a book written by somebody else or a character I'm writing, but I'll never know what it feels like to be another human being. Even though in my stories about my childhood my parents would actually say some of the things they did, they're not in the stories. It's my adult memory of my childhood perceptions of someone I've never really known. When I wrote the stories about my childhood, I no longer felt as I did as a child. So it's a difficult question to answer. Peter Jackman is an adult quasi-autobiographical character in that I made him into a divorced father and had him experience some of the things that I've experienced as a divorced father. But I took away from him two gifts that I have received: I took away his vocation, and I took away his spiritual life to see how he would struggle.

Edenfield: So without his spiritual life, he struggles harder?
Dubus: I think so, but I feel equally close to all characters I write about—or try to become close to them.

Edenfield: Do you feel just as close to Polly [in "The Pretty Girl" (1983)] as you do to Raymond [in "The Pretty Girl" (1983)]?
Dubus: Oh, yeah, sure. It just depends on the point of view I'm in—which is like life, isn't it? Have you ever listened to ex-spouses talking? Boy, you get a lot of different stories! They're all true. [Laughs] Each point of view is true. What are you going to do with that? I read to little teenagers on Monday nights. I was reading them an Isaac Babel [1894–1940] story about him getting bullied, and I said, "Look how many points of view you could tell this story from. If you read the story from the bully's point of view, you wouldn't feel bullied." You can do that to any story.

Edenfield: You have called yourself a realist. What did you mean by that?
Dubus: I did?

Edenfield: Yes.

Dubus: That's funny, because the other night I was lying in bed wondering what a realist is. [Laughs] It's true! I don't believe I can answer. What's a realist?

Edenfield: That was *my* question to *you*. That's how you defined yourself at one time. It was when you were talking to Kennedy.
Dubus: I've finally outgrown thinking in those terms. I'm not sure what a realist is. If a realist is someone who puts out life as we recognize it, then most writers are realists, right? I really don't know what it means anymore. I'm serious.

Edenfield: You also told Kennedy that you believe in absolute honesty.
Dubus: As a man or as a writer?

Edenfield: As a writer.
Dubus: I absolutely do as a writer.

Edenfield: Are there any characters who you feel come across as dishonest?
Dubus: Dishonest? You mean through their workings with other people or through themselves?

Edenfield: Either.
Dubus: I can't think of one, but there must be some. The problem with an interview is that I finished this yesterday [points to an essay on the table] and it's already leaving me. It's a process and I hardly ever look at it again unless I get paid to read it. That's why I'm drawing a blank.

Edenfield: So Faulkner [1897–1962] wasn't lying when he said [in Gwynn and Blotner, *Faulkner in the University*] that he forgot that novel and forgot that story?
Dubus: I don't think he was lying at all. I have an incident in "A Father's Story" [1983], and when *The Lieutenant* was brought back into print in 1986 and I had to read the galleys, I had the same incident there. I didn't know I wrote that before! My son Andre has noticed that I have a repetition of last names and first names.

Edenfield: How do you come up with names?
Dubus: It's difficult for me. Sometimes one comes to me really easily. When I was a teacher, I used to combine students' names. They're hard for me.

Edenfield: Why so?

Dubus: I don't know. Some people have title trouble, some people have name trouble. And, for me, men's names more than women's.

Edenfield: I tend to read a lot into your choice of names. I think of Jackman as being almost everyman.

Dubus: Jack was the name of a British fellow who was teaching dance at Bradford College [where Dubus taught creative writing]. That's where I got that. [Laughs]

Edenfield: We talked in my class one time about Anna Griffin's name ["Anna" 1981], how Griffin is half one thing, half another. We saw Anna that way.

Dubus: I forgot that was Anna's last name. That's her last name?

Edenfield: We thought it was a brilliant choice.

Dubus: [Laughs] Yeah, I read that statement by some professor from the South. He talks about Paul and all the symbolism in the name Paul. No. [Laughs] Wasn't so. In fact, a woman friend in Iowa told me, "Your names are really dull. You try so hard to choose names that don't have meaning that you have really flat ones." So I put her in the draft of a story; her name was Nancy. I called her up and said, "I can't use Nancy." She said, "Why?" I said, "Because I can't write 'Nancy glanced.' I get an interior rhyme I don't like, so I got rid of your name, pal."

Edenfield: What's wrong with an interior rhyme?

Dubus: They're fine if they're in the right place, but "Nancy glanced" bothered my ear. I really do try to choose names that don't have tags. Except in "Miranda Over the Valley" [1975]; I chose those on purpose. There are a lot of symbols stuck in that story.

Edenfield: And they're symbols that you said you hoped that maybe we wouldn't catch on to too much; you said you were just having a good time with yourself.

Dubus: Yeah, they'd just be in the way. Teachers get a little weird with that stuff. Students go around knowing symbols, and they don't know the story. They haven't experienced it. I'd want to shoot a teacher who went into the class and said, "She's named Miranda from Miranda of *The Tempest*—"oh, brave new world"—and he's named Michaelis because he's Lady Chatterley's first lover. And Miranda is reading *Antigone* because that's about idealism versus pragmatism, and the ghost comes out after she sees the OB [and finds out that she is pregnant] because it's the eve of All Saints' Day, and on All Saints' Day she decides to kill the child . . . they wouldn't get much out of that class. I'd want them to talk about why she felt so bad at the end. And why she is crying till it hurts.

Edenfield: Why does she?
Dubus: I think she was doing something out of love and fear and courage. The people she needed at the time to help her with it talked her into denying love, fear, and courage and opted for something safe and pragmatic, and it probably disillusioned her—or I should say hurt her.

Edenfield: Is there any character whose honesty you're most proud of?
Dubus: That's another one I can't answer. I have to think about all of the stories. I certainly like honesty. I like the honesty Edith comes to in "Adultery." I think people are being honest in *Voices from the Moon* [1984], but I'm not really sure about that.

Edenfield: If your characters are moving in a direction that you don't want them to (you have said that they have lives of their own, that you are following behind them sometimes), do you ever allow yourself to be led away from discoveries that you don't want to make?
Dubus: No. I also like the honesty of Louise in "The Fat Girl" [1978–79], at the end when she realizes that he never loved her and what she should do is get fat again. No, I don't. I wrote "Miranda" over and over because I was sad that she was so mean to Michaelis at the end. But she wouldn't change. No. I wrote a story once in which I did that, and it was terrible. I wrote a sequel to a story called "Separate Flights" [1970]. I had already decided what I wanted her [Peggy] to do, and she did it, but I realized that I was just as bad as her mother; I didn't give her any freedom at all, and the story was dead from the first word on. I tell people now that students in English composition should not write outlines, should not be taught to write outlines, should not be allowed to write outlines. They should write a draft of what they believe and then outline. Controlled papers are as artificial as controlled love. I don't think there's any truth to be found from it. When you can teach people to go through research, tear open an idea, and say I can support this—that's what lawyers do. But it's got nothing to do with the truth. It just has to do with what I said about lawyers; they aren't after *the* truth. They're after *a* truth

that they can fit. That's a whole different thing. I had a friend who wrote political science books, and he really surprised me; he said, "Nothing I do away from the desk does any good for my book; I only can really work when I'm in the act of writing." I said, "I thought you guys had a thesis, came up with this thing in the outline," and he said, "No, I sit at the book, and I start to write." And this is about political science! Walking around, thinking about it doesn't do anything.

Edenfield: You have said that a trace of Faulkner comes into your prose sometimes. How does it get there?
Dubus: For me he has a very infectious prose, and I cannot read him while writing. When I was really reading him in my twenties, I sometimes realized I was speaking in his syntax and inflections. It's just consuming. Sometimes when I'm writing one of those lines and I'm aware of it, I just say, "Well, this will just be a tip of the hat." [Searching for a paper clip] Boy, a wheelchair complicates every simple little thing. It's so different than being able to stand at something. I'm thinking of a little poetic essay that I want to write, "Advice to People in Wheelchairs."

Edenfield: What would you start with?
Dubus: Don't do it. There'll always be some biped who will say things like "No pain, no gain. You can do it." And so forth. And let me tell you what will happen if you spill it. While your groin is burning, you dial 911, and you will get to a shower if you are the kind who can get to a shower. You will take off your burning clothes and turn the cold water on your burning flesh and sit there, waiting for the paramedics, and you will not get better.

Edenfield: Let's go back to what we were saying about college teachers. You say that college literature teachers, next to the *New Yorker*, are the worst influence that there is on a writer. Would you discuss that?
Dubus: That's a generality. I've worked with some very good ones. I think the PhD program is probably the heart of the evil, because the burden of coming up with something original makes people quite naturally make things up. I had a close friend who went to the University of Wisconsin who was actually told by his advisor to read Cliffs Notes as the primary source, that there was no time to read the primary source. He said just read the criticism and the Cliffs Notes; he could read the books later. He's the one who told me, "Cliffs Notes were not made for freshmen. They're made for graduate students." And this comes out in the classroom. There are also those teach-

ers whose students I had to reteach when they took my courses. A young woman signed up for two of my courses back to back. I said, "You must like to read." She said, "Oh yeah, I had a course with so and so. I learned all about symbols." We were doing Faulkner's "Barn Burning" [1939] whereupon she told me that she knew this story, that the fire was a phallic symbol. I said, "How did it become a phallic symbol?" She said, "It's just power." That's all she'd gotten out of it. I said, "Look at what Faulkner said it is. It's his sword. It's his pistol. It's what he can do instead of duel with the aristocracy. It's right there on the page. It's fire." I used to tell my students, "Never trust an English teacher, including me, because we have to talk about something for forty to fifty minutes. Sometimes there's not that much to say about something, but we will bullshit till the bell rings. Because there's not going to be some fool who says, 'Hell of a story wasn't it?' We're not going to do that; we're going to talk." Some people want to possess literature as if it were written by dried-up people: "This is Romantic; this is Neoclassical; got that in a category. Now I own it and possess it." Then they just start pointing out things that some other teacher told them happens in the story.

The only real reason to read a story and to talk about it with somebody is to experience life. In my literature classes, we talked about why the characters did this, what their options were, what was the moral, what was the complexity of their deeds, what other choices could they have had. And I wouldn't allow them to use the word *symbol* unless it started with a *C*. I said you may say dramatization of theme, but I don't want any symbol hunts. I said, "You have been ruined by all your teachers who find these symbols as if they have discovered something and never thought that Flannery O'Connor [1925–64] had written beautiful essays about that." The truth is when you are writing fiction or nonfiction if you are going critically, once you get into your theme, you can't escape it. That cardinal will take on poetic resonance, if you are up to about page thirty, that it wouldn't have anyway because it's like anybody else with a distorted view; you're only seeing what you're becoming in that story. So if the story is about loss, that cardinal's going to look evanescent. And if he's on the first page of a different story, then he's just a cardinal. I had a good friend, a Spanish teacher who'd been a school teacher once. He was angry reading *Madame Bovary*. He said, "That scene by the lake, the ducks: what do the ducks mean?" I said, "Maybe it's just called setting." He put the ducks on the pond. I put the stars in the sky. I try to do landscape. It don't mean shit, except to bring in the reader.

As Conrad said in his great preface in *Nigger of the 'Narcissus'* [1897], art is a communication from one temperament to all temperaments, and it has to be done through the senses, because a temperament is not amenable to persuasion. So the writer has to make the reader feel that he is there. Richard Yates [1926–92] did some editing work in his youth. *Esquire* magazine was having a contest for undergraduates, and they were going to publish two or three of the stories. Bantam Books was going to anthologize twenty. And they gave Dick the job to select them. He had never been an editor. So he came up with nothing. He went in and wrote twenty rejection slips. Sorry, no. Then he started reading a story. If he forgot he was reading the story, he stopped reading the story, and he set it aside in the keep pile. If he went through the whole story without forgetting he was reading a story, he attached the rejection slip and sent it back. To experience a story like that, you can't be looking for connections with Dante. You can't be thinking. You have to be drawn into it. You have to come away from your story and say, "Boy, that story made me hungry. It was hot where I was. And it was isolated, and the wind blew on the prairie." It's not a cerebral thing, writing. It's a very sensual, fleshy thing. Although our greatest thoughts appear in literature, they get there like everything—through the flesh. If you take that laughing, drinking, suffering, weeping Jesus out of Christianity, what have you got? Chinese fortune cookies. It's true.

Edenfield: This goes along with that, and you've answered it in part already. Kennedy says that in your fiction you find metaphors in the elements in which your characters and presumably your readers live daily. He says the meaning of the events is within the events. But I want to say that it's the reader's responsibility to understand how these metaphors are being used, that to connect them realistically to the character is finally to understand the character—whether she'll rebel by shooting, or by eating, or by fucking, or whether she'll do nothing but wait, looking through the screen door. O'Connor says the Misfit has on a large black hat because the Georgia sun is hot and typically the folks in the South wear large brimmed black hats to keep off the sun. No symbol. Just a hat. [Fitzgerald 334]. I want you to tell me what's a symbol and what's finally a hat.
Dubus: That's funny because I'm caught up in the fact that black attracts heat. [Laughs] But I'll agree with that in that context.

Edenfield: So what's a symbol and what's a hat? Are there no symbols?
Dubus: I hardly ever use them and hardly ever look for them. If I read a story about somebody wearing a hat, I don't think about that hat. Now if I read in a story that you have soft skin because you bathe in the water from

the cistern, and you live in Indochina and you wear silk, you say, "Well, this isn't a symbol; I'm not sure it's a metaphor." It's a truth which is also dealing in that story with not just the softness of skin and water but her sensuality, her eroticism, and probably some more levels too. So that line stands out. I noticed about the tenth time I read *The Sun Also Rises* [1926] that in Pamplona, Jake goes into the church one afternoon to pray, and he's thinking about what a grand church it is . . . and he starts to pray, and like most of us, he really can't, and he ends up praying for his friends and that it won't rain at the bullfight. Then he walks outside and his fingers dry in the sun. I used to point that out to students and say this paragraph's a poem, and what's happened is the holy water of the font is drying in the sun. I'll never know what gave Hemingway the idea, but the way I see the book is, let's have a character who cannot feel divine love in any fulfilling way, cannot in any way have erotic love, and therefore cannot have paternal love, let's see what he's got left. He's got his newspaper work; it seems to be fulfilling. He has enough money; he has friends; he has the flesh; he fishes, watches bullfights; he eats and drinks; he cries a lot. He drinks a little bit too much; he cries. He cries throughout that book.

He and his friend Bill go up to the mountains. I wouldn't call that a symbolic ascent, but I would say that because the book earned it, it's a thematic ascent. They go up into the mountains to fish, and it's the most pristine part of the book; but toward the end of that, they are lying on the bank of a creek, catching trout, and Bill says, do you believe in God, and Jake probably says sometimes at night—I'm not really sure what he says—and then Bill says, were you ever really in love with Brett, and the two great redeeming forms of love that he has been denied come right in. I would call that thematic, not symbolic. A symbol to me is something that represents something. You've got the guy in his spiritual and erotic condition; in this dialogue, he is very much in it. He is not removed from it, looking out from it. This is happening. Having said all that, I would say I guess you could call the holy water drying in the sun a symbol of the absence of spiritual love for him, religious rituals that may have pulled him through, and his willy-nilly commitment to sensuousness his reward.

Edenfield: But you just don't know why anybody would want to call it that?
Dubus: I'd call it a symbol. I can do a literary study of this! Isn't it great! I just realized that this is holy water drying in the sun. Get it! Church isn't working. The sun works, but he drinks too much when the sun is down, and he cries.

Edenfield: How did you go about choosing which stories to put into *Selected Stories*?

Dubus: That was mostly done with my editor's help, and we had hard choices to make because of the length. The great thing was that he said he wanted to put "Voices from the Moon" in there because nobody has read that. He said, "I don't want to showcase it; I just want to put it in the middle"—so that cut out a lot of stuff. It was a length thing. At one point, the boss said, let's just cut all of the Marine stories, let's cut all my Brother stories, so I left out some I would like to have in there. There were some long ones we really wanted in there. There wasn't anything painful about it. If I were the kind of writer who composed a five-hundred-page book, I suppose we would have done them all—and I would have sold six copies.

Edenfield: *Selected Stories* begins with a young girl who fails herself in "Miranda Over the Valley"—she chooses inauthentically—and it ends with a mature man making what he feels is the authentic choice, and talking to God even, in "A Father's Story." What should we learn through this progression?

Dubus: I don't know. My editor wanted to start with "Miranda Over the Valley." He said, "Of course, it should start with 'Miranda Over the Valley.'" I never asked him why. And he said it should end with "A Father's Story," and I never asked him why. This was conversations over the phone; it wasn't an artistic endeavor. But as an editor, I'm sure he would know the answer to that. I don't know the order of the stories. If you had asked me what the last story was, I would have had to stop and think. But I'm sure he had something in mind. He divided it into sections, and he is a very wise man, and I'm sure he knew what he was doing. It wasn't chronological. I wasn't any help on that one, but it was the truth. [Laughs]

Edenfield: There are a number of your stories that make a lot of references to a character's proximity to water. Is this suggesting anything?

Dubus: Not in my mind. I love water, and except for Iowa, I have always lived near water; therefore, I tend to put it into my stories.

Edenfield: At the beginning of "Killings" [1979], after the service, Matt is standing where he can't see the water. As the story progresses, little by little, he can start to hear it; he can start to smell it. Right before he kills, he can see it in the distance. He throws the gun and the keys into the water. At the end, he is above the water. My students and I saw this as a progression of his getting his life back, reclaiming what was taken from him.

Dubus: Let me give you a message. He didn't get his life back. He violated nature. He's out in the Neverland. I only use water in that story because the actual location of the story is a real place I can write about. It seemed an obvious place to bury a body and dispose of a gun. It's called "Killings" because everybody is getting killed in that story. He doesn't gain his life; he does something terrible. Of course, I didn't know that he would do it. But I knew during the scene when the shooting was imminent that if that boy would just turn and beg, he would have been saved. I also noticed the buddy never pulled a trigger either. But I put the water there because they drove along the river there. That wasn't symbolic. I've never that I can recall in my life used water as a symbol. I refuse to see Frederic Henry [Hemingway's *A Farewell to Arms* (1929)] swimming across the river to get away from the war as a baptism either; it looks like a pretty good escape route. [Laughs]

Edenfield: Can't it be both?
Dubus: It can. But if it's a baptism, what's it a baptism to?

Edenfield: You also pay close attention to weather, to seasons. I'm thinking about "Miranda" and "Killings" and "Waiting" [1979].
Dubus: Yep. I used to teach Dick Yates about putting the weather in because he grew up in the city. I miss the weather when it's not in stories. I noticed rereading Chekhov that in most of the stories I read that in the opening paragraph we learn what day it was and what season almost right away. I need that as a reader. That's one of my hardest efforts as a writer, to pull the reader away from herself, make her cold. I think a lot of people don't understand that much of the labor of writing is trying to get tactile. While somebody is reading this and looking for clues, you're saying, "No, man, I busted my ass to try to make a tree. Do you know how hard it is to make a tree?" I think Conrad said, "All I want you to do is see." That's everything. If I can remember a time I used weather as a symbol, I'll tell you.

Edenfield: In "Miranda Over the Valley," you mention again and again—and also in "Leslie in California" [1983]—feeling dry inside. Miranda refers to herself as a piece of chalk.
Dubus: She does?

Edenfield: Yes.
Dubus: I like that.

Edenfield: She says, "I'm a piece of chalk." What is that dryness?
Dubus: Beats me. I must have been in a state when I got that line. I really like that line—"I am a piece of chalk." I bet I said, "Yippee!" when I got up with that one. I don't know. Who else is dry?

Edenfield: Leslie. She has dry crying.
Dubus: Dry crying. Is she trying to conceal it?

Edenfield: No. "It feels like dry crying," she says.
Dubus: It sounds like a simile for sorrow. I don't remember why Miranda felt dry. I wrote that in about 1971 or 1972. My temptation is to say Miranda comes to dryness of the soul. But, boy, I can't testify to that. I don't know.

Edenfield: Miranda also identifies with the yellow dog that has recently been hit by a car, doesn't she?
Dubus: See, I forgot the yellow dog. He runs across the road on a hurt leg?

Edenfield: He does. He's also yellow.
Dubus: I don't know if the yellow means anything, but she must have been having empathy for something. She must have. That's the trouble with interviews; I'll just bullshit like I did teaching. If it comes at a time when she's sad, then I'm going to have to assume as a reader that she was feeling empathy caused by her own pain.

Edenfield: I wondered if it were a commentary on the availability of abortion, what it does to women once they've had one.
Dubus: I don't even remember the availability when I wrote that story.

Edenfield: They went to New York.
Dubus: Okay. That must have been the availability.

Edenfield: Is that the watching eye? Women especially feel watched in your stories. Is that God?
Dubus: Probably not. I got to the end [of "Miranda Over the Valley"], and I was thinking, boy, I was working hard that day. [Laughs] I got something done. I don't understand that story. And I didn't change it.

Edenfield: What do you mean you don't understand it?
Dubus: I'm not sure where it goes. I'm not sure what it says. I'm not sure what it means. I must have gotten to some depth that I don't ordinarily get to, and so I left it—right or wrong. When you're doing something you're not in harmony with, you watch yourself. That's all it is. Especially love. Well, anything. Like when you're shy at a party, don't you feel like you're watching yourself? She's making love out of harmony. And her heart is not in it. Her heart is watching her. "What are you doing to me?" her heart is saying. You understand that, right? Especially sexually.

Edenfield: Oh, yes. These questions are about "The Winter Father" [1980]. Why is it that the younger child, Cathy, is the one who understands the pain instead of her brother, who is older? To quote: "His urge was to turn away. She looked at him for a long time. Her eyes were too tender, too wise, and he wished she could have learned both later and differently. In her eyes he saw the car in winter, heard its doors closing and closing their top and the sound of heater and engine and tires on the road, the places the car took them. And she held his hand and closed her eyes."
Dubus: And you think she's feeling pain more than the boy?

Edenfield: "'Before I loved the beach,' David said. 'So do I,' Peter said. He looked at Cathy. 'You don't like it, huh?'" Her answer seems to be more sensitive, more thought through.
Dubus: The father is looking at a girl who has experienced the pain of divorce. Didn't the boy throw rocks at the car when he was leaving?

Edenfield: So it's just a different way of dealing with pain?
Dubus: I'm not sure. It sounds like a really tender moment on the beach. And I was so into the point of view of the guy who was writing it. Ask me the question again. Why does she feel the pain more than the boy? My gut is telling me she doesn't feel it more than the boy. But the camera is focused on her at that moment. Back to the point of view: if the whole story were told from the boy's point of view, just the boy's, you'd never say that, right? Point of view is very important. It's what screws up our lives, right? It very often dictates what we feel as readers in a story. You can tell that story from the point of view of the wife and you've got a whole other story. You could actually make a convincing story that the dad doesn't have to fight with them for the bed and all that. He could be just a nice guy taking them all over the place. To him, it's pain. To her, you'd believe that if you read it. And it would

be true. His is true. Hers is true. Right? But I certainly could have done that from her point of view. Oh, great. Went to the beach with Dad again, huh? Now, will you clean up your room? [Laughs]

Edenfield: Sometimes point of view can work against a character, though, can't it?
Dubus: Oh, yeah. Absolutely.

Edenfield: Someone could tell his own story and end up sounding worse than if someone had told it for him. I'm thinking again about Raymond [in "The Pretty Girl"], the casual way that he talks about taking rabbits that you come across in the forest and picking them up and bashing their heads against trees as if we all do that.
Dubus: Live rabbits? I wrote that? You're kidding me! He caught live rabbits?

Edenfield: He just says it matter-of-factly, like "Don't we all do this?"
Dubus: No. It must be rabbits he's shot and he's doing the death blow, right? I hope so. I cannot conceive that I would write about a guy who would catch an absolute live rabbit. Only somebody deep in Mississippi would have that kind of skill.

Edenfield: These are rabbits that he's trapped?
Dubus: No. When I rabbit hunted with bird shot, very often the animal wasn't completely dead; so what you did to take care of the pain was lift it by the hind legs and then whop it on a tree.

Edenfield: He's talking about raping Polly: "I got to her once back in June. She was scared like a wild animal, a small one without any natural weapons, like a wounded rabbit. The way they quiver in your hand and look at you before you pick them up and knock their heads against trees and rocks."
Dubus: They certainly do. Yeah. Okay. So he shot a rabbit, picked it up, and finished it off. I just lost the question. I was so astonished. I forget a lot, but I don't ever remember writing about some guy who could sneak up on a rabbit. So what was the question? It was about point of view.

Edenfield: But I make a judgment about this character that he can do this to a rabbit that looks at him like that.

Dubus: Oh, that's okay. I would say, as a man who used to hunt, what the rabbit wants is not to be shot, but once he is shot, he's better off in the hands of someone who's going to pick him up and kill him quick than stand there and look at him twitching and dying and say, "I'm sorry." Haven't you ever gone back and run over a broken-backed animal? I came across a broken-backed squirrel, and I thought, oh my God, and I went back and aimed the tire at the head. But I don't mind that judgment. I don't judge Ray; I love Ray. My editor said, "This horrible man." I thought, all right, I've created a good one here. But I love Ray because I became him to write him. I can't not love him. I can't write about someone I don't love. I forget that he raped his wife and all that.

Edenfield: Would he call it rape?
Dubus: I don't think he did.

Edenfield: He said, "They call it rape." Isn't he lying to himself? Doesn't he believe it's rape? What else is taking a woman by force at knifepoint?
Dubus: I call it rape, but I guess he didn't—but I was in his point of view.

Edenfield: He's not lying to himself.
Dubus: We're all shaped to an extent by our environment. I don't get beyond that. Within that, we are morally responsible. I'll tell you the only thing that I really remember sharply from writing that section other than getting into the voice was how excited I was when I found out why he was sad. I learned something: that he was not sad because of memories of the past. The present had become unbearable because she had dumped him for no reason he could figure out, and she was happy in the same world he was. Now, do I feel that way about human beings? Nope. But he felt that way about her. So probably in that context he said it wasn't rape, just as I've noticed throughout my life [that] I think people really want to be good because most people try to justify what they did. You hardly hear people say it was a wicked, evil thing I did and I loved it. They always say, "He deserved it." Or "Everybody does it." Or "It wasn't wrong." Or "I did it because of this." Should he have done it? No. He raped at knifepoint.

Edenfield: He was going to do it again.
Dubus: Not at the end.

Edenfield: He's not going to rape her at the end?

Dubus: No. I wish she would have listened to him. He was making sense. He says what's the difference, Steve or me. See, he went to her. If he hadn't gotten drunk; that did it. She shot him because she thought he was going to rape her. He wasn't going to rape her.

Edenfield: He took his clothes off.
Dubus: Oh yeah. He was in love. [Laughs] Would I advise him to do what he did? Nope, but he was not going to rape her. That scene is from her point of view, isn't it?

Edenfield: She doesn't really get a point of view. She doesn't get a voice, anyway.
Dubus: That's because I'm not confident about the first-person woman's voice. I've used it just in very short things—in "Leslie in California," in a little section in "Land Where My Fathers Died" [1984], and in a very little story with the name of a Beatle song, "In My Life" [1971]. But I never try to sustain it, and I don't trust it. That's why I went third person with her. She has a point of view; she just doesn't get first person.

Edenfield: So it's not Polly you don't trust to tell her own story, it's you.
Dubus: Yeah. Maybe I could have gotten the female voice, but I didn't feel I could. I think that in "Finding a Girl in America" [1980] Lori has a section that I think is in first person, though it may be in third. I don't know. That was the whole thing. It's her story. She's the one. She's my heroine. But as fucked up as she is . . . .

Edenfield: Why does Alex [Raymond's brother] get the last word in "The Pretty Girl"?
Dubus: That was a surprise. I was working my ass off that semester. I taught a seminar in *War and Peace* [1865–69] and *Anna Karenina* [1878]. I thought it wouldn't be real hard, but it was like leading Marines uphill; everybody was just exhausted. I thought reading a hundred pages a week of Tolstoy [1828–1910] would be idyllic, but I'll never do it again. And I had three other courses—and I was writing that novella. Near the end of the semester, I wanted to do some errands on a Saturday morning. I had a feeling it would end that afternoon, in that sitting. I was playing *La Bohème* [1896], and I was writing that last scene, and it was breaking my heart. I was in her point of view, but I could hear him because I had been in his point of view, and she hadn't. She had never been in his point of view. I had. There were

things about him I liked. There were things he could have given to Polly. He knew how to deal with depression. He knew how to get through the day. He thought he knew how to love. And, I felt tenderly about him. I was just hoping she wouldn't shoot, but she did. Next thing I knew, Alex was out in the boat. [Laughs] I wrote the last word, and *La Bohème* ended.—"Well, this sucker's done."

My agent sent it to *Esquire*; it was going to be a book anyway. Rust Hills [1924–2008; fiction editor of *Esquire*] called, that little butcher, and he said, "God, I like this. Why don't you add forty pages to it?" I said, "Why should I do that?" He said, "You could make a lot of money. Nobody writes about this Catholic blood and guts. I don't think you can switch that point of view, though. There's no precedent for it." I said, "Well, I did." [Laughs] That's what happened. Someone, not a reviewer but a critic, wrote an essay I read in a quarterly; he went crazy. He did this whole thing about the Fisher King and Christianity and Christ on the water. I said, "I don't read T. S. Eliot [1888–1965], I don't plan to read him in the near future, but I read him in college, and this has nothing to do with the Fisher King or Christianity. This is a grieving brother who's lost one in Vietnam and one to a woman. The story is about the curse of being pretty." My favorite moment in that story is when her foot sinks in the snow. She's got her own apartment and she's out in this great grown-up world; whatever that promises, she realizes this is it. There's really nothing out there. I kept wanting to say, "Polly, a good liberal arts education would help; you don't need to get a job but you might start understanding history. You might start understanding life."

Edenfield: You say that you love Polly very much and that you are struggling very hard for her to know herself. Isn't that what she's trying to do at the end?
Dubus: No, I wasn't struggling for her to know herself; I was struggling to know her. My emotions, fatherly, were, "If she only knew herself." Things aren't that bad. She didn't have to end up being somebody who, instead of calling paramedics, would call her daddy while somebody who didn't have to die bled to death. It's funny I would end up getting run over by a woman who ran across the street and said, "I didn't do it." I didn't ask for that either, thank you, God.

Edenfield: Isn't that what she's trying to do at the end, know herself?
Dubus: At the end, yes. I don't remember the story—but I think she's thinking maybe she'll ice skate again. There are things that she can do.

Edenfield: She thinks about going on long walks by herself.

Dubus: Yeah, I forgot that.

Edenfield: Isn't she trying to disarm herself of this prettiness? She only talks about pretty being worth anything if it's an active pretty, if it can make men change their lives. She says her sister, Margaret, is pretty, but she doesn't have the kind of pretty that makes men change their lives. But walking by herself in the woods, getting sick, she's not pretty when she's ill.

Dubus: You know why she's sick? One night I got up to take a leak and the wind was blowing hard, and I thought, I never put wind in a story. I'm going to put wind in a story. So "A Father's Story" got very windy just for that reason; I wanted to write about wind. One time I thought, I get the flu all of the time. I've never given a character the flu; so the next time I write a story, I'm going to have a character have the flu. That's why she had it; I wanted to write about the flu. [Laughs]

Edenfield: It's more than that, isn't it? Illness as metaphor?

Dubus: No. From the time I started that story, I thought, I don't know what's going to happen, but it will end at this lake with the flu on Labor Day weekend because it's so shitty to have the flu in hot weather. There was a man terrorizing his wife, and somebody told me the story, and I wanted to write something with the tension of a suspense story just to see if I could do it. Of course, I got introspective as always. But that's what I wanted to do. Feminists can grind their teeth on this one. I may be absolutely wrong, but I made a choice of a gender. I thought about having a man being the one who was being terrorized. That's not scary enough. You just tell him, "Hell, lift weights, buy a gun." [Laughs] I thought that must be why it's always the woman who goes up to the attic to check things out because it gets everybody more scared. What if Kevin Costner [b. 1955] goes down in the basement? You know old Kevin can always kill somebody with his fists. So I made that choice. I wanted the biologically inferior one to experience for me and for the reader to experience more terror. So I got me a woman with a body builder who owns guns.

Edenfield: She says her beauty is more of a weapon than his strength.

Dubus: Do I say that? The only preface I remember starting with is her physical beauty. And her father's approval of her allowed her to be lazy, to expect that something would happen. Because she was an American white high school girl who was just the prettiest girl in class, that gave her an expectation. There's the cultural comment. [Laughs, collating copies] It's good to have finger work to do. Gets me over my interview shyness.

Edenfield: You told Kennedy: "Polly is morally lazy and it's connected with her being a pretty girl, not a woman, but having grown up pretty and with a father who loves her very much." What's wrong with the way her father loves her?

Dubus: Nothing. I don't think there's anything wrong with the way he loves her or anything he does to help her, but having his love and approval and having the looks combined with whatever other elements in her character make her a bit spiritually slovenly. There were no demands. If she had had a different kind of a father and the same pretty face, maybe a father she felt she had to prove something to: "Maybe he'll love me if I go to medical school." I'm not saying that's good. Who the hell wants that kind of father? I'm just saying she had what looks like good luck, which combined with her soul was dangerous. No matter what she did she was loved at home, and out on the street she can make a man fall in love with her—which in another character could be only blessings.

Edenfield: The way Louise's father in "The Fat Girl" loves her?

Dubus: Yeah. And if Polly's character were a little different. . . . Her sister seems untouched. Her sister's very different from her. Her sister's a daily communicant, a jock.

Edenfield: Maybe I'm sounding a little too Protestant when I ask this: Did you give Margaret a more Catholic name than Polly on purpose?

Dubus: No. I didn't even think about the Catholic implications of Margaret. I liked Comeau because I never get to write about Cajuns anymore because I don't go to Louisiana. But the phone book up here has a lot of names I grew up with, and there are a lot of French Catholics here—so let me get a dark-skinned Cajun girl in, I won't miss that opportunity. So I worked with the rhythm to come up with Polly. Then I had to get a French name that people could pronounce. [Laughs] Margaret: I finally just read it off the left-hand side of the desk in passing.

Edenfield: You've already said all of this, but I'm going to ask it again. When the story ends, you say, "I was hoping that Raymond and Polly would get together." Instead, she shot him. What would you have her do instead of shoot him?

Dubus: I don't know. I've never had that choice. I'd shoot him. If it were my daughter, I guess I'd say shoot him. For anybody else, including myself, it's better to be raped than to kill somebody. Somebody asked Tolstoy about his nonviolence and said, "What would you do if you found somebody naked with your daughter?" He said, "I don't think I can live in the world I believe we should have." That's wrong to ask him that. I would hope I would never kill somebody to keep myself from being buggered, but I don't know. Maybe I would. I don't think it's worth taking a life. A little kneecapping might help.

Edenfield: Wouldn't Polly be like one of those wounded rabbits eventually? Wouldn't he eventually pick her up and knock her head against a tree and have done with her? Isn't that what this is going to lead towards?
Dubus: I don't think so. I think if he were that violent, he would have harmed her father and he would have harmed her.

Edenfield: He harms the father in another way.
Dubus: Yeah, but the whole time isn't he worried about him having a heart attack? This big, huge man with the older man that he strips of his arms does him harm—does it psychically—but he does not hurt his body.

Edenfield: He makes a horrible comment. He says that Polly says, "Once you get the clothes off, the rest is easy."
Dubus: I love that comment. I thought it was poignant. I've always wondered—not always, because I don't think about it anymore—but I didn't have the answer to his question [when he asks Polly's father, "Now what the fuck does that mean?"]. I know he was saying it out of pain and adrenaline, but I wondered, what did she mean?

Edenfield: Didn't he say it just to wound the father?
Dubus: I don't remember, actually.

Edenfield: What a cruel thing to say to somebody's father.
Dubus: Yeah, but I don't go in as a judge. I go in to become, and if I can't become, it doesn't work.

Edenfield: Raymond [in "The Pretty Girl"] equates physical strength with power: "It helps to be big in this world," he says. Is he right?
Dubus: Yeah. That was my experience. I used to be small, and then I lifted weights and got bigger. When guys bump into you in a bar they look at you

differently. They say "excuse me" in a different voice. It feels a whole lot different.

Edenfield: Isn't that the same as Polly's beauty? Isn't that why she works at being pretty? Because it makes people look at her in a different way.
Dubus: I don't know.

Edenfield: Doesn't it help to be pretty in this world?
Dubus: I do know that when he is lifting weights, he says, "I don't know how I feel until I hold that steel."

Edenfield: That's a great line.
Dubus: Andre got that off of a gym wall in Austin; he said, "I'll never give you another line again." Had a hard time translating that into French. I don't know what they did with it. [Raymond's] big because he lifts weights, but he doesn't lift weights to be big, if I remember this correctly. He really loves working out, the way I do, and the way I miss it. I never did a bit of exercise in my life for my health or to look good. I did it because I got off on it.

Edenfield: But he does it to have power, to be strong.
Dubus: I don't think so. I was going to say it's because he's male and he's normally big anyway, that it makes him big. I don't ever remember him saying that he worked out to be big so he could feel powerful. I don't ever remember him feeling powerful except when he was doing mischief. I remember him feeling kind of dumped and helpless. No, I don't think he should have beat up the boyfriend either. Some woman at a community college was pissed off at me about "A Father's Story." She said, "I wouldn't do that. It was wrong. My daughters wouldn't want me to." You wouldn't? Well, we could use some ironic distance. I don't read that kind of story. I don't recommend it. If you see Robert Duvall [b. 1931] in a movie, you wouldn't want him to think ironic distance between him and a character. So why would you want a writer to do that?

Edenfield: Throughout the story, Raymond speaks in absolutes. And he expects absolutes from Polly. The way he speaks, everything starts with a concrete image—"I do this. I do that. This is me." Everything is a concrete when he talks about himself. When he talks about Polly, he says, "You ever marry a woman who doesn't know what she wants and knows she doesn't?" So he expects her to be absolute. For two people who seem to be so alike, both controlled by their physical appearance—Raymond's bigness and physical strength, Polly's beauty—rather than any moral virtue or goal, why is Raymond so sure and Polly so unsure?

Dubus: I don't really know the answer. What comes from the gut is she was unhappy, and he wasn't before she left. For me, he is a limited man, but as I recall getting inside of him, he was a simple man.

Edenfield: When Raymond tells his story, he switches from "I" to "you." Is that further to suggest his unwillingness to accept responsibility for what he has done to Polly?

Dubus: Where's the switch? Probably I picked it up from Hemingway.

Edenfield: He starts using you—"you do this, you do that"—even when he's talking about working out.

Dubus: Oh, that's getting his voice. It's probably not just a New England thing. You know how it is: you go down the road, you get a flat tire, you get out your spare, your spare is flat, you try to use the car phone to call AAA, and your battery is dead. That's common in American speech.

Edenfield: I've got a thing about it. I think people use it to distance themselves from the responsibility of what they are talking about. Never "I do this" or "I do that." He switches from "I do this, I do that" to "you do this, you do that." I wondered if it was because he feels guilty.

Dubus: Not in my head, but I don't mind it being read that way.

Edenfield: Good. Is it foreshadowing that Raymond lives in a dead man's house that faces west?

Dubus: No. What would it be foreshadowing? He's in his dead brother's house.

Edenfield: Yes. And it faces west.

Dubus: I don't even remember why the brother's in there. I just kind of got into him, and he told his story. I don't know if I have the Vietnam brother in there because of the fear he knew. You go through a lot of logistical things to write a story. You see the cabin; I may have during the gestation period written notes and said, "Okay, I got to get my place to live. Where? Where did he live?" I don't know. Facing west, the way I write, may have been so he could see the sunset. That would be my guess.

Edenfield: Can we go further, though, and say that the sunset foreshadows his death?

Dubus: It can't be foreshadowing because I didn't know when I wrote that that he was going to die. At least it can't be a conscious foreshadowing. I also believe that when you really write as well as move through the world, you get in touch with things you don't know you know. I don't mean just writing. I mean a really harmonious person can be walking through the supermarket, picking up a head of lettuce for the family, and be absolutely fulfilled and peaceful in the realization of the moment that this is an eternal sacrament, and that he is not simply walking through a supermarket in Statesboro, Georgia, but that this is the feeding of flesh that has gone on and on and on forever. And it's not an errand anymore. The clock isn't running anymore. This is very precious. If I am writing in concentration, harmony is going to hit on universals and mysteries that we spend most of our cultural energies trying to avoid. I always want everything I write to be deeper than it looks. But the last way that I could achieve that would be to make up symbols.

Edenfield: But it's okay if it works, if we talk about them that way, isn't it?

Dubus: Yeah. There's no other way to do it.

Edenfield: I don't know if I can go back and teach your fiction and not talk about the things that I want to mean more. I'm thinking about the screen door at the end of "Leslie in California," with Leslie looking out. She can see out, she wants out, but she's trapped inside that life that she has in California.

Dubus: That's fine. I've got a draft of an essay on [Hemingway's short story] "In Another Country" [1927] that I had to rewrite and rewrite and rewrite; but I had that story knocked, understood, until I ran into these little Monterey girls several years after my accident, and now I see it completely differently. That's valid. There's healing in Hemingway's story. He doesn't commit suicide. The act of getting out of bed and putting on his uniform is healing. It's choosing. And this means to me, especially with the war and the flu epidemic and all those dead boys, that there's going to be another Italian wife who won't forget this one. But he will be all right. Until that, I could always see him forever with his hand in the machine. Now, I don't see him with his hand in the machine. But I had to get knocked all over the fucking highway to come up with that view. And I don't know if Hemingway saw that view. He was pretty young when he wrote that. I think if stuff is written really well, it has a life, and it's going to stay alive. I noticed in teaching literature that for some people a story was about one scene that really hit their lives; that was that story for them. That's honest. Look at me. I don't remember any of these things about "The Pretty Girl." I just remember her foot going into the snow when she's carrying in the groceries, thinking, "So, this is it. This is grown up."

Edenfield: This is Raymond: "It gets down to what is happening to you right now. And if you're hot and wet and itching, that's what you deal with. You'll end up tripping a mine anyways, so you might as well fight the bugs and stay cool and dry until then." It sounds existential, but the way Raymond says it, it sounds pretty damn selfish too.
Dubus: How come you don't like that man? Just because he beats up an occasional person, rapes an occasional wife? [Laughs] Awww. It's just sins. It's not an evil way of life. So what was your question?

Edenfield: Well, it wasn't really a question; it was more of a commentary. I wanted to know if you agreed with me. It's existential, living for the moment, living day by day, and being aware that we are all going to die eventually, so we better make the moment the best we can at all times; but it sounds pretty selfish the way Raymond says it, I guess, because I think of what he does to other people around him. I'm grieving, so let me go take back what is mine for a while. You can carry that philosophy in the wrong direction.
Dubus: Like most of them. I guess you could even take the Golden Rule in the wrong brain and turn it into something wrong, couldn't you?

Edenfield: It sounds pretty self-serving to me.
Dubus: You wouldn't want a masochist to follow the Golden Rule: "Here, crash. You'll like this." [Laughs] Well, I wouldn't characterize Ray as a gentle, loving man full of altruism and agape. I certainly wouldn't want him to marry Suzanne [Dubus's oldest daughter].

Edenfield: How is a pretty body a dangerous weapon?
Dubus: I don't know. Who's talking now?

Edenfield: Polly. She says it's even more dangerous than strength or a gun. I think it's when she's shooting with her daddy. Why is her face on the gun permit ugly? She looks at the picture and thinks that she didn't know what it was, but that it was very serious and not pretty.

Dubus: Oh, well, I would guess she's a little screwed up at that time. Hasn't she just been raped? I think that's what she's seeing. She was getting a gun to protect herself.

Edenfield: But in everything after that, Polly starts to change. I think she is different. I think that rape damages her. She's not just pretty anymore. I don't think she wants to be pretty anymore. I think that's why she sees herself out by herself in the woods where prettiness doesn't do her a lick of good. She's tired of it.

Dubus: She looks serious and not pretty. I'm just guessing that's the way she feels. The rape is from her point of view. Isn't it from his, too?

Edenfield: No. It's from her point of view. What commentary are you making about the elementary schools next to the graveyards?

Dubus: Was he making a joke, or was he thinking about life/death?

Edenfield: Just thinking about how strange it is. He didn't come to a conclusion.

Dubus: That was it, just children and death. But no, not elementary schools. I've got no beef about elementary schools. That's probably a true landscape; that's probably where it came from. There's always doctors' offices across from cemeteries. We joke about that.

Edenfield: I keep coming back to this, but she gives up an active beauty to be alone. Isn't that progress? She's making progress, isn't she, towards the end when she imagines herself doing those things and waiting for something to happen?

Dubus: I forgot that she was, yeah.

Edenfield: She says, "It'll come to me where I'm going to go." While she waits out her time there, I think, she'll get to know herself. Who's watching Bobby in "Graduation" [1977]? She says she feels like she's always being watched. Who's watching her?

Dubus: I would think that comes from having a reputation. That's a 1950s story. It was written much later.

Edenfield: She goes to California. That's a conscious choice on your part, starting a new life?

Dubus: I think so. It must be because the further she was from Port Arthur the better.

Edenfield: I think of California, "the land of opportunity," as where you can start your life over again.

Dubus: Well, probably if I had served most of my time in the Marines on the East Coast, I would have put her on a naval base on the east coast. That's the truth. I know they have sailors in San Diego, and it would be very likely for a guy from Tulane to go to sea and end up on the West Coast. I really choose places because I've been there.

Edenfield: And that's why you put Leslie in California? That's not some kind of ironic bad dream?

Dubus: That's where I got the letter [from Suzanne] from and it was about those hills and about those rattlesnakes and a bobcat and being married to a fisherman. So it was pretty ideal. I couldn't have placed it in the South because I don't remember the South well enough to do the landscape.

Edenfield: But it works ironically, doesn't it?

Dubus: I don't think of California being the golden land. We used to say it was where old Iowans went to die.

Edenfield: Are we supposed to see a connection between Bobbie and that absurdly alone Jesus in the nativity scene [in "Graduation"]?

Dubus: No. She's just grown up being scornful, maybe even pitying, of her parents.

Edenfield: She's not a hometown martyr?

Dubus: No. Well, she is, yeah, although a martyr actually gives up a life.

Edenfield: She did, didn't she?

Dubus: I don't know if I'd call her a martyr, but I would certainly say she was treated unjustly—the target of a lot of little meanness. But that's just her perception. Look at this. This is home. These people. You know that same feeling that you get for your parents at a certain time in your life. When you're hearing enough from them, you start to think they're kind of dumb. [Laughs] I've heard from people who took meaning from that story in modern times. One college girl wrote me and said she was going to do that—become a virgin again.

Edenfield: Why does she conceal her orgasm at the end of the story?
Dubus: She wants him to think of her as some pure virgin. But I had forgotten that there's child abuse in that story. I wasn't aware of child abuse when I wrote that, but I must have heard a story. Doesn't she say an uncle took her virginity?

Edenfield: That's what she says.
Dubus: Didn't that happen to one of her friends, so she incorporated the story? Yeah. But she does that to pretend that she doesn't enjoy fucking. [Laughs] She's going to let him believe that she's going to take a liking to it.

Edenfield: He's going to teach her about it. That's what I figured.
Dubus: Yeah. She was doing a very good job of what would now be called surviving abuse—just this tentative little girl in bed. I didn't know when I wrote that that somebody who had been abused by her uncle would be frightened. And she's fooling. We used to want them to be pure. Everybody in those days when I was a kid lost their hymens to Schwinn bicycles or horseback riding. I never knew a man who made love to a virgin, and all husbands said that the Schwinn Bicycle Company sure got a lot of cherries. [Laughs] We all married virgins, and nobody bumped into any membrane at all. "Oh, it happened on a picnic when I was riding a horse."

Edenfield: These women would explain themselves?
Dubus: If they were asked, yeah.

Edenfield: Who would ask? Seems like you wouldn't much be worried at that point.
Dubus: [Laughs] Haven't you ever heard the story, if it's true or not, about, in Italy, hanging the sheet out the next day? That's the story that's been told. I don't know if it's true or not. I can certainly believe it. And there had better be blood on it. The Japanese sold a little capsule women could insert so fake blood would come out. A guy designed it; he took pity on them. That was in the last twenty years. I remember reading about it in *Time*.

Edenfield: Who's the shit of an usher in "Waiting" if it's not death?
Dubus: Oh, I think it is.

Edenfield: She [Juanita] says it's not.

Dubus: She's going to commit suicide. That's her isolation. She says that she feels like she's sneaking into a movie. Well, she's going to commit suicide.

Edenfield: Is that why she goes out to the beach and just sort of waits to see what's going to happen?
Dubus: Yeah, at first. You know, A. Alvarez [b. 1929] has a great book about suicide, *The Savage God* [1972] and it's a great work because he committed suicide. He wasn't making a gesture for help; he committed suicide; it just didn't work. He is cognizant of that terrain, so that book is a study of suicide. And I had probably read that before I wrote the story because he says, "If somebody tries it, you should watch them because they're going to keep trying." Don't ever take it lightly. Don't ever call it a symbolic gesture. He was a friend of Sylvia Plath [1932–63] and puts himself down in that book because he had a feeling reading her last poem that her life was in trouble, and so, after she died, he thought, oh, God, maybe I should have done something, but that was before he tried it. He said the reason afterwards why people would say, she was so peaceful, I had lunch with her, is because when a person who has tried a few times decides they're really going to do it, they get real peaceful. So that's why I call that "Waiting." Because she's going to do it. I mean, she went out in the goddamn Pacific at night. [Laughs]

Edenfield: She leaves it up to fate at that point, doesn't she? Or maybe God? Or chance?
Dubus: Yeah, I think so. Like unbuckling your seatbelt and driving too fast. I've read that we'll never know how many car accidents are suicides. The book that story was in [*Finding a Girl in America: A Novella and Seven Short Stories* (1980)] got a terrible review from a guy at the *New York Times*. But he liked that story; he just didn't understand it. He said she was coping.

Edenfield: This question is about "Killings." I'm going to ask some more questions about Matt. I feel for Matt.
Dubus: I did too when I was writing it. You're supposed to. I want you to. [Laughs] But Matt and I don't like what he did.

Edenfield: What about the seasonal change in that story? It's powerful to me that most of the action is set in the summer, and at the end he's thinking about winter.
Dubus: I had it end at that time of year because I had to plot the murder, so they could pretend to go to a ballgame but listen to one. Then the leaves

would fall. And then the snow. And it used to be like this [deep snow, hard freeze] all the time. So by the time spring came there wouldn't be a trace.

Edenfield: It really is the perfect crime, isn't it?
Dubus: Yeah. It was based on that real woman's crime; it was the part of her driving the car to Boston. This guy, of course, had more of a reason to. The story's surely based on it. That guy did seven years, and now he's living in Haverhill with one of my former students.

Edenfield: Matt's a Congregationalist.
Dubus: Is he?

Edenfield: Yes. Is that to set us up for him taking the law into his own hands?
Dubus: God, I don't know anything about Congregationalists. He is a Congregationalist?

Edenfield: He is. It's perfect.
Dubus: I don't know what they are. [Laughs]

Edenfield: Each church has its own autonomy. It works perfectly.
Dubus: Well, that's great! That's a check-swing single. I think there's a Congregationalist church in town. I gave him a clothing store for his work. I gave his buddy a restaurant in town, and I probably just gave him the Congregationalist church.

Edenfield: Each local church has free control over its own affairs. The Congregationalists revolted against formalized worship and state control, and that is exactly what Matt does.
Dubus: Well, that's a check-swing single because he would have done it if he had been an agnostic or a Catholic. [Laughs]

Edenfield: I think his religion just sets him up perfectly for the way he takes everything into his own hands. Frank and Richard are foils for one another: Frank is a lifeguard; Richard is a bully. We're not glad that Matt gets rid of Richard?
Dubus: I'm not. That was a very sad scene.

Edenfield: He doesn't do it with ease. He doesn't take joy in it.

Dubus: No. At the resounding of that pistol shot I think at that moment he knew that he had forever violated nature and he would never be in harmony with it. He has broken his own harmony with nature; he is isolated forever.

Edenfield: Isn't he trying to give Ruth back some harmony, though?
Dubus: Yeah, he was, but killing somebody is not the way to do it. He's fucked up on the numbers, too. Now he can't tell the son and daughter; they have to believe something even worse, for them—that their brother's killer escaped and is living happily, like Polly with Ray. And now the lies are compounded and it's just worse and worse. He should have been a Congregationalist if that was his problem. To commit a cold-blooded murder, you'd have to believe that you could get away with it. You'd have to believe there is no spiritual life, no God, no victim to live with. And you'd have to have something deeply cold in you. Matt doesn't have that. Revenge and hatred and protection of children all feel very normal until you actually pull the trigger and kill somebody. It's not something that Matt Fowler can do with peace.

Edenfield: Is that why he can't make love to Ruth at the end?
Dubus: Yeah. She's a little more bloodthirsty, but of course she wasn't there. Another point of view. And it's fine with him, too, that's what I was getting to, until he's in the same house with the man, is in the same car with the man. That's why I knew, if this guy would just turn and say, kneel down and say, "Please don't," it'd be over with. He'd have never shot him. As a matter of fact, if he hadn't run—and I didn't plan that either. That comes out of the scene, and that's the movement that did it. If he had stood there, neither one of those men would have shot him. They couldn't have.

Edenfield: So even though most of us might do what Matt does, we're not right.
Dubus: No, I don't think they're right. I don't think most people could do it. I think a lot could plan it and a lot could feel it. The actual family certainly thought about it, the family who lives in this area. Somebody told me this story. Three different people offered to the father to do it for him. But he said no. And his wife tried to run the guy down. I ended up in a wheelchair years after I wrote the story, and after this happened, the woman who drove the wheelchair van was the sister of the dead boy. I said, "Oh, my God," so I told her about my story. The man who shot the boy apparently did all right. There was a civil suit, but he got out of serving his time in prison. He did

five to seven years. He said on the witness stand, "I'm glad I did it; I'd do it again." I used to have fantasies of driving by and shooting him, and I didn't even know the people involved.

Edenfield: To shoot Frank in front of his boys?
Dubus: He did that, too.

Edenfield: That just tells everything there is to tell about him in a sentence, doesn't it?
Dubus: Or at least it was enough for Matt until he went into his room and decided there was a lot more that he didn't know. That guy was so nice. I never knew him, but the people his age—he was about twenty—I heard they thought he was homosexual, and he was so nice to the kids.

Edenfield: So was Frank.
Dubus: Yeah.

Edenfield: And so was Matt.
Dubus: Yeah. I get pissed off talking about this, but I hope that this pissedoff-ness would never lead me to shoot somebody. Of course, if someone came in and blew Suzanne's head off, I'd be unpacking these fucking guns, wouldn't I? [Laughs] I'm glad you react this way. I want the complexity there.

Edenfield: You've got to go to mass.
Dubus: I missed it; it started at four. I'm peaceful with that. I know this is what the Lord would want me to do. You're up here to work. Don't worry about it.

Edenfield: I am so sorry.
Dubus: I knew what I was doing. Next question.

Edenfield: Is "The Pitcher" [1979] a story about connecting and controlling?
Dubus: An athlete can control a baseball. Connecting and controlling?

Edenfield: And can control an emotion.
Dubus: What I did to become a pitcher is I wrote about what it's like to be a writer. It's about somebody being consumed by a vocation. When I wrote the scene of her breaking up with him, to me it was a little bit comic. I ac-

tually had fun writing that story. I have never had that much fun writing a story. I was actually happy writing that story. [Laughs]

Edenfield: Why?
Dubus: I got to be nostalgic, to write about baseball. I didn't take the marital breakup seriously; I could get off a line like, "A dentist?" because I was writing about a guy being possessed by his work. And there was no tragedy there. It was just a guy who waits every fourth day to pitch.

Edenfield: He says, "If we can cause it instead of having it happen": this is what it takes to hit the majors, if we can cause it instead of having it happen?
Dubus: Is he talking about staying in shape or something?

Edenfield: No. He's talking about his emotions, about dealing with his grief over losing his wife.
Dubus: What does that have to do with causes?

Edenfield: He says if we can cause it; he's talking about life in general more than anything.
Dubus: This guy Stanley gets everything together for one swing. But it's not something he can make happen. It happens to him. If Stanley could cause it rather than having it happen to him, he would be in the major leagues. This guy did not have that kind of talent. But because he was up there swinging all the time, once in a while it worked. Like a bad dancer will once in a while get off some graceful stuff. That's all that's about.

Edenfield: It's about more than that, isn't it?
Dubus: Not much more. You can go deeply into philosophy, I guess, if you talk about harmony and the bat and the ball and all that. But that's also about somebody who can't make that happen. Most of us can't hit a baseball. That's why he's in the minor leagues. Some can make that happen. With him, it simply happened.

Edenfield: His marriage is like that.
Dubus: This is not the pitcher, though. This is Stanley.

Edenfield: But he's perceiving all of this from watching Stanley.
Dubus: I don't think so. I don't know if he understands his marriage.

Edenfield: I think that's what I mean. He can't make it happen. It happens to him.

Dubus: He's just a young man not really looking at that. He's looking at the majors. It's a pretty old theme. What does a wife do when the man has work that is a lot more important than anything he'll ever feel for her? What's it like to be married to a man who wants to be perfect? To me, it would be boring. That line is about that.

Edenfield: What makes Quintana go crazy?

Dubus: I don't know. We [the Boston Red Sox] had a pitcher named Rogelio Moret [b. 1949], and he went down to Texas and went catatonic in the locker room. It was a lot worse than I wrote about; I didn't think anybody would believe how many shots it took. I thought, I'll just see what I can do with these guys. I don't know what happened to him. I called my doctor and asked him and he said, I don't know, but it always means psychosis, catatonia.

Edenfield: What's he looking at?

Dubus: Nothing. There was a nurse in my workshop at Bradford when I read it, and she had had a catatonic patient. She said they are so strong that you can't take anything out of their hands.

Edenfield: This is from "Cadence" [1974]: Paul rejects his friend and chooses the herd. But in the end, certainty descends on him, and you say this warmly like the morning sun. So the connotations contradict the feelings of regret that the reader might have about the choice he has made. Could it be that each boy has chosen authentically for himself?

Dubus: I think so, and I want the reader to feel ambiguous. I like what Toby [Tobias Wolff (b. 1945)] said about that story. He said, "Seems like always when you have to be a man, somebody else has to be a not-man." [Laughs]

Edenfield: Why is "If They Knew Yvonne" [1969] dedicated to your sons?

Dubus: I wrote that when they were very young. I had a priest friend, and I had a lot of dialogue with that priest friend, and I told him the philosophy of that story before I wrote it. I said, "I'm going to tell them it's theirs. If you want to play with it, play with it, but don't hurt somebody else with it."

Edenfield: Is Janet right to receive?

Dubus: She knows there's no reason not to. A Jesuit told us when I was in high school; I wasn't in Jesuit school [he came to visit]. "None of you in your lives have known anyone who has committed a mortal sin." They are as rare as capital punishment. The monsignor there said nobody can ever tell you when to receive.

Edenfield: Not even a priest.
Dubus: That's right. How can somebody know what's in somebody else's heart?

Edenfield: Why don't they tell the boy from Chicago in "Rose" [1985] the power that he has?
Dubus: I don't know. I don't remember when I was writing why they did it. And I don't remember how I wrote it in *The Lieutenant* and I don't remember what we did when it really happened at Quantico, whether we told everybody or not. If the narrator in "Rose" doesn't tell why they didn't tell, then I can't answer.

Edenfield: He doesn't say; he just leaves that blank. So is "Rose" a story about the perception of power?
Dubus: It's about human possibility, mothers who lift cars off of children. That can happen spiritually. Rose is better than she believes she was.

Edenfield: She has that same self-doubt that Anna ["Anna" (1981)] has, doesn't she?
Dubus: I remember Anna being poor, uneducated, and not having much of a place to go. And being very much in love.

Edenfield: She wants to be a bartender, but she says she couldn't remember all of the drinks.
Dubus: Right, right. But Rose is a lot deeper than that. Anna's a lot more normal. I felt the same way before I went to tend bar, too. You can learn that in one night; it just doesn't look like it from the other side. [Laughs]

Edenfield: I wonder why she drives away from that confidence that makes her go back and forth over the body.
Dubus: I think she's killed him good. This time he really tried to kill the kids. She'd been sitting on that shit a long time. I was fascinated by the silent partners who so often show up in the news. But I had to get a very distant

narrator who heard it from somebody who was a silent partner years ago because I could not get close inside or be anybody who would do that. But I think now and then it dips into their points of view.

Edenfield: Why does she lose her confidence after that? She has the confidence to kill him but she . . .
Dubus: What kind of confidence?

Edenfield: In herself, as a good mother—because she acts correctly in killing him.
Dubus: I think that's because she allowed it to happen, and then the state took her children away. Wouldn't that be enough?

Edenfield: She couldn't have gotten her children back?
Dubus: I think a wealthy woman could have. I'm not sure. I haven't investigated this, but a doctor at Iowa was the first one who told me about children being actually injured by their parents. He said with the rich ones you can't do anything about it. He said poor people are prey to social workers. A social worker shows up and can get in the house. A social worker shows up at a mansion, they're not getting through the door. That's from the 1960s. All of that's true, but I wasn't thinking about her financial situation or anything. That's the answer that comes now, ten years after writing the story. I would think that Rose knows, but she let it happen, and she lost them. Looking back at it from this distance, it seems normal to me that a woman knowing she had allowed somebody to brutalize her kids and then had them taken away from her would feel unworthy. The narrator, from his point of view, says, "Wait a minute. She saved them from the fire. She finally acted."

Edenfield: Now we're to Louise [in "The Fat Girl"]. This is a quote from an article called "More Than Ideal: Size and Weight Obsession in Literary Works" [by Elizabeth G. Peck]: "Size and weight obsession so powerfully control women's lives in our society that it not only inhibits one's actions, but alienates us from our bodies, ourselves, and each other" [71]. Is that what this story is about?
Dubus: Amen. There are only two people who really love her in that story: her father and her friend.

Edenfield: She [Peck] says it's a story with open-ended possibilities.
Dubus: How so?

Edenfield: That we are not sure what Louise is going to do at the end.
Dubus: I always thought of her as the one who would end up owning the house, the car, the lake, the dope, having the boy, and eating Baby Ruths.

Edenfield: Did you choose cherry pie for a reason?
Dubus: Doesn't she do something with the syrup?

Edenfield: Yes, she spears that one cherry and rubs it all in the syrup.
Dubus: Maybe I was wanting cherry pie. I gained ten pounds writing that story.

Edenfield: Did you really?
Dubus: I got rid of all the Tabs and Frescas and stuff at my house. I used to be on a very lethal diet to stay slender and years later realized I was really good at that—so that twenty or thirty coeds for just a few hours each week would see me differently?

Edenfield: Were you different?
Dubus: I don't know. It affects men, too. A friend of mine taught that story, and he argues with me that there is a breakthrough in the marriage and the husband is going to be fine now. And I said, "I don't think so. No way."

Edenfield: He's not going to stay with a fat woman.
Dubus: My political science friend who thinks on writing said, "Maybe deep down he's just shallow." [Laughs loudly]

Edenfield: We've already talked about Anna's last name. This is a story about capitalism isn't it?
Dubus: It sure is. Or: money doesn't make you happy.

Edenfield: I love that scene in the bar, in Timmy's, when she's so happy for a little while when she's buying drinks.
Dubus: On the night that they robbed the place or the next day?

Edenfield: The night they rob the place.
Dubus: That scene is when I realized the most that they really loved each other. It wasn't supposed to be that. It was supposed to be a betrayal story. I got it out of the *Boston Globe*. A guy robbed a bank; he went to a phone and

called his girlfriend in Florida, and she said, "Where are you?" He told her; she told her boyfriend, and he called the cops in Boston while she kept him on the phone. So that was why I started that story.

Edenfield: So Anna was going to betray him?
Dubus: Yeah. But in the bar scene I realized that these people loved each other; so I said, "I don't know what the fuck the story's about"—and that's when it started to move.

Edenfield: She's the happiest when she's giving her money away, buying drinks for everybody. In *Voices from the Moon* [1984]: "We don't have to live great lives; we've just got to understand and survive the ones we've got." That's a great line.
Dubus: That line got quoted in a lot of reviews of that book, and it puzzled me. It made me wonder if the reviewers were trying to live great lives as hard as they should be because it is spoken by a woman who has given up. I wouldn't take it as gospel. She's got her space in her apartment designed so that a child of hers can't even spend the night. She doesn't see much of the young boy. Everybody in that book comes through for everybody in the clutch in that one day, but I would not want to be living inside that woman's body.

Edenfield: I thought she was cold, but she was able to tell her son what he needed to hear.
Dubus: Yeah. She married a stallion and got broke, I think, and anybody taking that line should think about the context. Out of context, it means something entirely different. Out of context, it's all right, but I didn't write it out of context. I think her boy could do more with his talent, but I love her. What am I going to do?

Edenfield: In "Now They Live in Texas" [1987], what is she waiting for?
Dubus: She's waiting for faith, for a spiritual experience. That story dropped in my lap. I wrote it on the airplane going to Louisiana and on the airplane coming back. It was two sittings with a week of work in between down there, reading. A friend of mine, while I was there, used to always talk about Barbara Hershey [b. 1948]. He said, "Didn't she used to play in those movies where the alien thing at the end says, 'This is a true story. Now they live in Texas.'" I said, "That's a good title." Within a week or two, somebody told the story of this experience to my wife. I said, "My God, I've been writing long

enough that I can recognize when someone drops a crumpled napkin in my lap. I can fold it. I've got a story." The truth is that story is a Barbara Hershey movie.

Edenfield: She [the protagonist whose name we never learn] is waiting for some kind of sign.
Dubus: Yeah. It's spiritual hunger, that's all.

Edenfield: That's what I thought. In "Townies" [1980], is there a change in Mike at the end of the story?
Dubus: I don't know. He is giving up, right?

Edenfield: He is going back to wait to be arrested.
Dubus: Yeah, he's going to jail. And through some hurt.

Edenfield: Is that a change? Or is he just the same?
Dubus: I don't know if it's a change. It fits the circumstances. I don't know if he's a changed person. Like most people who kill, he's not really a killer.

Edenfield: Do you think he regrets what he did?
Dubus: Oh, sure.

Edenfield: Does he regret it because he's going to jail or because he killed her, because she's dead?
Dubus: I think both, and there's something else, too: the condition of having killed. There was an editor at Clearwater [a publishing house] who wanted me to reverse the sections, and I said no, but in that letter he also asked if I would change "asshole." I wrote back and said, "That's why he killed her. Because he feels like an asshole." If she had called him a son of a bitch, a cocksucker, or anything else, it wouldn't have hit the same spot.

Edenfield: I think he acts without will when he kills her because he doesn't mean to keep kicking her until she's dead.
Dubus: Right.

Edenfield: But that's a pretty willful thing to do at the end, to go back and wait and to accept himself. But maybe it's a positive change.
Dubus: He's going to do some time.

Edenfield: You're tired, aren't you? We can stop.
Dubus: I know, but we've got to get it done.

Edenfield: We can stop. There's only a few more stories.
Dubus: Maybe we ought to keep going. It might be harder to get back into it.

Edenfield: Okay. I'm trying to narrow everything down. Mitchell won't tell the story to the end in "The Curse" [1988]. He keeps starting the story, but he doesn't finish it. Is that because he doesn't like the way that it ends—because he doesn't do anything? He starts to tell it in the bar when all the regulars come in curious and want to know about what happened. He starts to tell it, but before he gets to the end, he moves off somewhere.
Dubus: I forget. It sounds like he's busy.

Edenfield: He *is* busy. And it works that way in the story.
Dubus: I found it hard to finish a conversation when I was tending bar.

Edenfield: I thought maybe he was glad that he didn't get to finish those conversations because he doesn't like the way that story ends. Someone asks him, "Did you really end up in the hospital?"
Dubus: But the main point of that was, nobody tells him he did anything wrong.

Edenfield: But he knows that he did.
Dubus: And the guy he shuts off over-tips him. Everywhere he goes, he keeps getting blessed, blessed, blessed. He must be cursed. But I'll take a look.

Edenfield: You've answered the question.
Dubus: He wasn't threatened with theft either. He should have tried to stop this rape.

Edenfield: And he knows that.
Dubus: Oh, yeah, he knows that.

Edenfield: At the end of "Sorrowful Mysteries" [1983], when he's driving back into town, the dark starts to fade to green. Is that some suggestion that there's going to be hope?

Dubus: I was just trying to get the landscape. In that story, it's a little bit too subtle, but it's the best I could do. And the whole point of the ending was [that] there was no place to drive where there wasn't racism. They finally had to go home.

Edenfield: But it makes sense when he comes back into his town

Dubus: No. I think it was in his town that he held a knife against a guy's throat. They aren't unique, Southerners, but they're the ones I was writing about. And they do want out. When they are in the car alone together, there is no racism.

Edenfield: But he does the right thing in turning around and going home, don't you think?

Dubus: Oh, yeah. They weren't running away anyway. It was just being away.

Edenfield: I just wondered if that dark changing to green, if you were making a connection between—

Dubus: No, I always keep an eye on the physical world in a story.

Edenfield: In "Delivering" [1978], the boys are glad when their mother got slapped. And he [the oldest of the two] says that she started to cry; he makes the point that she didn't cry very long. The little one says, "'Good.' Then she cried a little, not much. And then they drank some more beer and talked quiet again." She's pretty selfish, isn't she?

Dubus: You sound like the boy. I don't know. I don't really feel a story that way when I'm in a story. It's point of view again. I don't know if she was faithful all those years. I'm assuming that what she tells him is the truth, that this is the first time. Yates said something great about that story. He said it was great that you only brought up a shotgun in the last paragraph. If you would have brought it up earlier, it would have just hung over the story. I didn't even know there was a shotgun there until the last paragraph. The father's not going to kill himself. But it's on the boy's mind when the father goes in.

Edenfield: He doesn't mean to hit his brother in the head, does he?

Dubus: No.

Edenfield: That's an accident. Is the older brother going to take on his mother's role in his little brother's life? Because he tells his daddy that it's all right, that it's going to be okay.

Dubus: I don't know. I think they're just trying to get through this moment. Something bad has happened.

Edenfield: I'm to the last story.
Dubus: Wooooo! [Shouts]
Edenfield: In "Adultery," the priest begins to die in the fall.
Dubus: I wouldn't have known that if you hadn't have told me.

Edenfield: It has a winter setting.
Dubus: I remember she slips down bringing shrimp scampi. I had a friend who began to die in the fall. That may be why. There were seven drafts of a total of four hundred pages written over a number of years—so I don't really know. I know the first draft really sucked. [Laughs] And God knows what's in there. I was reading Mailer [Norman Mailer (1923–2007)] at the time, rereading him, and I wanted to put everything I knew about God, women, love, and death in there. That's why it's so short. [Laughs]

Edenfield: It's not the last story. There's one more, but I've got one more about this one. I know you're tired because I'm getting tired.
Dubus: [Laughs] It's hard work. It's not you. I just get so bored talking about my work. Some poor bastard interviewed me against my will; he kept coming up here every night, and he sent me the interview last fall. He finally got it typed after a year or something—and it's thirty fucking pages! I read about seven pages and I got furious. I sent him a card: "This is boring and tedious—not you, me. I can't read this." I was also pissed off because he said, "Who is your first love?" and I told him about her, and I said, "This can never be in print." I said, "What happened to the girl in 'If They Knew Yvonne' happened to her." I looked in the interview and there the fucking story is. I'm going to meet that woman next week; she's still there. Why did I deal with this creature anyway? But I still don't know if I'm being objective.

Edenfield: I think that this may be my favorite, what Edith says to Hank [in "Adultery"]: "You're dying, too; I can feel it in your chest just like I could feel it when I rubbed him when he hurt. And so am I. That's what we lost sight of." Will you just talk about that a little bit?
Dubus: Well, it's such a simple truth, but if we treat one another the way we would if we knew the other were terminally ill, we'd be a lot kinder to each other. That's beautifully done in both the book and the movie of *Bang the Drum Slowly* [1956]. Sometimes when I'm impatient with a student or some-

thing, I will look at them and concentrate and think, "she's gonna die"—and it helps. In *Bang the Drum Slowly*, they stop picking on the character [Robert] De Niro [b. 1943] played in the film when they find out he's dying. Everybody just stops harassing him. That's all that happened. Everybody gets real kind. She says, "We forgot," right? What Hank was seeing was a little more smoke in the alley, away from the bandstand. The picture in my mind was one of musicians—with the dancers. He's off fucking around. He's fucking—for himself.

Edenfield: Why is he so pleased that she does have an affair of her own—because it relieves him of his guilt a little bit?
Dubus: Yeah, I think so. I never liked him, that's why I put him, the protagonist, in the third novella, and broke him. I said, "It's about time you feel some pain, you son of a bitch." He's an isolated, unloving man. I guess if he wouldn't have got caught, it would have never come up; but when he gets caught, he says, "Well, you're free too, you always were." How come I didn't know? [she must be thinking].

Edenfield: Is that why she says she's only known him in the last three years of their marriage?
Dubus: Probably. This is just a guess, because I did write that in 1976. I would think also that his not wanting her having lovers also means that he does not in the length of that story achieve the depths and brilliance of love that she does. She has to get that from the priest. I had dinner with a woman who's an architect; she says it's safe to say that she was looking for her soul and found it with the priest and he was looking for his body and found it with her. I said, "I never heard that one, but yeah, I'll take it. Yep."

Edenfield: Okay, now the last story, "A Father's Story." I said a little bit about pantheism, but is that why the pine is taller than the steeple?
Dubus: No. I was just getting in the landscape. [Laughs] He wants to tell his daughter that Catholicism and pantheism are like potatoes in a stew. I think it's to show the growth and solidity of the pine if there's any design there at all. It's a big old solid tree he chooses.

Edenfield: So it's just for practical reasons.
Dubus: Yeah, the religion in there is very blatant. It's not a sapling. And I doubt it's a tall steeple. It's a pretty simple church. But I'm really answering a question I can't answer. Why did I choose the size of the tree? I know it

wasn't for pantheistic purposes. And it may just intimate he was taller than the steeple. Maybe it was to make it stand out. Tactile stuff in writing is the hardest. If you can get the tactile, you will get the metaphysical. And one of the best ways to not get the metaphysical is to avoid the tactile. I don't think Hemingway was bullshitting at all when he said that in *The Old Man and the Sea* [1952] that he was just trying to make a real boy, a real old man, and a real fish. And if he did that, he did it all. [Baker *Selected Letters* 780]. I guess the critics went crazy with that one.

Edenfield: You said that sometimes Faulkner sneaks in. I thought this was possibly one time he did.
Dubus: Probably.

Edenfield: "Jennifer's car sat twice damaged, so redeemed."
Dubus: I can point out one, and I know as soon as I wrote it, and I thought oops, but I left it.

Edenfield: I did want to ask you about your new story ["The Colonel's Wife"] too.
Dubus: You can do that.

Edenfield: I'm just so impressed with his [Robert's] ability to forgive her.
Dubus: Good. Did that story work for you?

Edenfield: Oh, yeah, it worked for me.
Dubus: It's a really strange story. I don't know how I feel about it yet. My daughter Nicole [b. 1963], who lives in California, called me up a couple of years before I wrote that story and said, "How're you doing?" and I said, "Not well; another story threw me. Ever since my accident, I don't know why but when I write fiction, I just can't get it done." She said, "Well, your life has changed so much, I don't know how you could imagine a fictional world." She said, "You keep writing essays about your change and maybe some-day you'll write a wheelchair story. Maybe someday you'll be selling a story about a wheelchair." Psychologists and other people had tried to explain this thing, but nobody had cut through everything. Then she said, "When I write, I put my pain on the character." She said, "I have no way of knowing this, but you look at your stories closest to your first divorce," which would have involved her, "you'll probably find that you're closer to your characters, and as the years go by you've grown away." She was right about that. It took

me ten years after the divorce to write a story about a man and woman who trust each other. I had tried to write this story; I got it out on paper. It was about people in Los Angeles hiring private detectives to check up on their lovers' erotic pasts; but after the lead, the reporter wrote about all these juicy marital stories of private eyes. I started thinking, "If you have to hire a private eye, is there a marriage left anyway?" That was what I started with, but I couldn't get anywhere. But a few months after Nicole told me that, I thought, "Okay. I'm going to break his legs. Then it will work for me." All that kept me going writing that damn story, which was very hard to write. I thought, "I'm going to get to a point where he's going to get off of that chair, painfully, and I know the pain. He's going to go up the stairs on his butt with his legs aching. He'll go into the bathroom, open the diaphragm case, it's going to be empty. She'll just come back from her walk, come up the stairs, see him there with the empty diaphragm case, and she's going to say, 'How am I going to get you down the stairs?'" I said, "Then something will happen."

The morning that I thought maybe the story would end, I went to mass. I believe it was a Thursday. I was driving home, and I said, "I got to get food in me," and I ate at the desk; and all of a sudden, it wasn't a voice, but it came to me: "He's not going up the stairs," this voice said. "They're going to Arizona." I said, "They are?" [Laughs] And they did, and I thought—I read it aloud twice at a reading—that's an abrupt ending. But I think that there's something happening in that story that I'm not aware of yet. And that is certainly not realism. If realism is what I think it is, then we would have seen the dialogue. And it wouldn't have made that leap it made. I think something spiritual happened there. The act of writing itself is like dying if dying were a good thing to do. But something went out. And I wouldn't expect anybody to believe that this is the way things really happen. But I would want a reader to believe that this is what happened. [Laughs] But I thought it was going to work out too easy. He mirrored her story.

Edenfield: Is that why they lie down together on that bed to talk? Because there's going to be something spiritual between them?
Dubus: Oh, yeah. His spirit doesn't know his body is broken. He almost goes to get a cigarette. He sees her grieving; he wants to get up and hold her, but he can't. So he says, "Lie down." That's when he realizes, she's always been here. It doesn't matter where the hell she was, but she was always here. What she was doing when she wasn't here doesn't really matter; she was always here. She's going to die. I'm going to die. It's the same thing. He starts seeing her as a little girl, as a dying woman, and he says, "What the fuck. What's

it matter? She loves me. I love her. The sun's on the martini. What more do we need?" Chris Tilghman, who's in the workshop [that Dubus held in his home], read that draft and said, "If he'd been younger, he would have been up those stairs, right?" I said, "Sure. If he had been a younger man, he'd have been up those stairs, looking for that diaphragm." He couldn't have reached this point, I don't think. It's about being broken, too. I don't really know. Feeling other people's pain. Getting rid of horror and shock and fear of oneness instead. That's the metaphysic. I'm not sure the physical trappings of it support it, but *Playboy* took it.

Edenfield: So you're not going to write those stories that you can't write anymore?

Dubus: No. "The Curse" [a short story] was an idea before the accident, and I wrote it after the accident because I wanted to try to write. I was in a hospital bed—no, it was actually in this bed—I was still in the cast, in a lot of pain, and I said, "I know how to write this story." It took me twenty years to learn how to write this story, but I know how to write the kind of story that starts after the action and just focuses in a compressed way on what the action means to the character who was in the action. I learned that from a heavyweight [Richard Yates], and I know how to put one step after the other. That's why I chose to write that one. I heard about a rape in Rhode Island; it was during that whole trial, which I didn't really watch. I did hear that one guy tried to get to the phone, but somebody stopped him. What's he feel like? She got killed in a wreck in the middle of the morning in Florida; she'd had a few drinks, too. Anyway, I had a big notebook full of ideas. I've got enough notebooks, enough stories, to last the rest of my life. Well, the notebooks are still here, but they can be your notebooks. I know what they mean, they're clear, but they don't seem mine. I couldn't write about Polly [in "The Pretty Girl"]. Maybe if I cut her legs off. But I'm not there anymore.

Edenfield: Because your struggles and hers are so different?

Dubus: I don't know. I'll just go right to what Nicole said: "So many changes." I don't even try to understand it anymore. It's actually getting interesting now that I only have a few ideas for fiction, and when they come, I have to gestate them a year or more. That's always been the way I work. I don't regret that anymore. It's just become interesting. I'm really loving the essays. One I just finished [not named in the interview] to me is structured like a story, it was written like a story, so the act of writing hasn't changed.

Edenfield: What's the difference then?
Dubus: I'm not sure there is one.

Edenfield: I'm not sure there is either. I enjoy your essays just as much as I ever did your stories.
Dubus: I'm glad to hear that. I called Toby [Wolff] in 1990 in May and told him I couldn't write anything but essays. I was down. He said, "Andre, I think you and I are snobs about fiction. That's all it is." I said, "You're right." Not anymore. Just as soon as I put that sunset in there you'd try to figure it out: it's because the house faces 30 degrees west of north. [Laughs] I put that sunset in a lot of stories. I noticed maybe twenty years ago that all my stories seem to end with a woman and a man lying in bed talking to one another. I said it kind of self-deprecatingly, and my friend said that seems a good enough way to end a story. [Laughs]

Edenfield: How does it make you feel when you read all of these articles by people who try to explain every concrete detail in your stories?
Dubus: I haven't read many. The reviewers don't usually go into it. Kennedy's [Thomas Kennedy] I liked. The Fisher King thing [that Dubus referred to earlier] is kind of silly. Guy's got a good reputation, no kidding. Kind of a big gun. I was laughing. This was a long time ago. This guy's probably getting fifty thousand dollars somewhere; he's telling students this bullshit. [Laughs loudly]

Edenfield: As long as we don't work against the story, is it all right to find meaning in those things?
Dubus: You're supposed to find meaning in the stories.

Edenfield: I didn't phrase that right. I meant meaning in all those concrete details.
Dubus: It would have made absolute sense if he had said, "It reminded me of the Fisher King" and then began to wax poetic about him and Christ. But he didn't. He had the arrogance to say that's what this is, and he's wrong. A little humility, a little light-heartedness, would be better. There would have been nothing at all wrong with him saying, "Because of the proximity of swimming animals, I began thinking . . . . " It's hard not to bring your whole history into something. Larry Woiwode [b. 1941] has a new book about the Acts of the Apostles [*Acts* (1993)]. He says that biblical scholars are a lot like literary critics that have begun to think that their interpretation is more

important than the original source. I usually call it jazz. I say, "Now we're getting into the jazz; we're doing variations on the theme. We're not with the melody anymore, students. The melody's over here. Now we're doing our interpretation. It's not his. It's ours. It's what it reminds us of." You can go all kind of places. I remember a student once said, "I don't think we're in Kansas anymore, Toto." [Laughs] We went all over the place. But the melody is over here. We were doing this and that. [Pats a manuscript] That exists to make us do this. But this is not part of that. It's not in that. That's the melody. We're doing this because of our own histories and our own reasons. I didn't realize it until you asked me that, but it would have been fine if he had had the wisdom and the humility to do that rather than to say this is like that. That is not what he read; it's what he read that kicked off something in his mind. That's a whole different thing. If you apply that to a marriage, think about the danger. Your husband starts saying, "No, this is what you said, this is what you meant—rather than what you said. And what you meant made me think, say and do this." It's all back to point of view, isn't it?

Edenfield: That's the thing about dissertations. It's not about humility.
Dubus: Well, that's fascism. Those guys at Iowa: for little women who couldn't pass the orals, it was like a ritual: just wait another year in the Quonset hut. The MFA program was honest; we didn't have to do that shit. I'd see these poor bastards studying linguistics, and it became very clear to me that this was some kind of system. You're supposed to fail the orals the first time, be a graduate student with children in the Quonset hut for another year, and then come back. Because how is a PhD supposed to mean anything if you can get it the first time. You can't get a publishing PhD to teach a class. When I was at Iowa, the rhetoric teachers told us to put our names on the board and a phone number. They said, "You are the last teacher these students will know in their four years." And we did. We gave them our home phone number and our name: "You call us if you need help or something." I had buddies who would teach the sophomore lit course as graduate assistants. I guess there's teachers and there's scholars, but that whole publish/perish or get out of the classroom, whatever good it's doing, I don't think it's enough to justify it. Some like to defend the dissertation. They say, "You have to show your colleagues that you can communicate." That's when I came up with the idea of a book-length manuscript of essays about literature; that should suffice. My last year as a graduate assistant, they gave me a kid to work with. He had his first graduate assistantship; he was in the literature program so he could grow up to be a PhD, and he was a star. We started talking about

Salinger [b. 1919]. I said that the one story that I didn't like a whole lot is "For Esmé, with Love and Squalor" [1950]. He said, "But you don't understand. It's Salinger's answer. What does the little boy keep saying? What does one wall say to the other wall? See you at the corner. That's his answer. Eastern and Western philosophy must come together." I thought, "Oh, my God! Poor Salinger. Poor students this guy is going to have." [Laughs] He was a product. I had to get hurt and then have somebody say something nice for me to feel that story. I said, "All right. You can give somebody a watch and make them feel better." That's what I didn't believe. But this poor guy, he didn't give a shit about the emotional part. He found a topic.

Edenfield: I bought one of those great big clumsy Timex watches after I read that story and wore it for a long time.
Dubus: [Laughs] I like that story.

Edenfield: I'll turn this tape recorder off now, and I swear to God I won't turn it back on.

A Conversation with Andre Dubus

Lori Ambacher / 1993

Image 3 (Spring 1993): 40–55. Reprinted in *Leap of the Heart: Andre Dubus Talking*. Ed. Ross Gresham. New Orleans: Xavier Review Press, 2003. 215–34. Reprinted with the permission of the author.

Andre Dubus is a fiction writer and essayist, and the author of nine books, including *Adultery and Other Choices, The Last Worthless Evening*, and *Broken Vessels*. As a young man, he was a captain in the Marine Corps. Later he taught at Bradford College in Massachusetts. He has been a Guggenheim Fellow, a MacArthur Fellow, and was the 1991 winner of the PEN/Malamud prize for Short Fiction. In 1986, Dubus stopped to help two people on the highway who'd been involved in a car accident and was himself hit by a car. As a result of the accident, he is confined to a wheelchair. He writes every day, exercises while listening to opera, attends Mass regularly, and is passionate about baseball, movies, his children and grandchildren, his many friends, and the work of other writers. Lori Ambacher talked with Andre Dubus about his life and work one afternoon during a blizzard.

Image: In your story "Deaths at Sea," the character Gerry, an officer on an aircraft carrier in the Pacific, is lonely for his wife Camille, but his loneliness seems to go deeper than that. He talks about feeling things at night more deeply than in the daytime; he also talks about feeling lonely during Mass, or watching the sun set. Can you talk about that loneliness? It seems to recur in characters in other stories.

Andre Dubus: I feel things at night I don't feel in the day. Hemingway wrote beautifully about things being different at night than in the day. When I was teaching at Bradford College, we were talking about that in class once, and one of the female students said, "I have a rule that I don't mail any letters I write after eleven at night."

For me, it's primordial. The sun goes down. I see less of the world. Everything becomes more interior. You look in the window and you see your reflection. The world becomes limited to the range of the light that you're in. I think that tends to be frightening, lonely. I wonder whether bars would be as popular if people worked from midnight till eight, whether people would drift in during the day.

The summer of 1970 was the first summer of my first divorce. I had never really been without a family before then. I was living at home in college, I got married in college, and then right away was a father. At one point I was aboard ship, but I still had a family. So loneliness was a big problem that I had to deal with. I also had no car. It was a very tough summer. But I learned, and it surprised me, that I was only really lonely between cocktail hour and dinner. I wrote to Gina Berriault about this. I didn't know her, but we exchanged letters. I was puzzled; I asked her why this should be so. If I could just get through cocktail hour and dinner, I could watch a ball game or a movie, and I was all set. And she wrote back—I'll paraphrase it, it was twenty-three years ago—"it's primordial, the sun goes down, day ends, it's a little death, it reminds us of death, remorse and other feelings come in, and we need company at that time." And I think that's true. I usually like solitude in daylight, and do not at night.

They also taught us in the Marine Corps, never put a marine alone in a foxhole at night. Americans do not like to be alone at night. Put somebody with them.

Image: When he reviewed your novel *Voices from the Moon* for the *New Yorker*, John Updike wrote, "One of *Voices from the Moon*'s theological implications is that, in seeking relief from solitude we sin and fall inevitably into pain." To me this seems to apply in a broader sense to many of your characters. I'm particularly interested in two of them. Miranda, in the story "Miranda Over the Valley," is deeply depressed after she's had an abortion; and Molly, in the novella of that name, is incredibly sad after she loses her virginity. Molly feels that even though she's only sixteen, she has little to look forward to; she can already imagine Bruce going away to college, meeting someone else, and breaking up with her. And I don't feel as though Miranda does what she really wants to do.
AD: No, she doesn't.

Image: You may not have been trying to make a moral statement in these stories, but would you care to comment on these two characters at all?

AD: Those two stories may have been, at least in their inception, involved with moral statements, which then I have to try to leave before I get to the desk, so that the characters are free to grow. I agree with Updike's reading of *Voices from the Moon*, and that has nothing at all to do with my intent.

To me Molly's sadness is that because of her mother's love and friendship, she lost her childhood. So it wasn't so much the loss of the hymen as that she was suddenly granted adulthood by being able to share that with her mother, as though she were her mother's friend. It may have been absolutely different if she had a different mother and a father, or simply a different mother, and she had gotten drunk and stoned and performed fellatio, then the next night made love, and then gone back to that redeemed hypocrisy or redeeming furtiveness of what I think of as a healthy childhood: "How was the party?" "Fine." And continuing in your own home to be a child.

I don't think that it was the physical acts themselves that brought about the sadness. It was the little marriage her mother gave her—"your boyfriend can come over here and fuck you"—you know. The scene for that story was planted in me on a summer Sunday afternoon. I was pushing Cadence in a stroller on the Bradford College campus, which was empty of students. And there were three young girls sitting on the park bench, lovely, wearing makeup, with cigarettes, and they said, "Hi, Andre," and I didn't know who they were. I realized they must be neighborhood children who were maybe fourteen. And I thought, why are their parents letting them look like this? And that's where the story came from.

With "Miranda over the Valley" I was relying a lot on art—no, not relying a lot on art, but some of those themes came from reading and teaching Jean Anouilh's *Antigone*. I like Anouilh's *Antigone* better than the original, and it's a beautiful play to teach. In Anouilh's version, which is modernized to a degree, Creon and Antigone are ancient Greeks, but Creon refers to Antigone's brothers as wastrels who drive too fast and smoke cigarettes and drink. In that play, Antigone, when confronted by Creon, unveils herself as someone who doesn't believe in the religious ritual of burial; she wants to carry it out because he's her brother. And Creon says, I don't even know who's buried out there any more; I'm just doing this to keep a state going.

The play pits pragmatists against idealism. The Nazis allowed it to be produced in occupied Paris, because they thought that the play was on the side of Creon, and that it was pro-Nazi, or at least sided with their philosophy. Antigone finally tells Creon she's going to keep throwing dirt over her brother, and she doesn't know why, except she's saying "no" to his way. Miranda is reading that on the airplane going home. I didn't want any reader to associate that with the story; it was in there for me, to get me more deeply into the story. That story was first a one-act play, and to me it was about someone wanting to take a leap of faith, if you will; courage; fear—fear's very important. Miranda wanted to do something she was afraid of, and what she got from her parents was, "Be safe; be safe; be safe." To me, that wasn't just advice about a pregnancy; it was advice about living a life. I named Miranda's boyfriend Michaelis for Lady Chatterly's first lover, who I thought lacked commitment. If I remember correctly, he couldn't make her come, and I assume that was because he was selfish. So I was using a lot of literary and religious symbolism in that story, but just to get myself deeper into the story, and to have fun with it. So, what are the answers? I don't know the answers. I think artists just have to develop the questions and make them delightful for people. I would say as a layman, the general answer to Molly and Miranda and their parents is to act with a more sacrificial, a more daring, a more truthful love. And to be less practical, shortsighted and pragmatic. Neither Molly's mother and of course not her father, who deserted her, nor Miranda's parents, have anything really vital to say. And both daughters would do a lot better listening to a good philosophy teacher on a summer afternoon in a college classroom.

I noticed one year teaching short fiction, though I forget which writers—I was teaching several collections—that nearly every character who went under at the end of the stories would have been better if that character had received what a humanities curriculum provides, and had been able to apply it. You know, if the characters had been aware that their action was taking place in a moment in history, and there were precedents, and causes and effects, and that their action was of extreme importance.

Image: Your character Claire, Molly's mother in the novella, calls love a vocation. Can you talk about that?
AD: That's from Catholic training. I mean, I've heard that all my life. And I've never met anybody who was not exposed to Catholic training who had ever heard of it. The Christian Brothers taught us there were only two vocations: the religious life, or marriage.

Image: What about you yourself? Do you see love that way? Did you always take love and marriage that seriously?
AD: I don't think I knew enough to go into it seriously. I certainly learned it's a vocation, but I had to get knocked down a lot to learn that. No; I think

I can speak for my generation; we viewed marriage as the glow of love, and never thought anything would happen to it.

Image: Can you tell me something about your time as a student at the University of Iowa Writers' Workshop, and what you learned there?
AD: R. V. Cassill taught me to read; that's one of the first things he did. The same way he taught me to read, he taught me to go more deeply into writing. Once in a bar he said to me, "You're good at writing down what people do, and say, and what they look like. But you don't have the killer instinct of a Catholic novelist to go deeply and find out why they're doing it." And that was the first time I knew that you were even supposed to try. I had read that way; I had read some of the books that he taught, but I had never thought about them, and tried to figure out why they were powerful, why they were painful.

Image: Was that where you met Richard Yates also? Was he teaching at Iowa?
AD: Yes, though I wasn't in his writing workshop; I learned from being in his literature seminar, and from being his friend. He had been Bobby Kennedy's speechwriter. And after the assassination in '63 of Jack Kennedy, Yates came to Iowa—it was in the fall of '64. I know he needed a job.

Image: *Broken Vessels* includes the essay "A Salute to Mr. Yates." I know that his friendship meant a great deal to you, and that his recent death affected you deeply. Would you like to add anything to what you said in your essay?
AD: Dick left a manuscript of his novel in his refrigerator before he went to the hospital. I don't know if that meant he thought maybe he was coming back, or if it was just habit. Either way I like the story. He used to do that so that if there was a fire the manuscript would be saved.

I wish that more people had read him. He always suffered from poor health. When he was feeling low one summer after I got hit, we were talking on the phone, and I said, "Can you think of any writer in the history of western civilization who has reached your age and gone through so much, so many physical problems, and is still producing?" He couldn't answer that. That made me feel good. He had epilepsy. His lungs were never good. He had pneumonia often. So for the last ten years I was expecting his death in a way—no, not expecting it, but I feared it. But he was so strong-willed that a big part of me thought that he'd keep going. He still inspires me. He wrote in conditions under which I could not write.

When I was in the hospital after I got hit, he told me over the phone, "When they bring you your tray of food, after you eat, keep the tray, turn it upside down on your knees and you can write." I didn't tell him I didn't really have any knees to function that way, and I was in traction, but that was sincere Dick Yates—thinking, my writer friend is in the hospital, I'll give him a little tip on how to keep working.

Yates had a reputation as a drunk—he drank, but he was not a drunk. He missed engagements sometimes, but that was because he was in the hospital so much. He wasn't the kind of writer who wouldn't show up.

Image: Is there anyone now you discuss your work with before you turn it over to your agent or editor? Or are you fairly independent?
AD: I'm fairly independent. Usually I just turn it over. Unless I'm married.

Image: Your wives have been a help to you in your work, then?
AD: Yes. As encouraging readers. They were good readers, too. Sometimes one of them would say, "You don't want this here," and "this is wrong," and "this needs more," and so on. But I usually just send things to my agent and wait. And hope that he likes them. And if he doesn't, he sends them out anyway.

Image: How long have you been working with him?
AD: Since 1973.

Image: You're written a fair number of stories dealing with racism. Can you see any difference between race relations in the North and South? Is there really a difference say, between Haverhill, Massachusetts, and Louisiana?
AD: I don't think I could tell you. I haven't been back to the South in so long. When I left it was segregated. I went to teach in Alabama in the fall of '85, and it seemed to be like paradise, compared to when I had left. Also compared to what I read about and hear about in Boston; but I really don't know firsthand. And I don't trust that view. I'd have to ask black people whether they felt that there was more equality in Tuscaloosa, Alabama, than I saw, or in Boston, Massachusetts. I don't trust my own feelings about that; I don't really know. I mean, that stuff's everywhere.

Image: Do you think you'll ever write about your childhood in Louisiana? Will you ever write a memoir?
AD: Memoirettes. Yes. I have ideas in my essay notebook.

Image: I think I remember having read that you were fairly close to your mother.

AD: Yes, though I had secrets from her. I wrote a note in my notebook for a fictional character who when she was younger, believed she was not close to her father, but as she grew older she realized that only meant that she had secrets from him. That may just be my attitude towards post-sixties openness. But yes, I felt close to her. I miss my mother; I miss my father, too. I talk to them every day.

Image: You talk to them now?
AD: Oh, I pray to them.

Image: You said once that you felt you weren't really free to take off and become a writer until after your father's death.
AD: I don't trust that any more. I'll never know whether I would have resigned from the Marine Corps if he were alive, but as I'm older now, I think that because of the situation I was in I would have resigned anyway. I was writing when I lived with him; I was writing in the Marine Corps. He read my first story in the *Sewanee Review*. I think he would have been worried if I'd said I was going to graduate school with four kids, but I'm not sure that that would have had a big effect. I had one of those epiphanies in my twenties. The year after I was at Iowa City, I was walking down the street, and said, "It must be because Daddy died," and now I'm not really sure. I never have written about it, so I don't really know the truth of what I feel. That's one reason I write, to find out what I feel about something. Or to find out what one can feel about something, because obviously I don't always feel the same way about something as my characters feel.

Image: When did writing turn from being one of your interests into something more serious?
AD: When I got out of high school.

Image: Did you think it was what you were going to do for a living?
AD: Maybe not for a living, but for a life. My main purpose in going to college was to get a degree so I could earn a living to support me while I wrote. I would have had to go anyway, and I would have gone anyway, but that's what I saw its function as. That's why I went to graduate school, so I could get a teaching job. All six and a half years of education after high school did exactly what I wanted them to do.

Image: You were eighteen when you started writing in earnest? Do you think there's anything different about the way you write now than when you were younger? Do you still feel the same terror when you face the blank page?

AD: I was seventeen when I started to write. I think I feel more terror now. I think when I started I wrote when I felt like writing; I don't remember having a regular schedule. The funny thing is, I wrote at about the same rate. Three stories a year; that was about it. I wrote when it was brimming over. I learned pretty soon, probably my last year of college, that you had to start doing it every day. So that's probably where the fear of the blank page started. But not in the first exciting halcyon days. Writing a story. I remember writing one in college, in a library, longhand, while a guy sat there and I handed him each page as I wrote. That was hubris, wasn't it? Or I wouldn't even say it was hubris; it was happiness. And he was awed. I won a prize for that story. But I must have rewritten it.

Image: At one point you worked as a bartender to earn extra money.

AD: I did that part-time. I did that Friday and Saturday nights for a year in the seventies, whatever year it was they lowered the drinking age to eighteen. I was literally broke. I didn't have pocket money from one day to the next, to pay bills and this and that. I was a regular at this bar, and I asked the owner for a job. I didn't know how to tend bar. He said, "That'll be good. You might draw some students," because they had just lowered the [drinking] age. So I learned on the job. Friday was a twenty-hour day, with writing and teaching. I tended bar from five in the afternoon till two in the morning. And then the other bartender and I cleaned the place. We'd wait until after the bar closed, then we'd pour a big drink and clean. Then I'd go out with my kids on Saturday morning, and get back to the bar at five on Saturday night, and tend bar until one o'clock. And then close and clean the place again.

Image: Were your children living nearby?

AD: Yes. They were living in Haverhill. And Sunday we'd go to Mass and then do something. I was teaching five days a week. It was tough. I was in my thirties, though. I couldn't do that again. You get up on Friday and write and go run a few miles and then go teach two classes, have a conference, and get to the bar at five o'clock, close at two, and then sweep it and drink and talk until three or four—it was long.

Image: How did you get to know Tobias Wolff?

AD: We ran into each other a lot in one year. Maybe not even a lot; I was at an Ohio writer's conference with him. And I think one other. We had a good time. We first met at Syracuse, where he teaches. Though I was a fan of his before we met. I'd read *In the Garden of the North American Martyrs*. I actually called him a lot about that book before we met, as I was reading it. I'd heard about it the year before it came out.

Image: How did he come to write the introduction to *Broken Vessels*?
AD: That was an idea somebody at Godine had—I'm not sure who—and they told me they were thinking about it. So I called him and said, "You know, don't feel you have to." And he said, "I won't feel I have to. I'll read the manuscript and see if I want to." Toby's a good man; really a good human being.

Image: It's a beautiful introduction.
AD: I reread parts of it when I'm feeling low. Did you read Walker Percy?

Image: Yes. Do you like Walker Percy?
AD: I really liked teaching *The Last Gentleman*. My first year at Bradford College, I taught *The Moviegoer* and *The Last Gentleman* in the same year. It was great. My students used to talk about Percy's malaise.

Image: Since you mentioned Percy, are there any other recent or contemporary writers whose vision inspires you? Or anyone to whom you feel an affinity?
AD: I'm tempted to say everyone I read. If I don't feel an affinity to their work, I don't read them. Nadine Gordimer. Colette. Gina Berriault. Elmore Leonard. I love John Cheever. Malraux. Turgenev.

Image: In the past you've referred to yourself as a Catholic writer. Are you still comfortable calling yourself that?
AD: Yes. I can only see the world as a Catholic. I may imagine the world as a non-Catholic, but it's still the way I see it. We were talking earlier today about the movie "Alive." I remember when that event actually happened a priest, I think a Peruvian priest, said, "That was a sacrament." I had no problem with that. I still think of that event as that sacrament that happened in the Andes. And at Donner Pass. I don't care how the people felt about it; their feelings don't apply. In other words, if there was some dark person in

the Andes or in Donner Pass who thought, "This was a really good meal," I still say a sacrament was going on.

Image: You write about a lot of what I would call the dark side: rape, murder, child abuse, divorce, infidelity. Is there any particular reason for this? Would you say it's simply a reflection of the modern world?
AD: I think honest writers write about what bothers them.

Image: Have you ever found that members of the Catholic community respond negatively to your work because of its content?
AD: No.

Image: How about the opposite? Have you ever come across anyone who felt that your work was too religious?
AD: No. I'm sure there must have been people who felt both things, but I never got any letters about it.

Wait a minute, though. I came across two faculty women at a reading once who were angry about "A Father's Story" because the father in that story covered up for the daughter's hit-and-run. And I think they got a little more angry because I said, "I wouldn't do that. And my daughters wouldn't ask me to do that. I made this up."

That story began because I wanted to explore the morality of hit-and-run. Not what the law says, but the morality of it. That's how the story started in my mind. Then at the same time I was thinking of writing about a man of faith, so I thought why not have the man of faith be the father of the one who does the hit-and-run. I pointed out to these two teachers that the narrator says, "Feelings should be subordinated to actions. That is true love." But when the crisis comes he goes all on feeling. Now I don't know what's right or wrong. I don't think he should have done what he did, but I became him through fiction.

So one of the women said, "Well, some ironic distance would have helped us know that."

And I said, "I don't write stories like that, and I don't read them." Later, of course, I thought of a much better answer. I was watching Robert Duvall at a movie. I thought, you wouldn't ask Robert Duvall to create ironic distance between him and a character. Why would you ask a writer?

At the same conference, another teacher was disturbed for a different reason, when he found out that I did not espouse the emotions or actions of that narrator. He said, "Then what's the point, from Homer on?"

We got to be fairly amicable. I told him my approach to art is to become someone else in a situation which I construct and to try through imagination and gifts and other mysteries to go into the human heart. It's a mistake to think always that what's on the page has anything at all to do with what the writer would do in that situation. Although if you've read a lot of work by a writer you probably will not be largely surprised if you meet the writer. I've mentioned Gina Berriault, whom I did finally meet, though not for long enough to discover anything, but I think if I met Gina Berriault and spent some time with her there are some things I know she would not do. She would not call somebody a nigger. She would not denigrate someone for being poor. From having read her, I know where her spirit is.

Image: So for you a character starts from an idea, rather than being based on your own experiences? Where do the ideas come from? From the world around you? Do you ever start with something inside yourself?
AD: I've gotten a lot of ideas from newspapers. A lot from stories people told me. I think far fewer ideas for stories come from something I have actually seen. I tend to make those into essays. Ideas from myself; sure; a lot of those. Like, "The Fat Girl" you could say came from myself but it was from observing very large eighteen-year-old girls from time to time in my teaching career—silent ones, and wondering what it was like to be eighteen and female in the United States of America during the seventies. As I mentioned, with "A Father's Story," I wondered what about a hit-and-run; I wondered what about a man of faith, and started making up a situation. He was going to be a triple 'A' ballplayer who was a good fielder but couldn't hit, and a Catholic, and I was going to test his faith in that way—how long can you keep the faith in Pawtucket? And then I combined those ideas for a story. So it's obvious why I don't write novels. That took place over years. I had read *Fear and Trembling* twice. Then I asked this woman, a philosophy teacher named Peggy Walsh, if she'd like to do a free seminar on Tuesday nights. In the middle of the semester; we simply advertised it. Whoever showed up was our seminar. And we did it until we ran out. I think we ended up with one student at a bar. Then I read *Varieties of Religious Experience*. All for one story, which I don't think is thirty pages long. Probably a four-year process from the insemination period on.

Image: At one point in a long interview with the writer and scholar Thomas Kennedy, you mentioned that you were raising your daughter Cadence as a Catholic. But then you said that it didn't matter to you if a person didn't have a religion as long as they replaced it with a philosophy? What did you mean by that?

AD: Would you say Sartre had a religion? No, I won't even ask that question. If someone has a philosophy, understands that there are greater things at stake in their own lives, and that there are larger communal, social, and eternal values out there, and tries to live in that way in the human community, I think that's great. I'm disturbed by people who think the world started the day they were born, and that acquisition and nobility are somehow connected. At this point, Andre is my only churchgoing offspring. He goes to his wife's church. But it's in his spirit, too. I wish all six were going to Mass. I was very happy at Mass yesterday. I love Mass. But I don't think that's something God worries about, whether or not we're all going to Mass together. The gift of prayer, though, is a good thing to have. And I don't know how to give that to children. I mean, that keeps me going. I pray all the time. The worse it gets, the more I pray. I was in pain about one of my children last week—who did nothing offensive; it was just some suffering that she was going through, and I started thanking God for the pain I was feeling, figuring maybe this would take it away: thank you for the gift of this child and this love which is causing me this pain. Within three minutes I felt better. That's not the only way, but I know it's a good way.

Image: You seem to open nearly every book with an epigraph. What philosophers would you say have influenced your thinking?

AD: That's mainly because I love epigraphs. I like finding them, I like copying them, I like reading them in other people's books; I'm disappointed when a book doesn't have an epigraph.

I really love reading Kierkegaard. I love reading William James; I think he's great company. And I can't say whether or not I've ever learned anything from either one of them that I've ever been able to apply in my life. But *Varieties of Religious Experience* was a wonderful pleasure to read. I was reading *Manners and Morals* a while back. I like Dorothy Day; I'd call her a philosopher. I like the New Testament a lot. Antoine de Saint-Exupery. Toby and I were talking about him on the phone. That's something else we share: one of our favorite books is *Wind, Sand and Stars*. He's certainly one of my favorite philosophers. I don't know if he's categorized as one, but if he isn't, then I don't know what they are. That's one of the greatest books anybody ever wrote. It's arranged like a memoir; it's about different things. He was flying airplanes when they crossed the desert without radios. But it's about how to live, and why we're alive, and it's just beautiful. *Flight to Arras* is another nonfiction book in which he's going on a reconnaissance flight to Arras, and the Germans are sweeping through France, and he's certain he's going to be killed on a reconnaissance flight, because their planes won't climb higher than the German anti-aircraft, so he's trying to figure out during this reconnaissance flight why. Why's he dying? Why's he doing this? And he died flying reconnaissance from North Africa. He didn't come back. He was one of the reasons I joined the Marines. He and Malraux. I thought, boy, that sounds good, to be active, and in the world, and writing. I loved *Man's Fate*. I just bought Bernanos's novel again, *Diary of a Country Priest*. Because I don't remember it, but I was reading it when I was writing the novella, "A Pretty Girl." I remember getting up in the middle of the night and thinking, "*Diary of a Country Priest* is a masterpiece. Isn't that wonderful? I should always try to write a masterpiece." I started praying to Mary again because of that book.

Image: You have a reputation for being someone who is very kind to young writers. Is this partly because of your writing workshop?
AD: I've always tried to help other writers whose work I like. That help can be from getting them in touch with my agent. Or actually working with the manuscript, depending on where that person is. Or it can be as with my cousin Jimmy Burke, getting him in touch with my agent, who is our agent. That was a big change in his life which he talks about in interviews. You know, it's not a sacrifice. I love doing that. It's not like putting out a forest fire.

Image: Can we talk about what you're working on right now? You're working on a new book of essays? Are you also writing fiction?
AD: I'm working on a book of essays called *Meditations from a Moveable Chair*. But I hope at the same time I'm working on a collection of stories. I have the discipline to say—okay, I'll write nothing but essays till this book is finished, but I'm not comfortable with the lack of freedom. The second thing I can't do is control where anything I write goes, so yes, I'm working on a book of essays and a book of stories.

Image: Do you have a preference for the short-story form over the essay form? It seems like when you talk about your essays you think of them as a lesser genre.
AD: Yes, but I think that that's subjective, and it's all in my mind, because when I'm actually at the desk I feel no different and I get just as excited about

the work. I talked to Toby Wolff in May of 1990. I was feeling very gloomy about writing and telling him I wasn't getting any ideas for fiction, and he said, "I think you and I are snobs about fiction. There's nothing wrong with writing nonfiction." I'm so glad he said that. He may not have felt that, either; he may have just said that to make me feel better. But that really started loosening the crust for me, the outer crust that I had to break through, and I realized I did have a snobbish attitude which has nothing to do with writing or reading essays, only some idea. I used to, when I was younger, wonder why Hemingway ever took the time away from writing fiction to write *Green Hills of Africa*, and *Death in the Afternoon*. I never wondered that about *A Moveable Feast* because it's so magnificent. But I thought why not be writing fiction? Now I see how callow and naive I was.

Image: You've talked about how all of the ideas for fiction you had before the accident didn't seem to apply after the accident had taken place.
AD: Yes. And I'm not able to explain that. I mean, the notebook is there, the ideas are there. I know what the ideas are but I don't feel attached to them any more. They could be your notebook, and your ideas. Many people I've told this to understand immediately. They say, "Well, you've changed." I can't say I've changed. I've been through a change. I remember how things were physically, and I know how they are now. But I don't know if my mind has changed at all. I don't understand that part. It's becoming less sad for me and more interesting and more exciting to be starting over with new ideas. There's a flood of ideas for essays.

Image: You published a story recently.
AD: Yes. And I've been gestating a couple of ideas for stories. Which I have to do for a long time. I usually wait to start a story until after I see the first two scenes. Or at least I start seeing the story in my mind. I don't mean I understand the characters, but I see the story. Then it's time.

Image: You were very depressed after the accident. Would you say that you've recovered from that, for the most part?
AD: The title essay of *Broken Vessels* is affirmative. I'll always miss my legs, but I'm not depressed. I've got a bunch of children.

Image: People are always asking writers how women's roles have changed. It seems to me though that our entire culture has gone through some enormous changes. You've been a husband, father, and grandfather; a teacher and a Marine. Can you talk about how men's roles have changed in the past thirty years or so? Are things better or worse for, say, your sons, Andre and Jeb?

AD: I'm not sure. I have a lot of ideas about that question. Let's see. I don't like the way men have become. That's not about myself. That's age. No; it's just the old breed talking about the new breed. Erotic love used to be the fulcrum which matured us. And that's ancient. After the sexual revolution, boys of any age could experience erotic love and be free; free to be more frightened, to be less responsible, more narcissistic, to accumulate more toys for themselves because they weren't being breadwinners, and, in the worst case I can think of, to be single, promiscuous, selfish, and affluent, and then maybe in their forties find someone nubile and become a father. I don't think that that's a good force for our society. I'm not sure that men by nature want to nest and have children, although I wanted to. So I don't really know. But I don't see women getting any happier. And I see men getting more vain, and more involved with themselves.

Image: In interviews I've read previously, particularly in Thomas Kennedy's book on your short fiction, you speak of America in fairly pessimistic terms, as a rather greedy and selfish country. You said at one point that some "forced agape" might be good for America. Can you talk a little bit about that? Did you have any interest in the last election? Do you have any opinions about the direction of the country—you seem pessimistic in your outlook, or am I misinterpreting you?

AD: I'm pessimistic in my outlook, but I'm very much aware, especially while reading George Packer's *The Village of Waiting*, about his Peace Corps experience in Africa, that we have the freedom to be greedy and selfish and capitalistic and exploitative; that that is human nature. And it is because we are a democracy that we are able to exercise those freedoms. So I don't mean to criticize America as a system. I think it's a very materialistic country. I assume that much of the rest of the world is, too. I have very little faith in politicians. I would have faith in politicians, I think, if I did not see so many people out of homes, and see so much injustice. In general philosophical terms, I see abortion as I see any taking of a human life, as a homicide which is sometimes necessary, and sometimes justifiable, and sometimes good. The man I voted for was only a replacement for the man I voted against. That man executed a lobotomized black man in Arkansas. I would prefer to have a president, and his wife, who would say, at the risk of losing an election, "We all know that in this country if this lobotomized black man were a lobotomized white man with millions of dollars, he would never be executed, so we're not going to execute him." So I think of Clinton as the Dr. Death I helped vote in, who can sleep well, if we up the abortion rate to three million a year, and the capital punishment rate to whatever. But that's hopelessness either earned or just accumulated from the sixties when a lot of us thought that there were some idealistic people—I'm thinking specifically of Bobby Kennedy—who really meant to attack the problem of poverty and to do something about it. Robert Drinan, our ex-Congressman, a Jesuit, wrote in the *National Catholic Reporter* that he wanted Clinton in his inauguration address to speak about world hunger. Drinan said that we can produce on this planet three thousand calories for every human being on the earth, and that the earth has been waiting for a planetary leader, and that within four years we could be getting rid of world hunger. But I don't think the poor and the hungry are on anybody's agenda. Not on the agenda of the people with any power. Every time after I vote, I think, "Why did I vote?" I think I voted in the hope of health care and maybe some help for the poor. I think that it's a difficult culture to grow up in, but I suspect that all cultures are difficult to grow up in. But it is so hard, physically and spiritually, to grow up here. I love this crazy country. I think most people in it don't want people to be executed, and don't want people starving.

An Interview with Andre Dubus

John Smolens / 1994

AWP Chronicle 29.1 (September 1996): 1–6. Reprinted in *Leap of the Heart: Andre Dubus Talking*. Ed. Ross Gresham. New Orleans: Xavier Review Press, 2003. 244–54. Reprinted with the permission of the author.

I first met Andre Dubus in 1970, while he was teaching literature at Bradford College, which is north of Boston in the Merrimack Valley. At the time, Dubus had recently published a novel, *The Lieutenant*, and was working on the stories that would eventually become his first collection, *Separate Flights*.

For years the stories, novellas, and collections kept coming and Dubus's reputation grew; as the *Village Voice* said, "Like some of the most satisfying storytellers of the past (the Russians come to mind—Dubus has been compared to Chekhov), he is munificent, spinning out whole lifetimes . . ."

In July of 1986 Dubus was involved in a car accident that has resulted in numerous operations and the loss of one leg. Since then he has published his *Selected Stories*; a book of essays, *Broken Vessels*; and most recently a collection of stories, *Dancing After Hours*. In 1996, he received the Rae Award for lifetime contributions to the short story. He has received many other awards including the PEN/Malamud Award, and fellowships from both the Guggenheim and MacArthur foundations.

In July of 1994 I visited with Dubus at his home in Haverhill, Massachusetts, and, as in the past, we talked into the night while eating steamers and watching a Red Sox game.

John Smolens: You've recently signed a contract with Knopf for two books, a collection of stories and a collection of essays. Do you find writing essays different from writing short stories?

Andre Dubus: At best they feel nearly the same. But for me, the essay has a unique problem. When I'm writing fiction, I never really know what's going to happen in the story, spiritually or psychologically. And that's what keeps me going, keeps me excited—whereas with the essay, I sometimes have to force myself through the boredom because I know the action; there, the challenge isn't so much discovering the action but setting the action down right so I can discover what truths might be in there.

Smolens: My undergraduate students read *Broken Vessels* last spring and were really taken with the way the essays moved from pre-accident to post-accident. It was a pleasure to see that they didn't respond to *Broken Vessels* as a "book of essays," but as an account of someone's life.

Dubus: Some of them go back a long way—I hadn't read them since I went over the galleys for old issues of *Boston Magazine*. I was supposed to give them an essay a month, so I wrote some of those early ones pretty quickly—a lot more flippantly than I do with essays now.

Smolens: "Out Like a Lamb" touches a religious nerve that is evident in much of your work. Early in the essay you talk about growing up with the image of humans being a sweet, lovable flock of sheep in the arms of a tender, caring Christ. But as a result of caring for sheep on a farm in New Hampshire, you concluded, "We were stupid helpless brutes, and without constant watching we would foolishly destroy ourselves."

Dubus: Well, I didn't understand that essay until I read Toby Wolff's introduction to the book. I took my daughter Nicole to a horseback-riding lesson when she was a teenager. I had set aside the third or fourth Sunday of each month to write those columns—I was often thinking, I don't have any idea what to write about! And one Sunday on the way back she said, "Write about those sheep."

Smolens: There's one passage in that essay where, out of anger and frustration, you and the rest of the family are tackling the sheep as they try to escape and throwing them back into their pen. It's a moment of embarrassment, pain, and humor. And then a few pages later there's the grief of finding one of the sheep dying.

Dubus: *And* the fear of the owner finding out why it died! An artist friend of mine asked, "Why didn't you take the dead sheep to the butcher and eat it?" And I thought, God, I never even thought of that as a solution!

Smolens: You're presently working on stories for the first book in your contract?

Dubus; I think the contract with Knopf was intended to bail me out, to get me on their list. And my agent told them that I would have to get my confidence back to write a book of stories; I didn't want to be signed up just to do that. I actually submitted a proposal, something I've never done before; I opened my notebook of ideas and simply put them all in a letter. I had thirty-three ideas for essays.

Smolens: I remember years ago we'd be in a movie theater, or a restaurant—
Dubus: Or a bar.

Smolens: And you'd open your notebook and start scribbling. For the theaters you had one of those little pen lights—
Dubus: Which I think ceased to work when I spilled some beer on it.

Smolens: It should be noted that as we are speaking, he is taking his notebook and pen out of the leather bag that he always keeps with his wheelchair.
Dubus: So I do a lot of notebook preparation before writing an essay—though it's not as cool as that sounds. The notes have been coming. This Friday will be the seventh anniversary of my accident—see, I had a notebook full of ideas for stories, enough to keep me occupied for the rest of my natural life. But none of those stories mean anything to me anymore. So I had to start all over. There were the notes and I knew what the notes meant, but I had to start all over.

Nicole finally explained that to me. She said, "Your life has changed so much that I don't see how you can imagine a fictional world. You've had all these losses. Keep writing about people in wheelchairs, then gradually there'll be people in wheelchairs in stories, and then people out of wheelchairs in stories." But I don't really have the words to express what happened. I just know that some enormous shock happened, and after that those stories in the notebook made sense to me, but they didn't seem to be mine anymore. They could have been anyone's. You know, the notebook's in my room somewhere—but it doesn't matter. I had stories in that notebook that were meant to be sequels to stories I had already written. Those characters don't mean anything to me anymore either. Very strange; it's like a little death.

To tell you the truth from my heart, it depressed me for years. But lately it's become a little bit exciting that everything now is within the last seven years—all my ideas.

Smolens: Such as "The Colonel's Wife"?

Dubus: I'm up to about one story a year now, and two to three essays. "The Colonel's Wife" is a story I started in the summer of '89, and at first the retired colonel, Robert Townsend, was a biped. The original idea for the story I got out of the *Boston Globe*, where I get a lot of stories. They ran a piece about private detective agencies in Los Angeles, where people were having private eyes check their lovers' past sex lives—because they were worried about AIDS. The news story got into anecdotes about marriage and people's sex lives, and never really got back to the issue of AIDS. But it made me think, well, if you had to hire a private eye to check up on your mate, was there a marriage left there anyway, no matter what the private eye told you?

That's how that story started, but I could not make it move. So some five months after Nicole had that conversation with me, I thought: I'll break this fucker's legs. So I had those characters, and I had written part of the story—and I also got a story called "The Lover" that was in *Ploughshares* out of that; it was a section about a character who was going to be the boyfriend of the wife. This is how things worked for me when I was in my forties—I'd start something, move away from it toward something else, all in the same draft, then get back to my original intent.

But before I got hurt I had really hit a nice peak. Most stories I started and finished in one longhand draft, working very slowly.

Smolens: Over twenty years ago when we first met, you were writing the stories that eventually appeared in your first collection, *Separate Flights*, and you were always talking about drafts, the importance of building a rough draft, typing that up, then writing another draft—again in longhand—and building through the drafts toward the completed story. So years later it amazed me when you started to say that a certain story was done in one draft. Somehow you had managed to eliminate the preliminary work and apply the oil directly to the canvas.

Dubus: From 1980 to 1986 I was working that way. Then, with the accident, I had to start over. Now I'm starting and stopping work on a story, and a lot of the time it looks to me like a failure, but I have to remind myself that this is exactly what I was doing in my thirties. It took me a good while to remember that. You know, after I got hurt I wanted everything to be the way it was two minutes before I got hit.

Smolens: One of the marvelous things about reading your stories is that they are so connected. Characters keep reappearing, and one story lends a shading to another. They all tend to know each other, or know about each other—as only husbands, wives, lovers, ex-lovers, and the parish priest can. They often share the same place, the Merrimack Valley, and we know them better as a result. There's a kind of accretion in your fiction. You're always looking to the sides: If this character's married to so-and-so, what's going on over here?

Dubus: That's how I feel about the story I'm presently working on—looking out at the sides. The thing about recurring characters, though, happened less by intention, but the character wouldn't go away. They keep coming back to say, "Look what I'm doing now!"

My Catholicism—whatever that is—is always there, whether it's evident or not. I make a decision whether I want a particular character to be looking at things the same way I do. Since the accident I've written six stories, but only one of those stories has a character that has a religion. She's a Catholic, named LuAnn Arceneaux, of French-Canadian descent. I've recently finished a second story about her.

Smolens: It seemed that early reviews of your work didn't note the religious connotations, and that it wasn't until a number of collections were published that the response was, "Here's a religious fiction writer."

Dubus: Yes, it took them a long time. They seemed to focus on the blue-collar aspect of this place, the Merrimack Valley. On the other hand, when I was a very young writer I avoided religion in my writing, even though it meant a great deal to me. Religion has always been a very intimate thing for me. Maybe that's why for a long time I was very interested in agnostics.

I've had interesting reactions from, you know—people! Ha! Not reviewers—*people*! After one reading I gave at a small college, the faculty wanted to talk about "A Father's Story"; some of them were angry at me. They said, "Luke Ripley ruined his daughter's life; he shouldn't have done it." I said, "I don't think he should have done it either." And they said, "You mean these aren't your opinions?" And I said, "No." Of course, a month later I realized what I should have said—because one woman said, "A little ironic distance would have helped," and I said, "I don't like 'em, and I don't write stories like that." What I should have said is: "You wouldn't ask Robert Duval to establish ironic distance. So why would you ask that of a writer?" So then another teacher asked, "If this isn't what you believe, then what's the point from Homer on?" Well, as the discussion went on, the teacher seemed to realize that writers write to experience something, and to see what truth might come out of it.

I would never do such a thing as cover up for a hit-and-run accident for one of my daughters, and none of them would ever ask me to do that. So I never said that what Luke Ripley did is good. But it's important to experience it—I think the character's good, but he's wrong.

Smolens: Is it possible that there's a change, not in fiction, but in the way fiction is perceived?
Dubus: You mean *imaginative* writing!

Smolens: There seems to be an impatience on the part of some readers.
Dubus: They're sometimes unwilling to grant the writer a certain freedom. I think they are poor readers. I mean, when I read I like to forget my name. I like to experience being another person—I get to love the character, if the writer is good. I learn something, and then I put the book down and I'm me again.

I think there are some people who have strong opinions, and they get offended by what a writer says. They seem dictatorial to me. Sean O'Faolain wrote an introduction to a big anthology of short stories, and in essence, he said, "If you don't like a story, consider it your fault. And read it again." Then he went on to explain eloquently why it may be your fault. For instance, you may be in moral shock: these characters may do something you never considered doing.

A while back I read about the actress Debra Winger in a profile Tom Robbins did for *Esquire*. He put it better than this, but the essential question he asked her was, "You're not really beautiful, so why are you so beautiful on the screen?" A hard question, which he stated politely. And her answer was, "The camera picks up the heart. To go before the camera you must open your heart, and get rid of all prejudices, all preconceptions, and be absolutely open. If you had twin sisters appear before the camera—where one did this and the other didn't—the camera would see it immediately." In effect, that was her response. To me, that's what writing is about, and that's what pure reading is about.

Smolens: We've previously discussed that a central problem in writers' workshops can be criticism that merely tells the writer how to rewrite the story, and that some writers bring a piece to the workshop and request just that: they want their fiction written by committee, so to speak.

Dubus: In my workshops we've discussed this, and there have been times when I've learned that I was not the only one who found it difficult to go back to my own work—that's how important this problem can be.

In my workshop we started to have difficulties; I had this explosion, then we took the summer off. Then Chris Tilghman came to the house to discuss how we should be when we came back together. If you go into a room with eight or nine very good professional writers and ask them to read your work, you're going to get eight or nine very good ideas, all of which would work. But it wouldn't be your story; it might be a story you could write, but it might not be the story you *should* be writing.

What we worked out for the new workshop—there were a number of new members who joined at that point—was that a writer reading should say, "I just want to hear about this. I'm concerned about the grandmother's character." Or the writer can say, "Go full bore and tell me whatever you want."

Some people enjoy a good debate, of course, but I started wondering: what is the reason for two writers arguing about a third writer's work in the third writer's presence? Too often they were arguing for their own ideas. It was exhilarating, but I'm not sure it's always a good idea.

Smolens: Do you find that at times discussion of writing becomes discussion of politics?

Dubus: Yes—the way the word *politics* is being used now. As far as gender goes, I try to keep the balance equal. There are more women than men in the workshop right now. I like to hear what a woman has to say, especially when I'm writing about a woman. Sometimes a man or a woman replies, "That's a lousy portrayal of my gender," but it hasn't been what I would call a problem in my workshop. Or a woman might say, "A woman wouldn't do that," about a character—that's not political.

Smolens: What about the argument that you can't write about something that you aren't, whether it's a matter of gender, race, ethnicity, or whatever?

Dubus: Whether you sit in a wheelchair, even. That's not true. I wonder if this notion is accepted by many writers.

Shortly after my accident, I was contacted by someone who wanted to include one of my stories in an anthology of fiction that would include stories about men written by women and stories about women written by men. I wrote back and said, "I don't want to be in it. You're celebrating what should be normal." Nadine Gordimer said, "All writers are androgynous." I've never read a published story by a woman about a man that didn't seem right to me.

That John Sayles movie *Passion Fish*, which was about a paraplegic woman, pissed me off—but that was a movie. It kind of left the body out. Everybody loved this movie, so I went to see it and I was furious. This soap actress in New York gets injured. No more soap acting. She goes home to the family house in a wheelchair, and the house is not wheelchair-accessible. She's paralyzed from the waist down. They showed some struggling scenes, they showed some anger, and in came the black, hard-charging nurse who was going to save her—but the film never showed many of the physical problems of being a paraplegic. I remember one scene in Louisiana, they're on a wharf and there's this little skiff, and she tells the nurse, "Get me in the boat." Now these are things I live with all the time. Next scene, she's in the boat, and I said, "How the fuck did she lower this woman from the chair into the boat in the water?" Show me that and you've got some story. And then he threw in a drinking problem, and that made me angry. Here you have a thirty-nine-year-old woman who's suddenly lost sensation in her sexual organs, her ability to walk—you don't need a drinking problem to make this a dramatic story. And the actress never achieved the depth the guys did in *Waterdance*, which was a great wheelchair movie. Which just happened to be written by a guy in a chair. I think if I had worked at it I could have written about somebody in a chair before I got in a chair, but I'd have to talk to the sucker, follow him around.

Smolens: You recently had a memoir in *Harper's* entitled—

Dubus: They changed the title. My title was "Imperiled Men" and they changed it to something like "The Quiet Siege" because "Imperiled Men" didn't fit the heading on the page somehow. I was happy to be in *Harper's* and I didn't fight for the title, though I had to fight for some other stuff in that memoir.

It was about when I was a Marine stationed on the aircraft carrier *Ranger*, and the commander of the air group—well, the essence of the piece was that there have been homosexuals in the military, as in other walks of life, and they have performed their duties well. I suppose if I wanted to I could write about every homosexual that was on the *Ranger*—and tell Mr. Aspin I'm going to make a career of it! I wrote that memoir when this debate came up shortly after Clinton took office because I felt it was time for an old soldier to tell his story. But when I got into the essay I realized there wasn't one line of opinion in it—what really excited me was writing about being twenty-five and being aboard a ship again. I was just trying to recreate that time. I didn't give my opinion, though toward the end I did make it clear that after this officer had committed suicide—because he knew the military authorities were about to question him about his sex life—that the consensus among his men was that they would have followed his command anywhere, any time. Even to Moscow in planes without enough fuel for the return trip. He was a good soldier. I do feel it's unjust to keep someone out of the service because of what he or she does in bed with someone who's consenting.

Smolens: The first of the two books for Knopf will be the collection of stories?

Dubus: I have six stories thus far. I'm including "The Intruder," my first published story (*Sewanee Review*), a story I wrote when I was twenty-five, and which was published while I was still a Marine. I included it because Dick Yates, through the years, told me now and then I should put it in a collection—he read it at Iowa City. I always told him I had outgrown it. Dick died in November 1991. 1 began thinking about my story and about Dick, and I pulled out the story and read it. It was like looking at a picture of yourself when you were twenty-five. I didn't *know*, but I didn't dislike it. So I sent it to Gary Fisketjon at Knopf, told him about Dick, and let him decide. So far, no one has disliked that it's a younger story. Gary wanted the book of stories first, but he doesn't care how long it takes. I think his not holding me to a deadline is good for me. Having to concentrate on fiction, avoiding essays, may have opened a door for me. The title story was the hardest to write: I had never handled six people in a room, all at the same time, in one evening—*not* in a story, anyway.

Smolens: One of the most effective stories I've ever had my students read is "The Fat Girl." We usually end with this discussion about the last scene, where Louise is upstairs with the baby, and Richard is downstairs; she gets one of her candy bars and goes downstairs with the baby, and she's surprised that he's still there. I ask my students to write about what they think will happen to these two people after the story is finished.

Dubus: I don't think they'll stay together. I think of her owning the house, the car, et cetera, and he moves on. And she remains very large—he never really did know her, and he can't love her. Because he's a shitty person!

That was a hard story to write. That story stopped on me after about ten pages, and I picked it up a year, maybe more, later. I don't know about other writers, but when a story stops on me I can't force it. Then one day I was walking down South Main Street in Bradford, passed the church, and something inside me said, "Get her married." And I finished it in two days.

It's a matter of patience and discipline. I do believe you have to go to the desk every day. But you have to understand how much waiting is involved. You can't always expect forward movement, but sometimes just sitting there reading and working on a sentence will cause something to happen down the line. But the writer has to remember it's very ungoverned. It's mysterious, and elusive, and you've got to be real patient. Patience includes discipline.

In other words, to get an idea for a story and then to write a bad story doesn't mean that the idea was bad. It may mean that sometime, say two years from now, you're walking down the street and you may hear a voice that says, "That story about Willy is really about his brother." You know, if a carpenter worked like this, he'd have maybe six unfinished, abandoned houses to get one that's finished—but he'd never get any work! I don't know of any other work that's like what we do as writers, as artists. One of the hardest things for me has always been to cheer myself up when things go terribly, so I have to remind myself, "That doesn't mean this was bad." Or it may mean that it's just taking me someplace. It takes some kind of faith.

Interview with Andre Dubus

Tom Grimes / 1997

From *excerpt*. http://www.english.swt.edu/excerpt1.dir/dubus1.htm. Reprinted with the permission of the author. Tom Grimes is the author of *Mentor: A Memoir*, which traces his long friendship with Frank Conroy and his own life as a young writer. He is also the author of five novels and directs the MFA Program at Texas State University.

Andre Dubus lives in Haverhill, Massachusetts, and is the author of nine books of fiction, as well as *Broken Vessels*, a collection of essays. He has received the PEN/Malamud Award, the Jean Stein Award from the American Academy of Arts and Letters, the Boston Globe's first annual Laurence L. Winship Award, and fellowships from both the Guggenheim and MacArthur Foundations.

Mr. Dubus jumped directly into his thoughts on writing fiction and gave them to us at length. He later took questions from the young writers who had gathered to hear him speak. But, we feel the way to enjoy the interview is to read it as Mr. Dubus's stream-of-consciousness riff on the writing life.

AD: I know as well as every laboring writer how hard [writing] is. I've been writing for forty years now, thank God, and I'm lucky I'm still around. I mean I was hit by a moving car on the highway—I was standing up, the last time I ever did that without assistance, but I'm probably one of the few people alive who've been hit by a car on the highway (laughs) and I still am not happy unless I write.

I have a friend, two friends, the woman is a writer and her husband is a math teacher. He was over watching a ball game.

I said: "How is she doing?"

He said: "Well. . . ."

I said: "Is she sending her stuff out?" (Because that's what she won't do.)

He said: "I guess writers have a self-esteem problem."

I said: "Well we get a lot of support for that lack of self-esteem because sometimes it takes years to publish a story—one of mine took seven years, it was in a brown envelope for seven years—there's always somebody ready to tell you you're no good."

He says: "Well (this woman has published a book), I guess a writer doesn't feel any better than his last book."

I said: "Skipper, I don't feel any better than what I wrote today."

And his eyes opened and my eyes opened—two epiphanies—and I got a look at that light and thought this guy actually does not hate himself at night for what he did today. He does not worry about getting through the night and getting back to the desk and getting something done tomorrow. I'm not happy if I don't write, but I'm always afraid to go to the desk. It's very simple because you're not sure you can do it.

A friend of mine, Chris Tilghman, has a wonderful book of stories, *In a Father's Place*, is working on a novel now, and he came by to visit and I asked, "What's it like?" He said working on a novel is different; writing stories is more painful. He said when my novel's not going well, I figure if I stay with this for five weeks or a few months things will get better. With a story, everyday you know you may just shatter it and never get it back. And he said maybe that's why Wallace Stegner said the short story's the young writer's form.

Teaching and writing are very similar in that [aspect]. I taught five days a week, and told my friends if you get three good days out of five that's a great week, 'cause you'll always fail teaching. There's a wonderful book, which still may be in print, called *Robert Penn Warren Talking*, it's his interviews. Keep it on your bedside table and read it—you'll feel good about whatever ails you. This is a man who was blocked and couldn't write a poem for ten years! We say, "That's no problem. He's famous. He's got a lot of awards and novels." That's bullshit. This is his life—the man who said, "I am a poet. If I'm writing fiction and get an idea for a poem, I stop the fiction and write the poem. Him not writing a poem for ten years was not like saying a shortstop had trouble going to his left for one season. That wasn't it at all. In two separate interviews he said different things: in one he said he and his wife had a child, a daughter, and he thinks that broke it. Ten years! Another interview he said he stopped writing stories the same time he got out of his block. He realized he was using some poem ideas in his stories. What he said in this other interview was "You have to write everyday, with your pencil or typewriter, or sit under your tree," which he did a lot of. He wrote a lot of

All The King's Men sitting under trees in Italy. [Robert Penn Warren] said you have to know that most days will be bad ones; he didn't say some, he said most days will be bad and you have to accept the awful responsibility of wasting time. I've also learned over these decades that most of the wasted time turns out to be something else sometime later, so I never throw away that stuff I hate. It may gather dust. I got a six-page story out of a novella I spent a year on—I got two stories out of that, but the rest is gone. So I know about that difficulty, and any writer who tells the truth says [this is true]. To a non-writer it'll probably sound like complaining; [writing] looks like a pretty cushy thing except there's no money in it.

I met a lawyer in Massachusetts at a party back in the seventies. He says, "What do you do?" and I tell him. He says, "What's the hardest thing?" Actually, this was 1980—I said, "I just realized this year it's concentration." I don't mean forgetting about the bills, or what's going on in the family, or where I'm going tonight, I don't mean that part. I mean actually concentrating so completely that I really get into the word. And we started talking about pitchers, and how you'd say about a pitcher who'd lost his concentration in the eighth inning with a three nothing lead in front of eight thousand people, where'd it go? And he said, "I'm a Zen Archer," which is a very good book for writers to read, *Zen and the Art of Archery*. He said, "My concentration's off lately. You know, in this country they forgive you losing concentration if you're pitching, or writing, or trying a case, or shooting bow and arrow, but there's one place they won't forgive you for losing concentration—that's in bed—they always say, "Don't you love me?"

Well, the truth of that is anybody who's been around a few ripe years knows you lose concentration in bed, too, and you come up with anything to keep yourself with that person. Concentration's a very elusive thing. I think when writers achieve concentration we do like the Zen person, or even these people who do Transcendental Meditation and get their teeth drilled and not feel anything. We get to this region where we don't live, and in that region we find truths we cannot live by. If I could live by lines that I have written and truths that I have discovered, I would not be thrice divorced—I may be in a wheelchair but I would have no troubles with any of my six children—we would have achieved absolute harmony, and I'd probably have some money in the bank. I think that concentration, and the little vision of that light, which I'm certain exists somewhere in the world that we don't perceive, is the main reason to keep writing. At your level of experience you're thinking in terms of the crust of the earth, and that's normal. You're in ambitious times, you think well, I'm going to begin with a call from that city on the eastern coast—that terrible city where the pinstriped ball players are, and Steinbrenner, and the publishing world, that cutthroat thing. You figure achievement is my name on the spine of a book, and if you really let yourself go, you get in the swampland and you'll think: and hundreds of thousands of people carrying that book home, and maybe even talk TV. I've never had any of those things, but I'm old enough to know they're not the reason to keep writing. I was complaining to a young writer, who has published a number of books, about the *New Yorker*, one of my favorite complaints which has nothing to do with the real truths of the world, it's an esoteric complaint. I've been published in it so I can put down the *New Yorker*, but they do try to tell you how to write your stories. We were talking about an acquaintance who had changed a story to be in the *New Yorker*, and I was appalled, and I'm not ashamed that I was appalled because I was more appalled than I am about Somalia and Haiti, it's a personal thing and that's not a very good quality of mine. I said, "What's the *New Yorker* doing? Why don't they exercise their freedom to reject? Why do they say, 'We'll take the story, if you change it'?" Would you take Mo Vaughn, a two-hundred-pound first baseman and say, "Our ball club likes first basemen that weigh one hundred seventy-five pounds and steal bases? And have him go on a diet and change his body? Would the ball player do it? And my young friend said, "Maybe if it meant two more years of triple A he might. I thought about that for a week and, when I saw him, I said, "You know, what you said is really wrong. There is no major leagues in writing. Major leagues in writing is at the desk with your pen or your computer—whatever you write with. That is the Major Leagues. The rest is something else. Think about baseball, think about movie stars, but don't apply that to practicing art. It happens at the desk. If we can sustain what happens at the desk we don't blow our heads off, and we don't get screwed up, we lead some kind of halfway contented lives. It's a deep and spiritual thing which has to be supported by the craft of all architects and sculptors. Conrad said in his great preface to *The Nigger of the Narcissus*, which you all should have memorized by now, or read enough times to feel like you have, "Prose has to have the plasticity of sculpture, and the colors of painting." He calls music the "Art of Arts." He doesn't explain it. I'm going to assume he meant because a human being can thereby put her and his emotions into sound, like the bird does, and you can hear this sound and you know what the person felt. And Conrad said, "Art is the communication between one temperament and the myriad temperaments and has to be done through the senses because the temperaments are not admittable to persuasion." That's why in workshop we say show don't tell. If you call up your aunt in Portland, Maine, and say, "I've had a terrible week," she'll say, "I'm sorry honey," and she'll be watching the TV and talking to you. But, if you're mainly abstract, if you start telling her, "The pain begins in my breast, it moves through my back and it burns. I haven't seen Harry in four days—I think he's at the trailer with a co-ed and some tequila. Little Liza has the flu and I really need somebody to make me some soup." She might turn off the TV, and that's what Conrad was saying. So you have to combine that concentration of getting what is really inside of you, willy nilly in some mysterious way—thoughts that you don't know you know, words that you don't use ordinarily and then—out comes that word from god-knows-where. If you do that and you are also trying to make it visible, audible, tasteable, and smellable, you've got enough challenge and what you have to do is not worry about whether there's a spine of a book in your immediate future, and not worry about people who don't understand what you're doing, and not worry about your family who loves you but thinks that you should be doing something that will make you some money.

I had to get older before I learned that almost every writer, including myself, had to tell their parents, "Well, yeah that's what I do want to do" and I always thought it meant I was smarter than they were and they were dumb. I got older and had children and realized that wasn't it at all; it was because they love you.

You can't expect anybody to feel the fire you were born with, and you can't expect anybody to understand that fire, and there are two things you can do: you can burn in it or you can run from it. I suspect most writers run from it because there are so many MFA programs and I don't think everybody who goes to an MFA program continues to write. I think in your early stages it is real easy to quit. I have taught students who have talent that I was never born with, and they never wrote a word after they got out of school. This is a good country to get lost in. If you get an education, get a job, and buy yourself enough toys, you can forget about it till three in the morning when you wake up.

There's a lot of commitment to writing. I wish I could bring more commitment to my life, but I can't because it is very draining to do that. I'm going to read a brand new story tonight, which I don't feel confident about but I'm going to read it, and there is a scene in there in which some physical action occurs, and I was writing that all during the month of August and I was writing it over and over and over again, not liking the way the scene was going. It was driving me nuts but what I was fighting most was the time between being at the desk. I learned when I was eighteen or nineteen, writing a research paper on Hemingway, the greatest advice anybody ever gave a writer and the only other writer I heard mention it was Márquez in an essay: Stop in mid-sentence in mid-scene when it is going well. Do some physical exercise, and forget it. Let the subconscious work on it and start again the next day by reading through from the beginning. I've used that method since I was a teenager. Take a pen. Start from the first word and read and read and read and get to that middle scene, middle sentence, and there you go. The only times I skipped doing that, I think twice in my life, I spent the morning staring at the page saying, "What's supposed to happen next?" Well how do I know? I was somebody else yesterday and since then I did other things—I was a teacher, father, husband, drunk, I lived twelve lives like everybody else and I get back the next morning and "WHAT IS THIS?" There's a lot of difference between leaving to go teach at 11:30 in the morning, high and feeling like you are in touch with God and the next morning drinking coffee, grateful to be alive and looking and saying, "What is this stuff?" So that was great advice.

I was saying to my son, Andre Dubus III, my impulse about this story is that I'm losing confidence, I'm afraid I'm going to blow it. I'm also excited and pumped to sit down and grind it out, and I know if I do I'll somehow lose it. I'll ruin it, miss the road, miss the path, nuance, shadow—miss something. I'm going crazy trying to keep from thinking about it or making sure it doesn't think about me. And I said—you know this is not true—one can make a case that my entire adult life, marriage and teaching has been something to keep me occupied between sittings at the desk. Now that's not true, but you could make a bizarre story out of that. Because the other side has caused more pain, pleasure, and joy than writing. Andre III said the truth is for years he thought we (the family) just existed between sessions!

That's hard to deal with. James Dickey once said the reason the writer drinks is to shut out the brain because it's a monster and it won't stop. I gotta take pills to sleep. That sucker just goes and goes—it's gone, like six little children—what are you gonna do? Channel it, concentrate it, and put your hand through somebody else's body.

I think you should be sending out stories at all times. I started at eighteen, and I knew they wouldn't be published but I knew I had to go through a period of rejections, so I said, "Why not start it now?" I figured it took Hemingway eight years, so I would be published by the time I was twenty-six and that's exactly what happened. I was sending to the *New Yorker*, *Collier's*, *Esquire*, the *Atlantic*, *Mademoiselle*, *Harper's*, etc. They'd come back, but it worked! I knew my stories weren't ready but it worked. By the time I got out of college I had become immune. I can say in all honesty that I have never been hurt or pissed off by a rejection slip since I got out of college. A book manuscript is something else, but a story, never. I just adopted an attitude which has nothing to do with honesty or reality: "The stupid sons of bitches." That's the point I've reached. This was a professional thing, like Wade Boggs, who checked in every day to the club house at the same time and did the same thing everyday, and I know watching him at bat that when that ball was coming he did not know his name—just him and that white thing, whoever he was at that time.

The *Atlantic Monthly*, when I was a senior in college at McNeese State, had a flier which said, "Subscribe to the *Atlantic*," and I had just finished a story so I clipped the slip to the bottom and wrote "You buy from me I buy from you." Ten days later, it was back. I've still never been in the *Atlantic* and I've never subscribed. On top of that, I needed an unreal attitude and it has served me very, very well. I think developing that attitude early has given me the brass to tell an editor: "It's more important to me to have my story the way I want it than the way you want it. Let me have it back." After your story leaves the desk, you enter another world where there are people who say they love your work and say they love you, but they'll never love your work as much as you do. You are the custodian of those two things: you and your work. When you reach that plateau, which you will if you continue to work, then you will deal with that part and you'll have to be a lawyer, which is not what you want to be. I haven't had a lot of this stuff happen—I took one back from the *New Yorker* and had this discussion with some others, but there are people who have given up themselves in order to publish, probably not so much for money but because we need it so much inside ourselves, that affirmation that this is good. And you know some of these people.

Q: What do you think about the criticisms of MFA programs which say they produce writing that is all the same?
AD: I think it's stupid. I've visited a lot of MFA programs and have seen none of this. You could make a case that MFA programs exist to give writers jobs, but you can also say science programs exist to give scientists jobs. That's all bullshit. MFA programs exist, I believe, because in any town you go into, you're going to find some genuine writers. I know writers who make a living teaching workshop in their homes—they just advertise. There they are. I think MFA programs are great. Paul Engle of Iowa used to tell us, "I had to fight so hard to get this going. To tell them my writers don't have to read *Moby-Dick*. They may read *Moby-Dick* in their fifties. Maybe they nev-

er will." When I was at Iowa it was a sixty-credit degree, fifty-seven of that in writing. Three in an allied art and I got that waived. Sounds like a gig? No. We were writing stories and novels and having conferences with some very generous teachers. I only realized how generous when I got out and started teaching and said, "My god, how do they put up with this?"

Q: I was reading the back of one of your books which compares you to Ray Carver.
AD: I don't understand that and I respect Carver, but don't see that comparison.

Q: What do you make of the whole concept of minimalism?
AD: I don't think I've ever read a minimalist. I have heard Tobias Wolff, who was a good friend of Carver's, say he did not like minimalism, he was not one, Carver was not one. Wolff said he liked Ann Beattie and he talked about minimalism but I still don't know what it is. But see, I learned long ago, because I was an English major, to get rid of romanticism, realism, and naturalism. I won't talk about any of those things. I don't think they ever existed. I don't think anyone ever writing thought, "I'm doing this." I was talking to a dean we had at school and I said, "I've been reading Zola," and the dean says, "You like that naturalism stuff, don't you?" and I said, "I don't see any difference in Zola and any other writing I like. All I'm seeing is people." I could be wrong and if I am I want to continue to be wrong in this way. I don't want to be called anything but a writer. I don't want to be introduced to anybody by saying, "You'll really like this baroque writer."

What is minimalism anyway? I visited a university to the east of here in the south and smelled a rat. All the stories were very short, with a lot of space breaks, and ended suddenly. The host wasn't there and I heard it was his mode not to attend a visiting writer's workshop because the teacher thought visiting writers were intimidated by him. He wanted to give them freedom to express themselves. Everybody wrote alike. That night I was drinking with a fellow from Jersey who said, "You're bringing an aerosol can of fresh air here." I said, "Is there some kind of thing about the *New Yorker* at this school?" He said, "That's the goal. The goal of this school is by the time you graduate to have a *New Yorker* story." If that was minimalism, maybe it was NewYorkerism. They didn't go deep, they didn't go far and they could have, and that was the sadness.

I don't believe in deadlines and I always told undergraduate students you don't have to finish a story to get an A in this class. I told them you'll be writing a story-in-progress. What I want to see is your work. I did have a woman work on the same story all year and then she rushed the ending and she blew it. I dearly believe if you assign deadlines you don't really respect stories because no story will obey deadlines. And, if you try to force it on them, you may as well pick up something else to do for a living. Deadlines are for the artificial world of rules which we have to obey to get out of school and go be free. You can't create on a deadline—women do, it takes nine months—and that's nature! But that's not a deadline. That's just following the flow.

Q: Do you have any techniques for figuring out what a story is about when you are writing it?

AD: I do. I started this in 1980 and since I got run over in '86 I've been trying to get it back. It's not been easy. Until '80, and I started writing in 1954, I wrote what I call horizontally; I tried to get five hundred words a day—you don't think that came out of the world of deadlines, do you? That meant I usually wrote five or six drafts for a story and the first draft usually told me what it was about, or the second or third. In 1980 I was working on a story called "Anna" and I was so lost and confused, I'd never written about anybody who'd held up a drugstore, never written about this particular kind of young woman, and I decided I'm not going to leave a sentence until I knew, physically, what it feels like to be "Anna." That changed everything for me. Oliver Sachs, after the filming of *Awakenings*, said Robert DeNiro doesn't know something unless he knows it with his body. That has always been true for me, I guess, but since '80 I've really focused on it. So in that story there were too many details, but I didn't leave until I knew what the glass felt like in her hand. I began to write what I call vertically. I'd actually go to the desk and hunch my shoulders and say, "Fifty words is fine, Andre, twenty is fine. Don't leave until you know what it is like to be her." It's a good thing I do that. Write one longhand draft, tape it, listen to it so you can spot things—internal rhymes you didn't want, words that sound wrong. The idea for the story came from the *Boston Globe*. A guy who had robbed a bank in Boston called his girlfriend in Florida and told her where he was. And she said to her other boyfriend, who was in the room, "Go call the police." They were still talking when the cruiser pulled up. I thought I'd write a story about betrayal, so I gestated for a long time and started the story. I wanted to be inside the woman who betrayed this robber. But that never happened. I realized they loved each other. This was a love story. So I followed them. What do you do after you rob a bank? You take some of the money and you get drunk in a bar. What do you do after the bar? Well you go home and go to sleep. What do you do after that? You wake up? Then what? Go to work, etc., etc. The way I try to find out is to go slowly and try to get into each word. I try to be so inside the character, I don't even know my name. Annie Dillard said in *The Writing Life*, if a story stops it's because the writer's not listening. You've got to listen. It weird isn't it? It's a wonderful thing, too.

Q: Is it hard to get inside a woman character?

AD: No, and I think anybody can write in anybody else's gender. If they want to. Nadine Gormier said in the introduction to her short-story collection, "All artists are androgynous." We've seen it in movies and on the stage with Linda Hunt and Dustin Hoffman. There are some physical things I can't do—you know, wouldn't touch childbirth. I have had a line about lactation because I asked a woman. That was a pretty easy sensation for her to say "This is what it feels like." But there are some things I can't touch.

I can't do that in my life—get inside the head of a woman. (laughs) One that I'm making up is easier.

Hemingway in *The Old Man and the Sea* certainly gets inside of that marlin. He gets inside of everybody in that story. There are times in that story—and I can't say how he does it—you can see old Santiago in the boat as though you are above him, and at the same time you are seeing through his eyes, you're feeling his back and his hand hurting, you're feeling the tug of the fish and at the same time you're seeing the fish underwater and the point of view of the fish looking up. It's amazing. Of course, he spent a lifetime living with that.

Paula Fox has a lot of wonderful novels. One of them, *The Widow's Children* is divided into sections "Hotel," "Hall," "Elevator," "Dinner." A widow and her boyfriend are going on a trip on a boat and the family is gathering and it's a mess. She is a wonderful unknown writer who's been confused in bookstores because she's also a prize-winning children's writer and sometimes her novels get put in there. This man who used to be my editor and her editor and I used to say, "After Flaubert, there's Paula Fox." Well, there is one scene where everybody is at the dinner table and I suddenly realized I knew where everybody was sitting, and I asked, "How does she do that? I've got to figure that out." She placed them physically by who spoke to whom. One asked for the butter, one for a light for her cigarette, one murmured something. And she conveyed this individually. That's the good thing MFA programs are for: to learn the architecture not only from your teachers, but I've always thought you can learn more from reading a story that's not perfect, that's not accomplished, than you can if you pick up *Dubliners* to learn the craft. If you pick up your buddy's story and you can say, "Oh, look here. I've got to avoid this. This doesn't work. This is something I do and I'm not going to do anymore." I think it is a good thing to share manuscripts, sharing flaws. It's a lot smoother than studying masters because we often don't know how the hell they did this.

Q: I like the idea of having a mentor to help me learn how to write and I'm curious how you found a person who became your first mentor.
AD: I was on the rifle range at the officers base in Quantico, Virginia, a brand new husband, a new lieutenant, and I was going back to get my targets and I heard a Midwestern voice say something about Aristotle. I said, "Are you an English major?" He was a writer named Mark Costello. We're still friends. We were about the same level, but very different, so he would see things about my work and could help me get into my stories. Even when I was thirty-two I would send a story to Mark before I sent it out.

But the real mentor was at Iowa. R. V. Cassill, who was a friend and a real mentor. He pushed and said to me once in a bar, "You know, you are very good at describing people and writing down what they say, look like, and do. But you don't have the killer instinct of most Catholic novelists—you don't go down deep and find out why they do it." I was pretty innocent and dumb. That was the first time I knew you were supposed to. He also taught me how to read. I had read many of the books on his reading list and when I met him and said, "I read a lot of these books" and he said, "What do you like about them?"

"Well, it's so sad and beautiful."

"Why?" he'd say.

That's how I used to read and write—sad and beautiful—and he taught me how to think. A lot of writers have had mentors. We think it's so romantic—all these guys in Paris. But I think the reason they were there because Paris was a good place to be and it was cheap. They were basically doing the same things you guys are.

Q: I really liked the quotation you used in *Broken Vessels* about memory and imagination and I could see how it worked for the essays. I was wondering, how do you use memory in your fiction?
AD: Usually fiction is about something I didn't see, and usually, if it happened, I write an essay. But certainly my life has to go into my fiction somehow, but I don't know the answer to your question, which maybe is the answer. I don't know, but I assume I use it somehow.

That quote is also about when memory is a possession. I'm starting to feel that memory doesn't have to be recorded faithfully in essays.

Q: So can you be more truthful in fiction?
AD: No. I really got shaken loose by Tim O'Brien's *The Things They Carried*, and I thought, there's no reason when writing essays to worry if Joe was really here and if that really happened. Just write it like fiction and try to get the truth of what was there—it doesn't really matter any more than in fiction. When I have written autobiographical fiction, specifically about my boyhood, then I can answer your question. I don't remember what really happened. That's why now, at my age, I distrust all stories about spouses. I don't care if he's my best friend and she seems to be a bitch from hell—I still don't believe it. Point of view is the whole key. You can write any story you've ever written, and any one you've ever read, from a completely different point of view and it's a whole other story.

Q: What story of yours do you feel most proud or do you feel is the most complete?
AD: None. What I get proud of is the work I've put into it. I can't look at the story and say, "Boy, that's the way I wanted it." But, I can look at it and say, "Boy, that one cost a lot," and be proud that I stayed with it.

Q: Do you always know when your stories are finished?
AD: No. I know when I've gone as far as I can and the next feeling is I wish I could have really finished it. I don't think anyone's ever done the work that she or he wanted to. So many people have said it, I feel the same. Faulkner and Penn Warren both said, and they weren't in the same room, that if a writer ever wrote the book he wanted to, he'd retire. Capote said something like that about Harper Lee. He said she had that one book to write and she wrote it. I would love to believe that and live happily ever after.

Interview

Jennifer Levasseur and Kevin Rabalais / 1998

Glimmer Train Stories 31 (Summer 1999): 39–59. Reprinted in *Leap of the Heart: Andre Dubus Talking*. Ed. Ross Gresham. New Orleans: Xavier Press, 2003. 255–75. Reprinted with the permission of the authors.

Jennifer Levasseur and Kevin Rabalais: For more than thirty years you have been publishing short stories almost exclusively. Your first published book, however, *The Lieutenant*, was a novel. In the past, you've said that book would have been better as a novella, even though it has all the characteristics of a novel. What would you have changed?
Andre Dubus: I looked at *The Lieutenant* in the eighties because a small press reprinted it, and I had to read the galleys. I wouldn't have cut it then because they wanted to print it as it was, and because I couldn't figure how to change it. I don't remember that novel, but I suspect I could have compressed some of it. I could not at twenty-nine have compressed more, though. If I had written it twelve years later, maybe I could have. Maybe I would have had fewer scenes. I couldn't have made it twenty pages, but maybe one hundred and twenty. I was learning while writing that novel.

JL/KR: You began a second novel, which was later abandoned, after the publication of *The Lieutenant*. Did any stories grow from that novel?
AD: I had actually written a novel before *The Lieutenant*. I finally burned it after eighteen drafts because I had outgrown it. After *The Lieutenant* was published, I started one, and I think I was on the second chapter when I read a story by Chekhov called "Peasants." It covers one family, one village, and one year in thirty pages. I went for a drive in New Hampshire, and when I came back, I read it again and thought, I have to learn how to compress. I never looked back again. No, I didn't get any stories out of that novel.

JL/KR: Shortly after the publication of *The Lieutenant*, you wrote a screen-play based on the novel.
AD: I wrote two drafts of a bad screenplay a year later and was paid.

JL/KR: What kind of exercise was that for you?
AD: It was so easy, and I think that is why it was such a bad screenplay. The producer said, "Go home and write the kind of movie you would like to see." After I finished, he said, "There is too much dialogue. You're thinking like a novelist. Ninety percent of this would be cut because the actors would express this with their bodies."

JL/KR: Would you have liked to see it made into a film?
AD: I still would. I think it would make a good movie, and I could use the money.

JL/KR: Several of your characters reappear throughout the stories. What do you feel are the advantages of having recurring characters in stories, rather than using these characters in a longer work?
AD: I do sometimes plan to have several stories with the same character, but I have never thought of the advantages. It could be a limitation; I don't know. I prefer reading stories. François Mauriac said, "I don't know why anybody writes long novels. You could always write another [short] novel about the same people."

JL/KR: How do you know when a character will stay with you for more than one story?
AD: Well, I wrote a series about a boy, Paul Clement, in Louisiana, and I knew I would write about him. When I got older and looked back at those stories, I realized those weren't my parents; those were my memories of how I saw them when I was ten. The stories always changed anyway. There were also those three novellas—"We Don't Live Here Anymore," "Adultery," and "Finding a Girl in America"—and I did not think there would be three. I wrote "We Don't Live Here Anymore," and I started worrying about the character Edith. I think she's the only one in those stories I liked. Then I wrote "Adultery." I was writing "Finding a Girl in America," a story about a man whose girlfriend aborts his child, and I decided to put Hank Allison in there. There were also some Peter Jackman stories. I don't think I knew

he would get three stories. There are several LuAnn Arceneaux stories in *Dancing After Hours*. Those were a mess to get going. I used her when I decided to write a story about how two people meet, because that always fascinates me. I knew I would try "Out of the Snow" with LuAnn. The idea for that one came from an experience I had when I was picking up my youngest daughters one day. I was in my wheelchair, and I saw a big boy pushing a smaller boy around. I started to drive away, but then I thought, I can't just let this happen. I drove back and said, "You stop that, or I'll call the police." What else could I do? Another guy came up and said, "It's okay, mister. Don't call the police. That guy said something about his sister." I said, "That guy's too big. He shouldn't be doing that." I then thought about how I shouldn't disturb the police over something so foolish. But a woman came up behind me and spoke before dispersing them. And then I thought, why not write a story about a woman dealing with violence?

JL/KR: Do you still read novels, or do you concentrate more on stories?
AD: I still read novels. I recently pulled out Mauriac and Balzac's *Cousin Bette*, but I got interrupted by baseball season. I like to reread novels. I'm in the mood to read some more of Graham Greene's novels. I'm not sure I like stories more than novels; it just depends on who the writer is.

JL/KR: Do you ever think about writing novels again?
AD: Oh, God forbid. No, no.

JL/KR: Your stories are driven by character, and you've said your characters often control the fate of the story.
AD: In my story "Miranda over the Valley," the character gets so bitter, and I kept rewriting the ending, but she kept doing the same thing.

JL/KR: It sounds like you feel your characters hold the ultimate responsibility.
AD: Yes. I only got nineteen words today and I don't even know what the characters are doing in this story I'm writing. I've got to take a couple days off until they show me something. If I would have finished that section today, I would have been screwed. It's a new section, and I don't know what's going on, so I'll take a few days off and then see what happens.

JL/KR: So do you see your characters as somewhere outside your mind? Where do they come from?

AD: I think they come from their actions and what they are thinking and feeling. My job is to figure out what they are feeling. I will have a physical description and some history in my head before I start a story. I'm writing a western now, and I know this character who is a black cowboy in Southern California. I know his family went from Chicago to California during the gold rush, and his father set up a church in Los Angeles. That's not the story but I know that.

JL/KR: Do you feel you know more about your characters, even things that don't get put into the stories?

AD: I want to know about their religion, their sensual habits, how they feel about death, life, where they are from, whom they are kin to. But that's not always what I get to know. I'm thinking about my story "Dancing After Hours." All I had with the female character was her age and that she thought she was not pretty. I don't know where she's from, and I don't know anything about her family. Since she doesn't mention much about religion, I assume that is not part of her life.

If I can finish this western, I'm going to try this one again: a Catholic family, French one side, Irish, the other, with a martyred nun. I wanted to have her martyred in El Salvador. I either copped out, or I made a tactical decision. I've never been to El Salvador, and I don't know any Spanish. I thought, why go through all that work to find a violent country when we live in such a violent country? I try to see the characters, to know some of their history. I will think about characters for a long time rather than just start the story and see what they do. I like to feel I can get inside of a character. I used to tell students to write sketches. I told them they should know if their character prefers a bath or a shower. I like to think I know that. Now, with this story I'm writing set in 1891, they don't take many baths. This is a sequel to one I wrote last year, and nobody has taken a bath yet.

JL/KR: One thing you do when writing a story is to read drafts into a recorder. When did you begin this exercise?

AD: I was at Iowa, and I don't know who told me about this wonderful idea. And then, one of my kids dropped the tape recorder, and I couldn't replace it. Several years later I got another one, and I've been doing it ever since. It's a great thing to do.

JL/KR: What do you feel this allows during your editing process?

AD: I think I see things I didn't see before. Sometimes I've read paragraphs a hundred times, but I think reading aloud allows me to get physical and use my body so I can see mistakes more clearly. I cut a lot this way. It helps to check dialogue: Is this the wrong rhythm? Are these repetitions? I hear things that I don't see when I do this. I read it in a very dull way. When I listen to it, it's even less interesting. It's not passionate. I don't read it dramatically. I just read it. If you heard the tapes, you would say, "This man's working." It's not like I'm reading my work in front of an audience.

JL/KR: How, other than reading into the recorder, do you edit your work?
AD: I write slowly, and I try to edit as much as I can while I'm writing. The next day, I'll read from the beginning, so I'm doing it all over again. I don't read it when I'm finished that day. I put it aside and don't think about it until the next day.

JL/KR: Your novella "Adultery" went through seven drafts before it was published. There were a total of four hundred pages from the drafts, and the final version appears at sixty pages. How did you compress this novella?
AD: The first draft was a short novel, and it was terrible. It was embarrassing. Nobody ever saw that one. It never got out of longhand. The idea came from two articles in the newspaper. I think I read them in the same summer. One was about a guy who was traveling on the highway with his wife at night in Massachusetts. He stopped to get gasoline, and while the tank was getting filled, he went into the bathroom. His wife woke up, and she decided to go to the bathroom, too. He came out, and he didn't know she had gone, so he drove away without her. The state troopers got him and brought him back. The other story was about a young guy who got an internship with the *Boston Globe*, and he was hitchhiking from Washington State to Boston. A trucker who was dying of cancer picked him up. The trucker was driving around drinking beer and smoking cigarettes and talking into a microphone to his family, but he didn't have it connected because he didn't want them to watch him die. So then I thought, let's put Hank and Edith in this story. I had them go to Mexico. He drives off the road to go to the bathroom, and she crosses the highway and hitchhikes back with a trucker who dies in Maine. There was a funeral scene, and the whole thing was just awful. And then I got to work, and he disappeared.

It was a long process. I thought I had a draft finished in the early stages, and then I realized it wasn't done. One time it was much shorter, and it almost worked on several occasions.

JL/KR: *Voices from the Moon* was also an idea that came from a newspaper story. Does this happen often?

AD: That story came from the *Boston Globe*, too. Maybe I should be reading the paper more now. I guess several stories have come from the paper. There is a story in *Dancing After Hours* called "Blessings," and I got that idea from the paper.

JL/KR: Do you do all your own research?

AD: Yes, I do. For this western, for instance, the next thing I have to do is call a music store and find out what would be a nice waltz to play on the gramophone in 1891. There's not a lot of necessary research in my work, but if I have to I do it. There's always somebody to ask, and people like to tell you about their work.

JL/KR: After over thirty years of publishing, how have your ideas of what fiction should accomplish changed?

AD: I want to use physical details and spiritual light and darkness in such a way that a reader experiences them and becomes the character, goes through what the character goes through. But when I'm writing, I always become the character. I just go through the story with the character to see what is going to happen.

JL/KR: You served in the Marine Corps, and in 1964 you left as a captain. Were there similarities between the community of men on the ship you were stationed on and the community of writers when you moved to join the Iowa Writers' Workshop?

AD: There was some immediate shock. It was very different. In the Marine Corps, I didn't talk about writing. Teaching was a lateral move. There were similarities between that and the Marine Corps. To be in a room full of writers and not hide that you were writing was a very exciting thing for me, and I hadn't experienced that until Iowa.

JL/KR: Had you hid that you were writing during your period in the Marines?

AD: Well, I didn't go around telling everybody. I had my first story published when I was in the Marine Corps, and there was nobody to tell. I couldn't just go knock on the major's door and say, "I wanted to tell you . . ."

JL/KR: Would that have been looked down upon at that time?

AD: No. Actually, that was some kind of narcissism in my head from school days. My son Andre III, who is a writer, and I were talking about this. We were the ones who thought the guys thought this wasn't a guy thing to do. The guys didn't think that. I told him, "Good athletes used to ask me to help them with their school work. All I had to do was ask them to help me throw a football, and they would have been happy to." And he agreed. There was a gunnery sergeant I was very close to, and he found out I sold the story and said, "I want to read it." It was just my own self-absorption. Of course it wouldn't have been a problem.

JL/KR: Were you thinking at that time that writing could be a career?
AD: I never thought it would be a money-making career. I thought I would have to stay in the Marine Corps for twenty years at that time. I thought I didn't want to teach, but then I resigned from the Marine Corps, and I began teaching, which I always enjoyed very much.

JL/KR: You taught modern fiction at Bradford College for eighteen years. What writers did you teach?
AD: There were many I enjoyed teaching. I did seminars, but they would change from time to time. Once it was Hemingway, and another time it was South African writers, but I couldn't find many in those days. Nadine Gordimer and Andre Brink I could find without a problem. I couldn't find many blacks, and the blacks I was able to find were not very good. I guess it was because they hadn't been able to read much. I can't remember his name, but there was one black writer I taught whose stories were not good because of the rage, but the rage was good. I had a Southern literature course I really enjoyed. I started with Faulkner's *Go Down, Moses*, and we spent six weeks on it. I wouldn't leave a page of "The Bear" until we all understood it. I went from pre–Civil War to *The Moviegoer*. I went from *Go Down, Moses* to Chopin's *The Awakening*, and then there was *Lie Down in Darkness*, and so on. The course went through time and place. I taught Chekhov, Joyce's *Dubliners*, Isaac Babel, Kafka's stories, Raymond Carver's stories. I stopped using anthologies at one point, and sometimes I would teach stories and novels I hadn't read. I certainly did teach Graham Greene.

JL/KR: Aside from the literature courses, you also taught creative writing. Did you enjoy teaching one more than the other?
AD: They're very different, and I think I enjoyed teaching them equally. Literature was scarier to teach because I had to hope something would happen

in the course. In fiction workshops, I just had to respond to what somebody else did.

JL/KR: What would you say you've learned about reading and writing through teaching?
AD: I could never list the things because the students were good. I learned to stop defining stories and telling people what they are about, because to each student, the story is what happens to her on that page. If she's got a good reason, then she's right. The students' writing was always stimulating. Every day I was hearing sentences that had never been written.

JL/KR: Many of your stories are written in third person. Is this a conscious choice you've made in your body of work?
AD: It is a conscious choice. When I write in first person, I tend to be too wordy. The narrators just take off. I think I need third-person narration. First-person narrators, when I'm writing them, tend to tell everything. I don't even know the last time I've tried using first-person narrators in stories, but I've written many first-person essays.

JL/KR: Do you approach the writing of essays differently than the writing of fiction?
AD: They are very different. The first difference is point of view. I've really got to squeeze it to make sure it doesn't wander all over the place. It's not the same kind of excitement with an essay. I always know what is going to happen because they've all happened to me, whereas with the stories, I don't know what is going to happen; there is an element of suspense. Other than that, when I'm writing the sentences it feels about the same. No, that's not true. If you write about a black cowboy beating up a white racist, it's a whole lot different from writing a sentence about something that happened to you and your children, as far as the rush is concerned.

JL/KR: It seems you use material from your life, judging by some similarities between personal essays and stories. I'm thinking of the essay from *Meditations from a Moveable Chair* titled "Giving Up the Gun" and a story from *Dancing After Hours* called "The Intruder."
AD: That's interesting. I wrote "The Intruder" aboard ship in 1961, and that's the story the *Sewanee Review* took while I was in the Marine Corps. Richard Yates read the story, and he liked it. Through the years, when my collections were being published, he would always say, "Why don't you put 'The Intrud-

er' in there?" A year after he died, I started thinking about "The Intruder" again. I said, "Dick is talking to me." I was working on *Dancing After Hours*, so I took "The Intruder" out and read it, and it was like looking at a picture of myself when I was seven. So I sent it to my editor, and I said, "This may look like I'm trying to fill up the book, but the truth is I think Yates is talking to me." Sure, I take raw material from my life, but that story was all made up.

JL/KR: Dialect is rarely dealt with in your stories.
AD: I don't use it, and I don't care much to read it. I have no dialect in this western I'm working on now. I decided before I started that the black man was going to speak normally; he would not have any kind of accent that would denote slavery or anything else; he's educated, and everybody in the story would just speak normally as they do in Chekhov. I like dialect in the right hands. Faulkner did beautiful things with language. Sometimes he wrote a line that sounded more like dialogue than read like it. There was a voice he developed that made this so, I think. No good writer's dialogue ever sounds good in a tape recorder.

JL/KR: What was your process in selecting stories for *The Selected Stories of Andre Dubus*?
AD: The editor selected most of them. He came out to the house one day, and while we were going through the stories, he said, "I'm going to put *Voices from the Moon* in there. Nobody read that story, and I'm going to put it right in the middle." He did the arranging. I don't have a clue about arranging stories. With the newest collection, all I knew was that I wanted "Dancing After Hours" last.

JL/KR: Were you happy with the way *The Selected Stories* turned out?
AD: Yes. I think he did a good job. I was looking through there the other day to see if anything is missing. I should talk to someone at Knopf about collecting some of the novellas and longer stories.

JL/KR: Speaking of *Voices from the Moon*, it was marketed as a novel upon publication, rather than a novella or long story.
AD: That was a very funny period. We had a gentleman's argument, and I could have said no to calling it a novel. But we had a debate, and you can't win that kind of debate. I kept saying, *Play It as It Lays* by Joan Didion is a novel. It takes about as long to read as *Voices from the Moon*, but my book is a novella." If we were in France, it wouldn't even be a debate. A woman in

my workshop said, "I don't know why you don't call yourself a novelist. You would be in Japan or France." *Voices from the Moon* came really nicely to me, not easily. It's never easy—but it just came out. I'm not sure it took longer than a summer.

JL/KR: Your novel *The Lieutenant* took about the same amount of time to write. Now you say your stories take longer. What is the difference in pacing between your writing then and now?

AD: I'm not sure if I knew how to bear down then. I'm not sure if full concentration came to me during the writing of *The Lieutenant*. I was writing what I call horizontally, making scenes go. In my forties, I switched to vertically, trying to get inside a world and inside a character. Of course, the book was based on a story that actually happened. I changed the events a little to make the novel. I told the story so many times, and somebody said I should write it. That started in first person, too. I gave a chapter to my wife, and then realized I was writing everything that happened as I remembered it, every detail from the ship. I started over in third person. First person feels like talking to me.

JL/KR: Your essays are all written in the first person, and they are very short.

AD: I really bear down with the essays. I saw a nice review in the *Philadelphia Enquirer*. The reviewer said, "Hemingway is an influence more than ever before in these personal essays." I said, "He may be right." They are very hard to write, and it's hard to keep from launching into a monologue about my life.

JL/KR: You've been critical of some fiction editors of magazines. You've also said, half-jokingly, you feel the two worst things for a young writer are literature professors and the *New Yorker*. What do you think is the role of an editor of a magazine?

AD: I think their role is to say yes or no and not try to change the story. Finding mistakes, maybe suggesting to cut a line, that's all right. I've gotten weird letters from editors. One place wanted "The Timing of Sin," but the editors wanted the whole story to take place somewhere else, cutting the story in half. They thought they wanted the story, but they didn't. They wanted the story they thought they saw. I think it's a bad thing to tempt a young writer because young writers want recognition, and the magazine is waving the check, which won't do anybody any good anyway in the long run. I had a friend who was studying at the University of Arkansas in Fayetteville, and he called and said a buddy of his had just sold his first story to the *New Yorker*. He said they made him change it from a Southern voice in first person to a neutral voice. I said, "Why did he change it?" He said, "Thirty-five hundred dollars." I said, "He's a graduate student. He can't go to Mexico for a year. He can't even buy a car. You know why he did that? Because nobody cares what anybody writes. You'd like to be able to walk into a bar in Akron, Ohio, and have the guy next to you say, 'What do you do?' and you say, 'I write.' He says, 'You been published?' and you say 'Yeah, the *New Yorker*?'" It's not the money that's a bad influence; it's their need to rewrite the story. And regarding literature professors, some of them go nuts on reading into things and, in turn, they ruin the spontaneity of readers. They make literature some removed thing.

JL/KR: How do you feel about taking advice from colleagues or members of your writers workshop?
AD: I like it if I respect the person. If the person is right, then yes. Gary Fisketjon at Knopf had some suggestions for *Dancing After Hours*. I had a story called "Andromache" that was in the *New Yorker*, and that was a good letter, a good editor. He sent the rejection, and I showed it to a wonderful writer named Thomas Williams who said, "I haven't read the story but this is a very interesting letter; maybe you should read it again." He was right. I had been reading too much William Styron. There were flashbacks inside flashbacks and vortexes and this and that, and I didn't need that. I wrote that story again, and it was better. I said to Tom Williams, "I wrote part of that story for myself. Some of it has nothing to do with anything, but what do I do?" He said, "Well, you just put it in the drawer and cry until you can use it somewhere else."

JL/KR: How do you feel about the market for stories right now?
AD: I think it's great. There are all these quarterlies. I keep telling writers, "If you keep it in the mail, somebody will take it." I was talking to a French literary agent in the eighties, and he said, "We don't have literary magazines for stories and poetry. There are only two, and they commission pieces." I don't know about other countries, but you just have to persist. I don't believe a good story will go unpublished.

JL/KR: Many publishers seem to be leery of trying to publish books of stories.

AD: It's hard to publish any kind of book these days. I have a friend who has worked in bookstores for years, and he says new books of stories come out all the time. I just endorsed one this year by Mark Slouka called *Lost Lake*, and it's wonderful. It's always been true that publishers would rather have a novel than a collection of stories. Americans, for some reason, don't seem to be reading books of stories, but is that really true? I think today Hemingway and Fitzgerald would publish books of stories between novels. I believe their stories would have been published anyway, as well as Faulkner's. But publishers have always preferred novels.

JL/KR: In a review of *The Times Are Never So Bad*, Joyce Carol Oates said, "The stories read more like excerpts from longer works than stories complete in themselves." What is your definition of a story?
AD: I stopped having them. I had a student named Michael Bussey, and my system for undergraduates was that every other week, they had to come in with five longhand pages and read them. I told the students they could go both semesters without completing a story, as long as they were working. I feel anybody who assigns three stories in a semester doesn't respect the form, because a story may take three years to write and you can't hurry it. I told them to keep working. As it turned out, around March the finished stories started coming in, and every other week, Michael read a complete story. In the fall semester, I started thinking of them as sketches. By the end of the year, I saw he had written nine beautiful stories, stories about a little boy and his brother, and he followed the boy until age nineteen. I said, "Michael, I'm never going to call a story a sketch again. I used to think these were sketches, but now I think a story is what feels like a story." So that's what I think, and I'm not sure what Joyce Carol Oates meant. Maybe they were excerpts from longer works and the rest of them didn't come to me; I don't know.

JL/KR: Themes run throughout your work, where the same idea repeats itself. Do you revisit scenes or sections of dialogue because you feel you've reached a new understanding of the matter?
AD: It's not intentional. I knew I had written about abortion, for instance, in "Finding a Girl in America," and I didn't look at it again. I didn't want to go back in that direction in "Falling in Love" in *Dancing After Hours*. I told a priest who is in the workshop about my situation, and I said, "I've got another abortion story, and I've already gone there twice in stories. Do I have to go back again?" He said, "Yes." So I did. That doesn't bother me. There's a

lot of repetition in a lot of writers I love, probably because of their passions, fears, what we love as humans. It doesn't bother me; it's just unintentional.

JL/KR: You've said you don't outline stories. Do you outline your essays?
AD: No. I'll do something similar to an outline, though, in the notebook I'm writing in. Take *Voices from the Moon*, for instance. Before I started it, I worked it out so it started one morning and ended later that night. I knew the sections would have alternating points of view, and I knew the young boy would control the point of view for every other section, because it's his story. I chose which sections would have which character's point of view. I wouldn't call that an outline, but I guess you could. I just said, "This is where people will be." I make notes in the margin when something comes to me.

JL/KR: In your essay "Selling Stories" from *Broken Vessels*, you say you became used to rejections from magazines at a young age, that you learned to accept them. However, you say it's different with a book publisher.
AD: The rejections that really hurt during that period after I wrote *The Lieutenant* were not the rejection slips that said, "I don't like the collection of stories," but the ones that said, "We'll publish this collection of stories if you write a novel." That hurt. I thought I was being told to be somebody else. I became immune to rejections by the time I got out of college, long before I had anything published. I started to send out stories when I was eighteen because I knew I had to develop a thick skin.

JL/KR: In that same essay you also say, "There is no one to sell out to as a story writer." Has this been one of the reasons you've continued to write stories?
AD: I just don't see novels. I still think *The Lieutenant* is an idea for a short novella. I've written shorter things about more complicated things, but I don't get ideas for novels, and that's why I don't write them. I don't know how anybody does. My son Andre does, and he goes off for five years into this world and then comes up with a new world he's made.

JL/KR: How do you feel about your son's decision to become a writer?
AD: I love it.

JL/KR: Much of your work is dedicated to your children. How do they respond to your writing?

AD: They tell me they like it. The young girls haven't read it yet. I think it's just something Dad does. My oldest daughter, when I published *The Lieutenant*, was nine years old. She was very happy and curious that her dad didn't go to work every morning, but that he went to classes three days a week and then came home and wrote, and I felt the same way.

JL/KR: You recently switched to publishing with Knopf after many years with Godine.

AD: I was in my last year of a MacArthur Foundation grant, and I wasn't going to be able to afford the mortgage. The accountant said, "This is real. You will lose the house." I was feeling very low, and then I realized I had to stop waiting for guys with suits to do something, that I needed to call my agent. I called and said, "I've got to go free agent. I can't be loyal to anybody. I'm going to lose my damn house." My agent said, "This will be fun." So I got a two-year contract, and my house is paid for. I'm glad I did it. I'm very happy with Knopf. As long as I had income, I didn't need to do it, but things change.

JL/KR: Every Thursday night since the fall of 1987, a writers' workshop has met at your house. How did this come about?

AD: In the fall of '87, a woman from south of Boston called. She said she had eight writers who wanted to pay a couple hundred dollars each for four nights of a workshop. And then ten writers gave a benefit for me that winter. I thought, Well, all those writers gave me that, so I'm not going to charge writers until I have to. I said, "Come up and I'll see what you are doing." So they came over, and I talked to each one, and I said, "It looks like we need a workshop." So that's how it began. There's been a major rotation over ten years. We have a twenty-seven-year-old who hasn't been here much because she's in Harvard at the business school. One woman has published a novel; another is publishing stories in quarterlies. There's another woman in her seventies who is publishing. They're pretty much in their thirties and forties, most of them, with jobs and families.

JL/KR: Bradford was a women's college when you taught there. You've said in the past that women are better writers than men. Do you still feel this way?

AD: Did I say that? I do read a lot of women writers. We came to Massachusetts for the geography. We had never been here. Women are the ones who read books. But I don't think women are better writers than men. They're different. I said in a class at Bradford, "Updike writes like a woman," and the women got upset. I said, "It's not an insult. A man goes into a room in a strange house he's never been to, and when he comes out he doesn't know what he saw. His wife will go in, and she will know the wallpaper, the curtains, the furniture, and every detail of the house. But the guy will come out and say, "Well, they were nice people." I didn't know what was in my house until I got confined to it. I couldn't tell you what color the walls were. Women are very sensuous. I have a group of abused teenagers I meet with every Monday night, and one of them asked to read some women writers. She said, "Let's read some Virginia Woolf." I said, "All the women writers I read are too complicated and lyrical and too sexy. I'm just not going to read them in here." In that group, we mostly read Tobias Wolff and Hemingway, stuff like that with sentences that are approachable. When a woman writer gets on a roll, boy, you get lost.

JL/KR: What have you been reading lately?
AD: At line yesterday while I was getting my driver's license renewed, I started reading Dennis Lehane's new novel, *Gone, Baby, Gone*. I was reading *Cousin Bette* and loving it, but something interrupted me. I hope it was something like swimming or baseball. I finally gave it up and put it back on the shelf. I read a novel in manuscript by my middle sister last week. So the truth is that if I can keep up with family and friends, that's about all I can do.

JL/KR: Are any of your other family members writing?
AD: My oldest daughter is working on a screenplay. She can write well. My fourth child, who is a therapist in Santa Cruz, has written two novels, but neither one has been published. They can all write. My sixteen-year-old came over with my eleven-year-old, and we were all in the pool. I looked up and the older one was gone. I said, "Where's Cadence?" My daughter Madeline said, "She's writing a story." I said, "That's a serious sixteen-year-old."

I got a little burned out reading. When I was teaching at the University of Alabama, I bought Marguerite Duras's *The Lover*. When I began reading it, all of a sudden it felt like it weighed two hundred pounds, and I had to put it down. I was going to reread *War and Peace* for the third time last fall. Then I thought, "It will be the World Series. You are going to read twelve pages a day." So I bought a six-volume video with Anthony Hopkins made for BBC, and it's the most magnificent thing I've ever seen in my life. I decided watching the film version wasn't a cop-out because I've taught the book and love it and always will. I'm lonely at night, and something about picking up a book at night makes me lonely, but videos don't. I don't know why that's true.

JL/KR: Are there any stories you are most proud of?
AD: They are mostly gone when I finish them. I remember the ones that were hardest to write. "Adultery" was hard, and I almost quit writing it a few times. "Dancing After Hours" was very hard, as well. I am fond of many of the stories in *The Last Worthless Evening*. I like "Molly" and "Deaths at Sea."

JL/KR: "Deaths at Sea" is one of the few stories that deals with racism. Did you make a decision to stay away from the topic?
AD: There should be more. This western I wrote last summer deals with it, and the sequel I'm working on now deals with it because the main character is black. But I don't know the answer. In the sixties and seventies, I shied away from writing about this topic because of the turmoil in our country. It probably just hasn't come up in the stories. I guess I haven't been writing about characters who are racist.

JL/KR: You just mentioned your story "Molly," which is a powerful story of a girl moving into adulthood and confronting her own sexuality. How did that story come to you?
AD: That story was hard. It started from the point of view of a fishing captain who first sees the mother, Claire. It started on his fishing boat off the New Hampshire coast. Claire invites him over to her house for dinner. He's the first one who sees Molly. I didn't know how to finish it, and then a couple days later I realized it was finished, and that I just needed an epilogue. I wrote that epilogue with my daughter Cadence, who was three years old at the time, on my lap.

JL/KR: In your essay "After Twenty Years," you say you've "always known that writing fiction had little effect on the world; that if it did, young men would not have gone to war after the Iliad." What do you feel a writer's role is in society?
AD: I hate to tell you. Somebody wrote me about that essay, and she said, "It helps those of us who do read to help those who don't." And I think that's what reading does, but it doesn't get things done. Caesar Chavez did more than six John Steinbecks could have done. Workers don't own their own lives yet. It must have helped in communist countries, but it doesn't help in

capitalistic societies. Have you ever seen any good come because somebody wrote a book of fiction? Individual good, yes. I think it's a limited effort, a beautiful effort that is a gift from God. I think people should do it and make music and paintings. I just wish the world would get better for everybody and there would be true democracy. Literature touches individual lives. It comforts, soothes, and delights. It turns us on, enrages us. I think the average life span in Haiti is forty or forty-five. Graham Greene wrote *The Comedians* about Haiti, and that's a wonderful book. When the day comes that a politician picks up a novel and sees the light, I'm just going to walk straight to heaven. I think art is for the individual soul. I never read Thomas More's *Utopia*. A woman I know read it, and she said, "There are no artists in there." I was educated by Christian brothers, and a wise Jesuit once told me, "If there were no sins, there wouldn't be art." At the least, stories are fun to read.

Interview with Andre Dubus

Greg Garrett / 1999

Art and Soul. 23 February 1999. Reprinted in *Leap of the Heart: Andre Dubus Talking.* Ed. Ross Gresham. New Orleans: Xavier Review Press, 2003. 276–77. Reprinted with the permission of the author.

Greg Garrett: Many of the stories in *Dancing After Hours* are told from a female point of view. Do you ever worry about taking on that challenge of writing across the gender line?

Andre Dubus: Writers should write the stories that come to them. I don't think it's experimental to write from the point of view of a woman. I think it's just imagining.

GG: Can you tell us a little about your writing habits? The where and when of your writing?

AD: I'm retired now, so it doesn't matter when I write. I can get up at noon and still write before dinnertime. When I was a teacher, then I had to keep a schedule. But I don't just write when it comes to me, because that might just be a few nights a year.

GG: How do you go about creating characters for your stories? Do you start with real people, or are they made up entirely?

AD: I don't use real people. I did once, when I was young. I used a friend of mine. But I realized that as well as I knew this guy, I didn't know him at all. I don't know if anybody knows how any body else feels. I have no idea what it feels like to be my kids. I have no idea what it felt like to be my parents. I do use bodies I've seen, like you might use a paper doll. But for me the character becomes real on the page through the imagination and through whatever gift it comes from.

I don't know what characters are going to do. I have to work to discover the character, and I do that by becoming the character and experiencing

247

that life. If I say that I know exactly what a character is going to do, then I've killed that character. The character has to surprise you, the way you should have a sincere conversation, not a rehearsed one. If you plan everything, it isn't a conversation. You've planned how you will feel and how you will react.

GG: One of your great strengths is dialogue. How do you go about writing dialogue that is so real?

AD: It's probably not real; maybe it tries too hard to be real. You should never write realistic dialogue. We all talk too much. Look at the short stories of Fitzgerald or Hemingway—they write lines that sound like human speech but it's purified. No one says that little. I try to get a poetic rhythm going and I try to write literary dialogue. We're not trying to be real. We're trying to be better than real. We're trying to be true.

GG: What is the relation between your beliefs and your writing? Are you a Catholic writer, whatever that means these days?

AD: When I'm making up those characters, I generally know before the story when I'm about to become a character who's religious or not or something in between. But I never know the answer to the question about Catholicism and my writing. I've been a Catholic all my life. That's the way I see the world. We all share in the universals, but my worldview is shaped by my being a Catholic just like yours is shaped by being a Baptist.

GG: How do you decide whether you're going to write fiction or nonfiction? What makes you decide to write an essay?

AD: Usually when it happens to me, I write an essay. To tell the truth, I'm not interested in writing about my personal life, but sometimes I feel that it's something that needs to be told. I'm very excited about being alive in my personal life, but I don't want to bring it to my desk. There I want to be someone else.

Some people have to write close to the bone. That is their demon. My fictional angel wants to take me somewhere else.

Appendix:
List of Additional Interviews

Print Interviews with Andre Dubus Not Collected in This Volume

Doten, Patti. "Pain, Yes, Rage No; Five Years after His Accident, He's Back from the Depths." *Boston Globe* 19 August 1991: 33+.

Flamm, Matthew. "Talking with Andre Dubus." *Newsday* 14 April 1996: C31+.

Fleming, Phyllis. "Andre Dubus Knows What Happiness Is, He Sold Book." *Cedar Rapids Gazette* 8 May 1966: 8B.

Hayes, Larry. "Interview: Andre Dubus." *AEGIS* 9.1 (Spring 1981): 17–26. Reprinted in *Leap of the Heart: Andre Dubus Talking*. Ed. Ross Gresham. New Orleans: Xavier University Press, 2003. 17–26.

Holmes, Jon. "With Andre Dubus." *Boston Review* 9.4 (July–August 1984): 7–8. Reprinted in *Leap of the Heart: Andre Dubus Talking*. Ed. Ross Gresham. New Orleans: Xavier Review Press, 2003. 60–67.

Howe, Desson. *Washington Post* 24 May 1986.

Kennedy, Thomas E. "Raw Oysters, Fried Brains, the Leap of the Heart: An Interview with Andre Dubus." *Delta* 24 (February 1987): 21–77. Reprinted as "Interview" in Thomas Kennedy, *Andre Dubus: A Study of the Short Fiction*. Boston: Twayne, 1988. Reprinted in *Leap of the Heart: Andre Dubus Talking*. Ed. Ross Gresham. New Orleans: Xavier Review Press, 2003. 89–121.

Kramer, Jerome V. "Double Dubus." *Book* March/April 1999: 43–46.

Lyons, Bonnie, and Bill Oliver. "Andre Dubus: An Interview." *Crazyhorse* 44 (Spring 1993): 90–101. Reprinted in *Passion and Craft: Conversations with Notable Writers*. Urbana: University of Illinois Press, 1988. 145–58.

"The Man in the Ascot." *The Quill* 27 January 1967: 4. Reprinted in *Leap of the Heart: Andre Dubus Talking*. Ed. Ross Gresham. New Orleans: Xavier Review Press, 2003. 4–5.

Nathan, Robert. "Interview with Andre Dubus." *Bookletter* 3.12 (14 February 1977): 14–15. Reprinted in *Leap of the Heart: Andre Dubus Talking*. Ed. Ross Gresham. New Orleans: Xavier University Press, 2003. 8–16.

Ross, Jean. *Contemporary Authors New Revision Series.* Ed. Linda Metzger and Deborah A. Straub. Detroit: Gale, 1986: 116–19. Reprinted in *Leap of the Heart: Andre Dubus Talking.* Ed. Ross Gresham. New Orleans: Xavier Review Press, 2003. 79–88.

Samway, Patrick, S.J. "An Interview with Andre Dubus." *America* 14 November 1986: 300–301. Reprinted in *Andre Dubus: A Study of the Short Fiction.* Ed. Thomas Kennedy. Boston: Twayne, 1988. 124–28. Reprinted in *Leap of the Heart: Andre Dubus Talking.* Ed. Ross Gresham. Xavier Review Press: New Orleans, 2003. 126–30.

Audio Interviews with Andre Dubus Not Collected in This Volume

Gross, Terry. "Interview with Andre Dubus." *Fresh Air*, NPR, 25 June 1991. (Rebroadcast 22 March 1996). Printed in "A New Gift." In *All I Did Was Ask: Conversations with Writers, Actors Musicians and Artists.* New York: Hyperion, 2004, 53–59.

Stamberg, Susan. "Romance, Core of Love." *All Things Considered.* NPR, 24 July 1980.

———. "Author Hurt in Car Wreck, Writers Helping." *Weekend Edition*, NPR, 25 January 1987.

———. "MacArthur Prize to Injured Author Dubus." *Weekend Edition*, NPR, 24 July 1988.

———. "Accident Victim, Author Dubus Keeps Working." *All Things Considered*, NPR, 23 July 1991.

Index